BIBLE THROUGH THE LENS OF TRAUMA

SEMEIA STUDIES

Number 86

BIBLE THROUGH THE LENS OF TRAUMA

Edited by

Elizabeth Boase and Christopher G. Frechette

SBL PRESS

 **PRESS**

Atlanta

Copyright © 2016 by SBL Press

Library of Congress Cataloging in Publication Control Number: 2016040613

Printed on acid-free paper.

CONTENTS

ABBREVIATIONS

AB	Anchor Bible
ACCS	Ancient Christian Commentary on Scripture
AIL	Ancient Israel and its Literature
ANEM	Ancient Near Eastern Monographs
AOTC	Abindgon Old Testament Commentaries
BHS	*Biblia Hebraica Stuttgartensia*. Edited by Karl Elliger and Wilhelm Rudolph. Stuttgard: Deutsche Bibelgesellsdchaft, 1983.
Bib	*Biblica*
BibInt	*Biblical Interpretation*
BibSem	The Biblical Seminar
BWL	*Babylonian Wisdom Literature*. Wilfred G. Lambert. Oxford, Clarendon, 1960.
CAD	*The Assyrian Dictionary of the Oriental Institute of the University of Chicago*. Chicago: The Oriental Institute of the University of Chicago, 1956–2006.
CBQ	*Catholic Biblical Quarterly*
CEB	Common English Bible
CurBR	*Currents in Biblical Research*
FCB	Feminist Companion to the Bible
HKAT	Handkommentar zum Alten Testament
HSM	Harvard Semitic Monographs
IBC	Interpretation: A Bible Commentary for Teaching and Preaching
ICC	International Critical Commentary
Int	*Interpretation: A Journal of Bible and Theology*
JAAR	*Journal of the American Academy of Religion*
JANESCU	*Journal of the Ancient Near Eastern Society of Columbia University*
JBL	*Journal of Biblical Literature*

JFSR	*Journal of Feminist Studies in Religion*
JSOT	*Journal for the Study of the Old Testament*
JSOTSup	Journal for the Study of the Old Testament Supplement Series
JTSA	*Journal of Theology for Southern Africa*
LCL	Loeb Classical Library
LHBOTS	Library of Hebrew Bible/Old Testament Studies
LTPM	Louvain Theological and Pastoral Monographs
NAC	New American Commentary
NCB	New Century Bible
NICOT	New International Commentary on the Bible
NJPS	*Tanakh: The Holy Scriptures: The New JPS Translation according to the Traditional Hebrew Text*
NRSV	New Revised Standard Version
OBO	Orbis Biblicus et Orientalis
OBT	Overtures to Biblical Theology
OTL	Old Testament Library
OtSt	Oudtestamentische Studiën
Phillips	*The New Testament in Modern English*, J. B. Phillips
RB	*Revue Biblique*
SANt	Studia Aarhusiana Neotestamentica
SBLDS	Society of Biblical Literature Dissertation Series
SBLMS	Society of Biblical Literature Monograph Series
SBLStBL	Society of Biblical Literature Studies in Biblical Literature
SBLSymS	Society of Biblical Literature Symposium Series
SHBC	Smyth & Helwys Bible Commentary
StBibLit	Studies in Biblical Literature (Lang)
TDOT	*Theological Dictionary of the Old Testament*. Edited by G. Johannes Botterweck and Helmer Ringgren. Translated by John T. Willis et al. 8 vols. Grand Rapids: Eerdmans, 1974–2006.
TSK	*Theologische Studien und Kritiken*
VT	*Vetus Testamentum*
VTSup	Supplements to Vetus Testamentum
WBC	Word Biblical Commentary
YNER	Yale Near Eastern Researches
ZAW	*Zeitschrift für die alttestamentliche Wissenschaft*
ZDMG	*Zeitschift der deutschen morgenländischen Gesellschaft*

Defining "Trauma" as a Useful Lens for Biblical Interpretation[*]

Christopher G. Frechette and Elizabeth Boase

In recent decades biblical scholars have increasingly come to regard the concept of trauma as a powerful interpretive lens, and that interest has begun to spark significant discussion.[1] The interdisciplinary conference "Trauma and Traumatization: Biblical Studies and Beyond," held at Aarhus University, Denmark, in 2012, brought biblical scholars into conversation with scholars from various disciplines, including anthropology, classics, history of medicine, patristics, psychology, and sociology. Subsequently, an important volume of revised conference papers appeared in 2014.[2] During the Annual Meetings of the Society of Biblical Literature (SBL) from 2012

---

[*] We would like to thank Corrine Carvalho for reading and commenting on an earlier version of this essay.

1. For a survey up to 2014 of works of biblical interpretation employing the lens of trauma theory, see David G. Garber, "Trauma Theory and Biblical Studies," *CurBR* 14 (2015): 24–44. Works appearing since 2014 include: David M. Carr, *Holy Resilience: The Bible's Traumatic Origins* (New Haven: Yale University Press, 2014); the first issue of volume 69 (2015) of *Interpretation: A Journal of Bible and Theology*, entitled "Trauma and Faith"; and Elizabeth Boase and Sarah Agnew, "'Whispered in the Sound of Silence': Traumatizing the Book of Jonah," *Bible and Critical Theory* 12 (2016): 4–22; and Mark G. Brett, *Political Trauma and Healing: Biblical Ethics for a Postcolonial World* (Grand Rapids: Eerdmans, 2016). Forthcoming works include: Kathleen M. O'Connor, *Genesis*, Smith & Helwys Commentary Series (Macon, GA: Smith & Helwys, forthcoming); and Christopher G. Frechette, "Two Biblical Motifs of Divine Violence as Resources for Meaning-Making in Engaging Self-Blame and Rage after Traumatization," *Journal of Pastoral Psychology*, forthcoming.

2. Eve-Marie Becker, Jan Dochhorn, and Else Holt, eds., *Trauma and Traumatization in Individual and Collective Dimensions: Insights from Biblical Studies and Beyond*, SANt 2 (Göttingen: Vandenhoeck & Ruprecht, 2014). David Carr reviewed the volume in *CBQ* 78 (2016): 179–81.

to 2015, papers presented across more than thirty program units explicitly engaged the concept of trauma (see the appendix on 249–50 below).

In 2013, the SBL inaugurated the program unit "Biblical Literature and the Hermeneutics of Trauma" for its Annual Meeting. Recognizing the range of ways in which the concept of trauma was being defined and employed in biblical interpretation, the organizers of the unit prioritized the following three foci for critical attention: the manner in which a given interpreter defines trauma, or a particular aspect of it, and the corresponding interpretive utility of such a definition; the relationship between individual and collective dimensions of trauma; and specific ways in which employing trauma hermeneutics in biblical interpretation can benefit other theological disciplines. All but one of the essays (that of Ruth Poser) in the present volume are revisions of papers presented during sessions of that program unit held in 2013 and 2014.

Thus far, biblical trauma hermeneutics has emerged in dialogue with diverse disciplines and theoretical frameworks. While *trauma* can refer to severe physical injury, it is psychological and social trauma, their reflexes in literature, and the appropriation of that literature that have garnered significant attention among biblical interpreters. Developments in the fields of psychology, sociology, refugee studies, and comparative literature have all influenced the manner in which they employ the lens of trauma. Biblical interpreters recognize manifold aspects of trauma, which include not only the immediate effects of events or ongoing situations but also mechanisms that facilitate survival, recovery, and resilience. Trauma hermeneutics is used to interpret texts in their historical contexts and as a means of exploring the appropriation of texts, in contexts both past and present.

By way of introduction to the present volume, this essay seeks to provide a conceptual framework through which to consider modes of applying trauma as a hermeneutical lens for biblical interpretation, as well as demonstrate the utility of doing so. Situating this framework within the wider context of trauma studies, the discussion proceeds in three stages. After a brief introduction to the multifaceted nature of trauma as a concept, we summarize key insights from the fields of psychology, sociology, and literary studies, in each case focusing on issues of particular significance for biblical studies. The essay then turns to its principal task of articulating a framework for biblical trauma hermeneutics. The concluding section explains the organization of the remaining essays in the present volume.

TRAUMA STUDIES AS AN INTERDISCIPLINARY FIELD

The 1970s witnessed, among psychologists, an increased recognition of trauma as a distinct type of suffering that overwhelms a person's normal capacity to cope. Research involving Vietnam War veterans and victims of sexual abuse sparked this development in a particular way, revealing commonalities among symptoms experienced by the victims and among modes for promoting recovery from those symptoms. This gave rise to the category of traumatic stress.[3] Recognition of this complex phenomenon built on a range of prior research, including Pierre Janet's investigation of the effects of extreme stress on memory, Sigmund Freud's investigation into certain psychological symptoms in adult women as linked to experiences of sexual abuse during childhood, and shell-shock observed in soldiers during World War I. First recognized by the American Psychiatric Association in 1980, the diagnostic category of posttraumatic stress disorder (PTSD) is evolving, with the most recent revision of the criteria occurring in 2013.[4]

As already noted, the concept of trauma traverses a multifaceted interdisciplinary terrain, and tracing its development is a complex and vexed task. Roger Luckhurst has helpfully described it as a conceptual knot that ties together "an impressive range of elements," which allows it to "travel to … diverse places in the network of knowledge."[5] The entangled lines that feed into and out of this conceptual knot make this field a contentious

---

3. For historical accounts of trauma studies in psychology, see Bessel A. van der Kolk, Lars Weisaeth, and Onno van der Hart, "History of Trauma in Psychiatry," in *Traumatic Stress: The Effects of Overwhelming Experience on Mind, Body, and Society*, ed. Bessel A. van der Kolk, Alexander McFarlane, and Lars Weisaeth (New York: Guilford, 2007), 47–74; Judith Lewis Herman, *Trauma and Recovery: The Aftermath of Violence—From Domestic Abuse to Political Terror*, rev. ed. (New York: Basic Books, 1997), 7–32; and Roger Luckhurst, *The Trauma Question* (London: Routledge, 2008), 19–76. For comprehensive discussions of the cognitive and physiological effects of psychological trauma and strategies for promoting recovery from those effects, see Herman, *Trauma and Recovery*; and Bessel A. van der Kolk, *The Body Keeps the Score: Brain, Mind, and Body in the Healing of Trauma* (New York: Viking, 2014).

4. *Diagnostic and Statistical Manual of Mental Disorders: DSM-5*, 5th ed. (Arlington, VA: American Psychiatric Association, 2013), 271–80. See also the *International Statistical Classification of Diseases and Related Health Problems*, 10th revision, 3 vols. (Geneva: World Health Organization, 1992–1994).

5. Luckhurst, *The Trauma Question*, 14.

one. These lines include diverse branches of learning whose theoretical frameworks are often at odds with regard to fundamental constructions such as identity, memory, the relationship between the individual and the collective, and the mechanisms of representation and semiotics.

There are, at present, three dominant threads informing biblical trauma hermeneutics: psychology, sociology, and literary and cultural studies. Psychology contributes to our understanding of the effects of trauma on individuals and on those processes that facilitate survival, recovery, and resilience. Sociology provides insights into collective dimensions of traumatic experience. Literary and cultural studies open pathways for exploring the role and function of texts as they encode and give witness to traumatic suffering and construct discursive and aesthetic spaces for fostering recovery and resilience.

Despite the unique focus of each of these disciplines, insights from each have relevance for the other two. Collective trauma builds on individual stress reactions, and social fragmentation can increase the susceptibility of individuals to traumatization. Insights from psychology and sociology inform attempts to recognize reflexes of trauma in literatures, and the use of literature can affect how individuals and collectives process trauma.

Insights from Psychology: Trauma and Recovery in Individuals

Within the field of psychology, the study of trauma focuses on the range of responses evoked by an experience perceived to pose an extreme threat and that overwhelms an individual's ordinary means of coping. The degree to which the person is conscious of the threat may vary. The experience may involve a single incident or an ongoing situation of captivity, disaster, or systemic oppression. Such perception is radically shaped by culturally specific factors. Moreover, since it is the perception of threat that is decisive, the experience may or may not involve actual physical violation. Immediate, largely unconscious cognitive responses to such experiences tend to cause profound and durable psychic effects. Such responses may also occur in persons who are not experiencing the overwhelming threat themselves but who witness others who are.

Sensory stimuli that occur during such an experience are processed differently than are normal experiences. The impossibility of acting upon natural impulses to fight or to flee a threat in many cases prompts dissociation, that is, withdrawal to some degree from both the disturbing awareness of the traumatic event and the intense feelings aroused by it. Such withdrawal serves as a survival mechanism protecting the victim from psychic collapse. Dissociation and withdrawal diminish the person's ability to recall what occurred or to create a coherent narrative to describe the events. Oftentimes memory of the experience may be available only in fragmentary ways, in the form of feelings or images, and these may intrude into awareness.

Even as the mind creates psychic distance from the overwhelming feelings and thoughts, it attempts to make sense of the experience. It does so in ways that are largely unconscious but that may also enter consciousness.

A range of cognitive theories point to the existence of unconscious structures in the human mind—labeled *core beliefs, schemas,* or *assumptions*—through which sensory input passes. The content of these unconscious assumptions shapes the specific thoughts and feelings that emerge into consciousness after sensory input, over time giving rise to conscious assumptions about self and world.[6] Assumptions that the self has agency and dignity, enjoys solidarity with trustworthy others (human and divine), and inhabits an environment that is relatively safe are fundamental to maintaining identity and a felt sense of well-being. Although such assumptions normally take shape gradually and resist change, the intensity of an overwhelmingly threatening experience that contradicts a core assumption can shatter it and leave in its place an opposite, toxic assumption. The experience of feeling violated can shatter the basic assumptions named above.[7] Threats that are personal rather than impersonal are more likely to affect assumptions of dignity, trust, and solidarity. Even if the overwhelming experience subsides, the toxic assumptions that have replaced the shattered ones can continue to filter daily experience in ways that produce a variety of negative emotions and moods, while reducing positive ones.

In addition to effects on general assumptions, an overwhelmingly threatening event often prompts interpretations of the cause of the experience in a way that places irrational blame on the self. Doing so serves as a survival mechanism; by providing an explanation and asserting a sense of

---

6. The present discussion relies principally on "Cognitive Appraisal Theory" as developed by Aaron T. Beck and Albert Ellis. For an overview, see Michelle G. Craske, *Cognitive-Behavioral Therapy,* Theories of Psychotherapy Series (Washington, DC: American Psychological Association, 2010), 39–47.

7. For a comprehensive discussion of the impact of trauma on one's assumptions, see Jeffrey Kauffman, ed., *Loss of the Assumptive World: A Theory of Traumatic Loss* (New York: Brunner-Routledge, 2002).

control, blaming the self helps a person to confront the imminent threat of overwhelming chaos. However, such irrational self-blame may have harmful consequences if allowed to remain unchallenged.

A number of responses and strategies facilitate a degree of recovery from the effects of trauma and can help individuals to develop resilience in the face of ongoing threats. As described by Judith Herman, three basic tasks for recovery from trauma are to establish safety, to mourn the traumatic experience, and to reintegrate the survivor into ordinary life.[8] All three tasks involve cultivating interpersonal solidarity. The task of mourning involves remembering, interpreting, and grieving the experience in an emotionally engaged manner. However, an inherent paradox emerges at this point: because of the dissociation that has occurred, traumatic experience frequently defies linguistic expression, yet recovery depends, at least in part, on the ability to access sufficient memory in order to construct a coherent trauma narrative. The establishment of safety is crucial in such efforts.

Constructing a trauma narrative is an act of meaning-making.[9] Its purpose is best understood in light of the way in which traumatic experience causes dissociation from thoughts and feelings associated with the trauma and shatters assumptions and beliefs that support identity and well-being. Broadly speaking, a trauma narrative has two aims, each involving a paradox: to recount honestly the full experience of the trauma, including what happened and the feelings associated with the experience, even though the memories and feelings may be accessible only in fragments; and to interpret the trauma in ways that confront and replace harmful assumptions and beliefs prompted by the experience. Such interpretation has the task of supporting a sense of order, identity, agency, well-being, and solidarity, while also expressing the impossibility of fully comprehending the trauma. It is precisely the capacity to preserve such paradoxes that prevents a trauma narrative from slipping into banality.

In addition to the creation of a coherent linguistic narrative, symbolic representations of the traumatic event in forms such as poetry, music, art, bodily movement, and religious ritual can also advance a process of

---

8. Herman, *Trauma and Recovery*, 3, 155.

9. For an overview of the literature on meaning-making, especially in the wake of shattered assumptions, see Crystal L. Park, "Making Sense of the Meaning Literature: An Integrative Review of Meaning Making and Its Effects on Adjustment to Stressful Life Events," *Psychological Bulletin* 136 (2010): 257–301.

constructing meaning related to the traumatic events. Such nondiscursive symbolic forms may be conceptualized broadly as part of the trauma narrative. The safe and supportive presence of others as witnesses and dialogue partners can be crucial for advancing the process of reinterpreting the traumatic experience, helping survivors to address factors such as an eroded ability to trust others.

Because the psychological study of trauma has occurred largely in cultures of the modern West, the question arises as to the applicability of its results across cultures.[10] For the purposes of the present discussion, the following fundamental distinctions are in order. All mammals have a tendency to withdraw in the face of a threat, if neither fight nor flight is possible, and in humans such withdrawal tends to involve dissociation as described above.[11] Certain responses to stress are common among all mammals as a result of their social nature. For instance, young mammals tend to seek security in bonding with a caregiver, and significant disruptions in such bonding cause acute distress that may alter brain development. Among humans it is common for traumatic stress adversely to affect assumptions of safety, dignity, agency, and solidarity, as described above. Nevertheless, culturally specific factors are significant in determining perceptions of what is necessary to ensure these things and, by extension, to threaten them.

Broadly speaking, Marten deVries has suggested that psychology is powerful for explaining immediate reactions to trauma across cultures, while culture and social support provide important explanatory paradigms for how recovery occurs after trauma.[12] The three basic tasks for recovery from trauma described by Herman correspond so directly to typical immediate reactions to trauma that their applicability across cultures seems reasonable, while accomplishment of the tasks occurs in socially and culturally specific ways.

---

10. On this issue, in the present volume see the discussion of Schreiter, which cites personal experience as well as the work of cultural psychoanalyst Vamik Volkan. See also David M. Carr "Appendix: Contemporary Study of Trauma and Ancient Trauma," in his *Holy Resilience*, 253–70.

11. The present observations concerning mammals rely on van der Kolk, *The Body Keeps the Score*.

12. Marten W. deVries, "Trauma in Cultural Perspective," in van der Kolk, McFarlane, and Weisaeth, 398–413, esp. 410.

Insights from Sociology: Collective Trauma and Recovery

As trauma was recognized and accepted as a psychological phenomenon, the concept began to appear in other fields of study, including sociology and refugee studies. *Trauma* occurs alongside *disaster* to name overwhelming collective experiences of suffering. Although there is reasonable consensus as to the processes of individual trauma and recovery, shaped in part by the development of diagnostic categories,[13] the description of trauma at the communal and social level is less settled. Two theories are currently influential, and while these theories define collective or social trauma differently, central insights of the two do complement each other.

Kai Erikson describes collective trauma as "a blow to the basic tissues of social life that damages the bonds attaching people together and impairs the prevailing sense of communality."[14] Jeffrey Alexander, by contrast, describes collective trauma as a social process by which a collective adopts a particular trauma narrative. This narrative does four things: it identifies a group that is perceived to have undergone grave suffering *as a group*; it describes the nature of the suffering experienced; it identifies the agents responsible for causing the suffering; and it appeals to a wider audience to identify with the victim group. Once accepted, such a narrative forms a basis of group identity.[15]

The two theorists are attending to different social processes. Erikson is more concerned with processes that fragment social cohesion, while Alexander is more focused on processes that (re)construct communal identity. The complementarity of the two descriptions emerges in light of analogies to the description of psychological trauma in individuals given above. The

---

13. Note, however, that there are dissenting voices with regard to the role of memory and traumatic stress. See, for example, Amir Kadhem, "Cultural Trauma as a Social Construct: 9/11 Fiction and the Epistemology of Communal Pain," *Intertexts* 18 (2014): 181–97; and Joshua Pederson, "Speak Trauma: Towards a Revised Understanding of Literary Trauma Theory," *Narrative* 22 (2014): 333–53.

14. Kai Erikson, *A New Species of Trouble: Explorations in Disaster, Trauma, and Community* (New York: Norton, 1994); Erikson, "Notes on Trauma and Community," in *Trauma: Explorations in Memory*, ed. Cathy Caruth (Baltimore: Johns Hopkins University Press, 1995), 187. For a detailed discussion of Erikson's work and an application of it to Qoheleth, see the essay by Browning Helsel in the present volume.

15. Jeffrey Alexander, *Trauma: A Social Theory* (Cambridge: Polity, 2012). For an application of Alexander's work to Lamentations, see the essay by Boase in the present volume.

immediate ruptures in social fabric that certain events can cause correspond to the immediate disruption to the normal psychic functioning of an individual. As the immediate psychic effects of an individual trauma occur largely out of the awareness of the individual, in like manner the immediate harmful social effects of a collective experience tend to occur out of the immediate awareness of the collective as a collective.[16] In individual trauma, it is the unease felt by the survivor that motivates engagement in the challenging process of reinterpretation of the traumatic experience necessary to create a narrative of the trauma. In a collective, it is a shared sense of suffering felt by the collective that motivates certain groups to propose narratives to name and account for the suffering and that also moves the collective to accept a given narrative. Erikson captures the reality that the social fabric of a collective can be severely ruptured, irrespective of whether the collective has adopted a common narrative to account for the suffering. Alexander captures the reality that, when the group accepts a narrative for its collective suffering, that narrative has a capacity to shape the identity of the collective. By way of contrast, events that may rupture the social fabric of the collective but lack such a narrative do not have such a capacity.[17]

Comparison with the description of addressing the effects of individual trauma also points to modes of addressing collective trauma aside from the process of creating a discursive trauma narrative as described by Alexander. A process of representing and interpreting individual trauma may include nondiscursive as well as discursive symbolic representation. The same holds for representing and interpreting events that rupture social bonds. Moreover, just as the establishment of safety and the cultivation of interpersonal solidarity are crucial in recovery from the effects of individual trauma, both activities can cultivate basic social bonds, especially when enacted on a large scale. Social bonds may be reestablished through

---

16. Note, however, that the social erosion identified by Erikson is something that only becomes apparent over time (Erikson, "Notes on Trauma," 187).

17. By way of example, Volker Heins and Andreas Langenohl ("A Fire that Doesn't Burn? The Allied Bombing of Germany and the Cultural Politics of Trauma," in *Narrating Trauma: On the Impact of Collective Suffering*, ed. Ron Eyerman, Jeffrey C. Alexander, and Elizabeth Butler Breese [Boulder, CO: Paradigm, 2013], 3–26) argue that the collective suffering that resulted from the Allies' bombing of German cities in World War II did not give rise to a cultural trauma, not because the suffering did not exist, but because it was not represented as such.

a variety of media, including texts (of all forms), memorial sites and practices, and participation in ritual. Religious ritual can cultivate safety, nur-
ture social bonds, and foster both discursive and nondiscursive modes of
representing collective suffering.[18]

Insights from Literary Trauma Theory: Reading Literature though the
Lens of Trauma

Trauma as an area of study constitutes a significant field within literary
and cultural studies, as well as within the wider domains of the humanities. Scholars in the field of comparative literature have studied writings
that emerged in the wake of horrific events of the twentieth century, such
as the Holocaust and the bombings of Hiroshima and Nagasaki, referring
to such literature as *trauma* or *survival literature*.[19] Literary trauma theory
is concerned with the ways that trauma may be encoded within texts, on
the ways that texts may function in witnessing to trauma, and on the ways
that texts may facilitate recovery and resilience.[20]

As already noted, people who experience overwhelming events may
have limited or distorted memory or knowledge of the events, and they may
have difficulty recounting what has occurred. Trauma, therefore, resists
expression because of its wounding impact on the psyche, yet the representation of trauma is central to the process of recovery and resilience. Literature is, of course, a form of representation, so, to the degree that trauma
is considered unknowable and unassimilated, the concept of a literature of
trauma seems an impossibility. However, texts can and do witness to trauma
and are thus responsive to the needs of individuals and communities.

Trauma theory as a literary enterprise emerged through the work of
the so-called Yale school, in particular in the work of its leading exponent, Cathy Caruth. Influenced by Freudian psychoanalysis, poststructuralist literary theory, and neuro-biological insights concerning traumatic

---

18. In the present volume, the essays of Browning Helsel, Schreiter, and West give
particular attention to the importance of ritual practice in facilitating processes of
recovery and resilience.

19. For an overview of the work of theorists Terrence des Pres, Cathy Caruth, and
Robert Jay Lifton and the characteristics of this body of literature that they discuss, see
Garber, "Trauma Theory," 26–29.

20. In the present volume, the essay of Poser offers a robust integration of literary
theory and psychological theory.

memory, literary trauma theory maintains as a cornerstone the unknowability of trauma. Because the traumatic event is not experienced as it occurs, there is an inability to construct meaning in the wake of events or to incorporate the event in normal meaning-making structures. Trauma is experienced only belatedly "in its repeated *possession* of the one who experiences it."[21] Literary trauma theory attends to the representation of delayed or unassimilated memory in language.

Texts witness to trauma through their encoding of the not yet fully known or fully assimilated memories that are present in the form of absences, gaps, and repetitions. Texts become representations of trauma as much through what is unspoken as through what is spoken. The form of literary expression—the gaps, repetitions, and aporias—bear witness to trauma. Shoshanna Felman places emphasis on literary fragments as (further) witness to trauma. In discussing testimony to trauma, Felman notes: "As a relation to events, testimony seems to be composed of bits and pieces of a memory that has been overwhelmed by occurrences that have not settled into understanding or remembrance, acts that cannot be construed as knowledge nor assimilated into full cognition."[22]

Because it is alert to the way that the unknown and unassimilated is encoded, trauma theory is able to "make sense" of gaps and disjunctions within texts, pointing to the impact of the often-violent disruptions that lie behind the textual world. Trauma theory is able to account for the form of texts cognizant of historical contingencies and sensitive to the way a text might enter into a rhetorical context. Texts may represent and interpret trauma, thus functioning as a means of facilitating recovery and resilience for both individuals and communities.

In considering the ways that texts might facilitate recovery and resilience, we return to the paradoxical impulses of language in the wake of trauma. Trauma both resists yet demands expression to facilitate recovery and resilience. Trauma leads to the disintegration of language yet relies on language in its more integrative capacity.

Ronald Granofsky holds these paradoxical impulses in tension through the exploration of what he refers to as *symbolization* in literature. Granofsky is concerned with what he has identified as a subgenre of the modern novel—the trauma novel—which he distinguishes from other

---

21. Cathy Caruth, "Introduction," in Caruth, *Trauma*, 4.
22. Shoshanna Felman, "Education and Crisis, or the Vicissitudes of Teaching," in Caruth, *Trauma*, 16.

novels by "the exploration through the agency of literary symbolism of the individual experience of collective trauma, either actual events of the past, alarming tendencies of the present, or imagined horrors of the future."[23] He argues that linguistic symbols, in pointing beyond themselves, effectively link individual and communal experiences and at the same time allow traumatic memories to be confronted "at a distance," thus allowing for a " 'safe' confrontation with traumatic experience."[24] He suggests that symbolism "breaks down order only to create a new or greater order."[25] In terms of literary form, this process of symbolization/symbolic enactment occurs through three phases or responses, which Granofsky argues bears some resemblance to the psychological impact of trauma: fragmentation (the attempt to depict what cannot be assimilated), regression (the avoidance of the trauma), and reunification (the integration of the trauma into a narrative scripts).[26]

Trauma Hermeneutics in Biblical Studies

Interest in the hermeneutical value of trauma as a distinct category of suffering represents a development in what began in the 1970s among biblical scholars as a turn toward a rich appreciation of the psychological, social, political, and economic dimensions of human suffering. Powerfully illustrating this turn, Claus Westermann's landmark article of 1974 recognized the theological import of the human function of lament in the Old Testament. In an especially pregnant statement, he observed: "The lament is the language of suffering; in it suffering is given the dignity of language: It will not stay silent!"[27] Perhaps most influential in the hermeneutical turn to human dimensions has been the emergence of liberationist perspectives that focus on an array of particular and related aspects of systemic oppression. A hermeneutics of trauma is convergent with such approaches while promising to bring fresh insight, especially at the nexus of individual, collective, systemic, and semiotic dimensions of experience.

---

23. Ronald Granofsky, *The Trauma Novel: Contemporary Symbolic Depictions of Collective Disaster* (New York: Lang, 1995), 5.

24. Ibid., 6–7.

25. Ibid., 9.

26. Ibid., 18–19.

27. Claus Westermann, "The Role of the Lament in the Theology of the Old Testament," *Int* 28 (1974): 31.

In the turn to trauma as a hermeneutical lens, what is emerging is not a single methodological approach but rather a heuristic framework. Through sensitivity to the nexus between historical events and literary representation, this framework has the capacity to bring into focus the relationship between traumatic experience and both the production and the appropriation of texts. Fundamentally, a hermeneutics of trauma is attuned to the fact that language can encode and respond to traumatic experience in ways that correspond to the effects of trauma as well as to mechanisms of survival, recovery, and resilience. Moreover, as already noted, the context of a trauma narrative may organize such language into narrative elements that are linear as well as nonlinear, logical as well as imagistic.

A hermeneutics of trauma holds promise for biblical studies in two fundamental respects. First, by attentiveness to insights into human experience that reveal meaning not captured by the plain sense of a text, a hermeneutics of trauma can complement a range of interpretive approaches. These include historical critical as well as more theoretically oriented critical methods. Second, this framework illuminates both ancient and present contexts. When considering texts in their ancient contexts, it may reveal new aspects of meaning and function. Related to appropriating the biblical text within present contexts of discourse and praxis, this framework may offer new insights on questions in the areas of systematic, moral, and pastoral theology, as well as inform pastoral praxis with those affected by trauma.

When biblical scholars employ trauma hermeneutics to explore texts that have emerged out of contexts of trauma, they attend to the historical realities of traumatic violence and the disruptive and enduring impacts of those events on individuals and communities. In doing so, they are able to build upon the results of historical-critical approaches by accounting for features of the text that reflect psychological, cultural, and sociological impacts of traumatic events. Of particular interest are texts that have emerged from experiences of collective devastation, exile, or oppression.

When considering such texts in their ancient contexts, trauma hermeneutics may bring to light rationales for asserting aspects of meaning not previously recognized or that may call into question existing interpretations. Recognizing the ways that texts reflect traumatic experience can illuminate a level of meaning other than the plain sense of the language. Attention to the way that trauma narratives may represent past events in fragmented or impressionistic images, sometimes utilizing affective or bodily imagery, disabuses the interpreter of the assumption that such imagery must be explained in terms of a plain-sense account of events. A trauma hermeneutic can offer a rationale for the manner in which such alternative meaning would have rung true with the ancient audience.

In a similar way, a hermeneutics of trauma brings new dimensions to literary approaches to texts that have emerged out of contexts of trauma by taking seriously their historical contexts. A literary approach to trauma hermeneutics may narrow its focus to ways in which a text reflects the trauma experienced by those who generated the text. Biblical interpreters, however, have found it particularly productive to consider the appropriation of the biblical text by traumatized populations in both ancient and present contexts. Literary trauma theory attends to the way that texts link experiences of suffering, "structures of subjective and collective experience, and discursive and aesthetic forms."[28] Because it is alert to the way that the unknown and unassimilated is encoded, trauma theory is able to *make sense* of gaps and disjunctions within texts, pointing to the impact of the often-violent disruptions that lie behind the textual world. Interpreters cognizant of the historical contingencies behind the biblical text can use trauma theory to account for certain textual features. They do so by being sensitive to the way the text might enter into a rhetorical context to represent and interpret trauma, thus functioning as a means of facilitating recovery and resilience for both individuals and communities.

In addition to texts that arguably emerged from historical situations of trauma, biblical scholars may apply a hermeneutics of trauma also to texts that contain themes or other features related to trauma but for which an origin in actual historical trauma is uncertain. Here one may consider narratives such as those in Ruth or Job as well as prayers, especially many psalms.[29] Even while bracketing consideration of the historical origins of a given text, interpreters may use insights from contemporary trauma studies to interpret characters in relation to situations of trauma as constructed in the world of the biblical text, drawing implications for readers both in antiquity and in the present.

Whether or not a text originated in a historical context of trauma, a hermeneutics of trauma inquires into how appropriation of the bibli-

---

28. Michael Rothberg, "Preface: Beyond Tancred and Clorinda—Trauma Studies for Implicated Subjects," in *The Future of Trauma Theory: Contemporary Literary and Cultural Criticism*, ed. Gert Buelens, Sam Durrant, and Robert Eaglestone (London: Routledge, 2014), xiii.

29. See the essays of West and Strawn in this volume.

cal text might have a capacity to affect individuals and collectives as they survive the effects of trauma or face ongoing (potentially) traumatic situations. Trauma studies affirm the importance of creating a trauma narrative, a coherent narrative capable not only of processing past trauma but also of fostering resilience against further traumatization. Such narratives serve to construct identity and solidarity in ways that can restore healthy assumptions about the self in relation to the world.

Biblical scholars have long recognized that an important function of many biblical texts in antiquity involved their appropriation for the purpose of constructing identity in relationship to God, especially in the wake of disaster. Trauma hermeneutics recognizes that trauma erodes aspects of identity and solidarity necessary for well-being. Individuals as well as collectives who have fragile identity and experience diminished solidarity are less resilient in the face of potential trauma. Trauma hermeneutics reflects upon the capacity of the text to support both solidarity and identity in ways that enhance well-being. In various circumstances, certain biblical narratives would have resonated sufficiently with collectives and individuals to be adopted by them as their own. While it is useful to consider the individual and collective dimensions of this process of appropriation separately, the two are intimately related.

Individual survivors of trauma typically require support from trusted others to assist them in the task of constructing a trauma narrative. The tendency of trauma to interfere with the ability of individual survivors to give voice to their experience underscores the value of the biblical text for offering words that resonate with the experiences of collectives and individuals. To supplement Westermann's observation that lament gives suffering the dignity of language, grasping the effects of trauma helps to explain why many who suffer have such difficulty finding the necessary language to express their experience. Understanding the effects of trauma on both memory and assumptions helps interpreters to recognize features in biblical texts that would have been likely to resonate with traumatized readers in the past and that might retain that capacity in the present.

Of particular concern within biblical studies is the way that texts may have been appropriated within communal contexts as a means of shaping collective identity, particularly in relation to disasters that may have fragmented the community. Sociological insights into the effects of trauma on the social body provide opportunities for interpreters to identify fragmentation of communal identity and, conversely, mechanisms that might have forged new identities. What is of concern is the way that meaning-making occurs within the social body, creating narratives of social suffering that shape collective identities through the ideologies and interests projected. Sociological approaches attend well to the social dimensions of texts and are sensitive to the function that texts might play within their rhetorical contexts. Such approaches are aware that collective traumatization occurs within particular ideological and symbolic frameworks that are intimately tied to the dynamics of power within the social group.

A primary location for the identity-forming appropriation of biblical texts from antiquity to the present has been ritual, understood as performance enacted in spaces and times set apart from the ordinary.[30] To the extent that any prayerful appropriation of a biblical text, whether in personal or collective settings, is set apart from ordinary activity, it may be considered ritualized. When survivors of trauma draw upon biblical resources in telling and interpreting their own stories, it is of vital importance to ensure that the ritual space for this activity is safe and that participants create a sense of solidarity. This recognition invites investigation into ways in which the safety and solidarity among trauma survivors may have been preserved in ancient contexts of appropriation and opens pathways for understanding the ongoing power of texts to address the needs of individuals and communities in contemporary contexts.

Because of the way it allows recognition of a rationale for the juxtaposition of seemingly disparate elements in a trauma narrative, trauma hermeneutics facilitates a nuanced interpretation of some of the more difficult and disconcerting aspects of biblical texts. Of particular significance is the amount of violent imagery in the text and the ways in which the overall coherence of certain texts can be difficult to ascertain. To grasp the ways in which language can represent trauma opens up new avenues for understanding violent imagery, especially violent depictions of God, and sheds light on organizing principles.

Among the seemingly disparate elements of the biblical text that trauma hermeneutics illuminates are depictions of the behaviors and atti-

---

30. On the liturgical/ritual character of contexts in which biblical traditions were appropriated, see Jon D. Levenson, *Creation and the Persistence of Evil: The Jewish Drama of Divine Omnipotence* (Princeton: Princeton University Press, 1994); Levenson, *Sinai and Zion: An Entry into the Jewish Bible* (Minneapolis: Winston, 1985); and Gordon Lathrop, *The Four Gospels on Sunday: The New Testament and the Reform of Christian Worship* (Minneapolis: Fortress, 2012). For the last of these references, we are indebted to John Baldovin, S.J.

tudes of YHWH that seem violent and even abusive, especially when considered alongside other biblical depictions that appear compassionate and merciful. A growing body of interpretation suggests that in many cases representations of violence in the biblical text, including those attributed to divine agency, can be accurately understood as symbolic representations corresponding to actual violence experienced by survivors of trauma.[31] As representations of trauma, they transfer causality from the sphere of human agency to the divine realm, and with that shift a variety of traditional narrative strands and rationales become available with which to confront harmful assumptions and beliefs prompted by the actual violations. In many cases, biblical texts attributing suffering to dehumanizing violations enacted by God as punishment can be understood as representations of trauma that serve as mechanisms of survival, recovery, or resilience. This observation has provided interpreters with a rationale for dismissing the conclusion that the texts accurately represent what is characteristic of God.[32] In other words, trauma theory allows interpreters who otherwise might feel compelled simply to reject such imagery altogether to recognize within the images a limited beneficial utility.[33]

To the degree that a biblical text functioned as a trauma narrative, its coherence does not depend solely on linear logic, in the form of either a single plot or explanation for what caused the trauma. The overall narrative may contain different and perhaps conflicting strands of narrative, and it may include poetic and imagistic representations. Coherence depends on the capacity of each constituent element of the overall narrative to construct meaning from the traumatic experience, as judged by the degree to which the element rings true with the survivors. For instance, Jeremiah, Ezekiel, and Lamentations have posed challenges for interpreters based on questions relating to their conceptual and formal coherence, and trauma hermeneutics has proven helpful in addressing these questions.[34]

---

31. In the present volume, see the essays by Boase, Frechette, Odell, Poser, and Stulman.

32. See, for example, Carr, *Holy Resilience*; Kathleen M. O'Connor, *Jeremiah: Pain and Promise* (Minneapolis: Fortress, 2011); and Louis Stulman, *Jeremiah*, AOTC (Nashville: Abingdon, 2005). In the present volume, see the essays of Frechette, Odell, and Poser.

33. Christopher G. Frechette, "The Old Testament as Controlled Substance: How Insights from Trauma Studies Reveal Healing Capacities in Potentially Harmful Texts," *Int* 69 (2015): 20–34.

34. See Stulman, *Jeremiah*; Ruth Poser, *Das Ezechielbuch als Trauma-Literatur*,

BIBLE THROUGH THE LENS OF TRAUMA

Each of the essays within this volume engages critically with hermeneutical questions, demonstrating the ways in which employing the lens of trauma offers fresh insights into a range of biblical texts. The essays are organized under three topics that correspond at least obliquely to issues of theory and method addressed in the essays. While many of the essays may address more than one of those topics, the present organization attempts to highlight a central concern of each essay.

Although it is helpful to distinguish between the individual and collective dimensions of trauma, the biblical text often blurs the distinction. In the first section, papers by Ruth Poser, Elizabeth Boase, Christopher G. Frechette, and Philip Browning Helsel integrate insights concerning the collective dimension of trauma to elucidate the way in which the biblical text, often by means of imagery involving individuals, would have addressed the collective trauma of the biblical community.

Of these essays, those of Poser and Boase delineate ways in which trauma is able to account for a variety of elements of form and content as responses to traumatic experience. The essay of Poser includes a précis of her argument that the book of Ezekiel has a three-part structure corresponding to the three major elements of a *trauma novel* as developed by Granofsky.[35] Poser reads multiple features of the book, including its violent imagery, as both a witness to its traumatic origins and a narrative that facilitates the movement beyond trauma. Boase's essay demonstrates how the whole of Lamentations corresponds to the elements of Alexander's social process for constructing collective solidarity and identity in the wake of collective suffering.

In his essay concerning God's violation of Daughter Babylon in Isa 47, Frechette offers a psychological explanation for the idea that God's *nāqām* (usually translated "vengeance") against Babylon represents the removal of Babylon as an obstacle to the realization of the hopeful message of Isa 40–54. Frechette explains this obstacle in terms of the Judahites' harmful internalized assumptions linked to their collective violation by the Babylonians during the destruction of Jerusalem and forced migration to Babylon.

VTSup 154 (Leiden: Brill, 2012); Kathleen M. O'Connor, *Lamentations and the Tears of the World* (Maryknoll, NY: Orbis, 2002); and the essay of Boase in the present volume.

35. Poser, *Das Ezechielbuch.*

Browning Helsel uses the lens of trauma to argue that the texts in Qoheleth advocating pleasurable experience are best understood not in fatalistic terms but rather as effectively addressing collective trauma resulting from chronic oppression in the ancient context. Such oppression would have severely eroded the communal solidarity necessary to engage in relating to God, but the shared bodily pleasure advocated in Qoheleth would have helped to establish communal solidarity.

Newer methods in biblical criticism sometimes meet resistance among practitioners of historical-critical methods. In the second section, essays by Margaret S. Odell and Louis Stulman demonstrate how the use of trauma theory can foster new insights into classic historical-critical questions.

Odell's essay offers compelling insight into the contested interpretation of particular phrases in Ezek 16 having to do with male images and the sacrifice of children. Odell reinterprets the problematic references to ṣalmê zākār and child sacrifice in Ezek 16:15–22 as fragments of traumatic memory of political subjugation under the Assyrian Empire.

Stulman's essay demonstrates that both prose and poetic sections of Jeremiah functioned to make meaning of catastrophic events. He argues that the representations of the excessive guilt of the people as described in the Deuteronomic prose sections of the book interpret the devastation wrought by the Babylonians to be punishment from YHWH. Calling into question the historical accuracy of such representations, Stulman emphasizes that they function as assertions of order in the face of chaos.

The essays in the third section of the book all engage questions relating to the appropriation of the text in ways that support survival, resilience, and recovery in the face of trauma. The essays draw explicit links between ancient and present contexts.

The essay by Brent A. Strawn demonstrates the restorative capacity of incorporating texts from the biblical psalms into one's own disclosure of the thoughts and feelings prompted by traumatic experiences. Strawn emphasizes that such texts in present as well as ancient contexts can function prescriptively by providing readers with language that, as a crucial step in recovery, leads them through a process of articulating traumatic experience in the presence of others and of God.

The essay by Samuel E. Balentine signals the importance of trauma hermeneutics for addressing problems that arise when readers employ a plain-sense hermeneutic to read biblical narratives that portray God as carrying out judicial penalties that involve enacting events that traumatize. The inadequacy of such a reading becomes clear in light of Balentine's observation that reading such texts in this way invites humans to model their interactions on God's example.

L. Juliana M. Claassens's essay employs Judith Herman's work on trauma and recovery to argue that several features of the story of the rape of Tamar in 2 Sam 13 point to Tamar's preservation of agency and her capacity for resistance, survival, and recovery. Claassens suggests that the story has the capacity to raise awareness concerning sexual violence and to challenge readers of any era to resist it.

In his essay, Robert J. Schreiter discusses insights gained from reading biblical texts through the lens of trauma and brings them into dialogue with a rich understanding of the concept of resilience. He offers several specific suggestions for the potential of trauma hermeneutics to open fresh perspectives into a number of theological issues, particularly in the area of soteriology.

The essay by Gerald O. West highlights the capacity of passages of protest in the book of Job to validate the voices of marginalized persons living with HIV/AIDS in South Africa. West's essay thus acknowledges the crucial importance of creating a safe ritual space in which to invite traumatized persons to share with each other as they articulate their own narratives.

Peter Yuichi Clark argues that the letter of 2 Corinthians might aid readers affected by trauma through its modeling of a way of thriving in the midst of trauma and suffering. Clark points to features in 2 Corinthians suggesting that Paul was able to draw upon his solidarity with fellow Christians as well as his relationship with God in order to foster both recovery and resilience in the face of (potentially) traumatizing experiences.

Semeia Studies has a tradition of interdisciplinary engagement, and in keeping with that tradition the essays in its volumes often include responses from scholars in fields beyond biblical studies. While the present volume does not include such responses, it embodies the tradition of interdisciplinary engagement in two respects. All of the essays by biblical scholars employ methods from disciplines outside of traditional biblical studies. Moreover, three of the essays were written by scholars from fields outside of biblical studies. Browning Helsel and Clark bring biblical studies into conversation with their specialization in pastoral theology; Schreiter, a systematic theologian, offers a lucid appraisal of what is happening in biblical hermeneutics of trauma regarding resilience and proposes pathways forward for how trauma hermeneutics, both biblical and beyond, can enrich constructive work in theology.

Bibliography

Alexander, Jeffrey. *Trauma: A Social Theory.*Cambridge: Polity, 2012.

Becker, Eve-Marie, Jan Dochhorn, and Else Holt, eds. *Trauma and Traumatization in Individual and Collective Dimensions: Insights from Biblical Studies and Beyond.* SANt 2. Göttingen: Vandenhoeck & Ruprecht, 2014.

Boase, Elizabeth, and Sarah Agnew. "'Whispered in the Sound of Silence': Traumatizing the Book of Jonah." *Bible and Critical Theory* 12 (2016): 4–22.

Brett, Mark G. *Political Trauma and Healing: Biblical Ethics for a Postcolonial World.* Grand Rapids: Eerdmans, 2016.

Carr, David M. *Holy Resilience: The Bible's Traumatic Origins.* New Haven: Yale University Press, 2014.

Caruth, Cathy. "Introduction." Pages 3–12 in *Trauma: Explorations in Memory.* Edited by Cathy Caruth. Baltimore: Johns Hopkins University Press, 1995.

Craske, Michelle G. *Cognitive-Behavioral Therapy.* Theories of Psychotherapy Series Washington, DC: American Psychological Association, 2010.

deVries, Marten W. "Trauma in Cultural Perspective." Pages 398–413 in *Traumatic Stress: The Effects of Overwhelming Experience on Mind, Body, and Society.* Edited by Bessel A. van der Kolk, Alexander McFarlane, and Lars Weisaeth. New York: Guilford, 2007.

Diagnostic and Statistical Manual of Mental Disorders: DSM-5. 5th ed. Arlington, VA: American Psychiatric Association, 2013.

Erikson, Kai. *A New Species of Trouble: Explorations in Disaster, Trauma, and Community.* New York: Norton, 1994

———. "Notes on Trauma and Community." Pages 183–99 in *Trauma: Explorations in Memory.* Edited by Cathy Caruth. Baltimore: Johns Hopkins University Press, 1995.

Felman, Shoshanna. "Education and Crisis, or the Vicissitudes of Teaching," Pages 13–60 in *Trauma: Explorations in Memory.* Edited by Cathy Caruth. Baltimore: Johns Hopkins University Press, 1995.

Frechette, Christopher G. "The Old Testament as Controlled Substance: How Insights from Trauma Studies Reveal Healing Capacities in Potentially Harmful Texts." *Int* 69 (2015): 20–34.

———. "Two Biblical Motifs of Divine Violence as Resources for Meaning-Making in Engaging Self-Blame and Rage after Traumatization." *Journal of Pastoral Psychology*, forthcoming.

Garber, David G. "Trauma Theory and Biblical Studies." *CurBR* 14 (2015): 24–44.

Granofsky, Ronald. *The Trauma Novel: Contemporary Symbolic Depictions of Collective Disaster*. New York: Lang, 1995.

Heins, Volker, and Andreas Langenohl. "A Fire that Doesn't Burn? The Allied Bombing of Germany and the Cultural Politics of Trauma." Pages 3–26 in *Narrating Trauma: On the Impact of Collective Suffering*. Edited by Ron Eyerman, Jeffrey C. Alexander, and Elizabeth Butler Breese. Boulder, CO: Paradigm, 2013.

Herman, Judith Lewis. *Trauma and Recovery: The Aftermath of Violence—From Domestic Abuse to Political Terror*. Rev. ed. New York: Basic Books, 1997.

International Statistical Classification of Diseases and Related Health Problems. 10th revision. 3 vols. Geneva: World Health Organization, 1992–1994.

Kadhem, Amir. "Cultural Trauma as a Social Construct: 9/11 Fiction and the Epistemology of Communal Pain." *Intertexts* 18 (2014): 181–97.

Kauffman, Jeffrey, ed. *Loss of the Assumptive World: A Theory of Traumatic Loss*. New York: Brunner-Routledge, 2002.

Kolk, Bessel A. van der. *The Body Keeps the Score: Brain, Mind, and Body in the Healing of Trauma*. New York: Viking, 2014.

Kolk, Bessel A. van der, Lars Weisaeth, and Onno van der Hart. "History of Trauma in Psychiatry." Pages 47–74 in *Traumatic Stress: The Effects of Overwhelming Experience on Mind, Body, and Society*. Edited by Bessel A. van der Kolk, Alexander McFarlane, and Lars Weisaeth. New York: Guilford, 2007.

Lathrop, Gordon. *The Four Gospels on Sunday: The New Testament and the Reform of Christian Worship*. Minneapolis: Fortress, 2012.

Levenson, Jon D. *Creation and the Persistence of Evil: The Jewish Drama of Divine Omnipotence*. Princeton: Princeton University Press, 1994.

———. *Sinai and Zion: An Entry into the Jewish Bible*. Minneapolis: Winston, 1985.

Luckhurst, Roger. *The Trauma Question*. London: Routledge, 2008.

O'Connor, Kathleen M. *Genesis*. Smith & Helwys Commentary Series. Macon, GA: Smith & Helwys, forthcoming.

———. *Jeremiah: Pain and Promise*. Minneapolis: Fortress, 2011.

————. *Lamentations and the Tears of the World.* Maryknoll, NY: Orbis, 2002.

Park, Crystal L. "Making Sense of the Meaning Literature: An Integrative Review of Meaning Making and Its Effects on Adjustment to Stressful Life Events." *Psychological Bulletin* 136 (2010): 257–301.

Pederson, Joshua. "Speak Trauma: Towards a Revised Understanding of Literary Trauma Theory." *Narrative* 22 (2014): 333–53.

Poser, Ruth. *Das Ezechielbuch als Trauma-Literatur.* VTSup 154. Leiden: Brill, 2012.

Rothberg, Michael. "Preface: Beyond Tancred and Clorinda—Trauma Studies for Implicated Subjects." Pages xi–xviii in *The Future of Trauma Theory: Contemporary Literary and Cultural Criticism.* Edited by Gert Buelens, Sam Durrant, and Robert Eaglestone. London: Routledge, 2014.

Stulman, Louis. *Jeremiah.* AOTC. Nashville: Abingdon, 2005.

"Trauma and Faith." *Int* 69 (2015).

Westermann, Claus. "The Role of the Lament in the Theology of the Old Testament." *Int* 28 (1974): 20–38.

1

Between Individual and Collective Dimensions of Trauma

No Words: The Book of Ezekiel as Trauma Literature and a Response to Exile[*]

Ruth Poser

The book of Ezekiel strikes us as strange. Readers find the enormous amount of violence contained in the text disturbing or even shy away from reading it altogether. The characters in the narrative appear only as people wounded, tortured, or devastated by acts of war; the catastrophe seems to have broken them all: the prophet himself, the people of Israel, the populations of surrounding nations. Even YHWH is portrayed as affected by the violence and brutality.

Over the course of time, interpreters have repeatedly seen this as an indication that Ezekiel was mentally ill, but simultaneously many have regarded the prophet as the (single) historical author of the ancient text as it has come down to us.[1] In recent years, several commentators have offered a diagnosis of posttraumatic stress disorder.[2] This disease-based approach tends largely to overlook the fact that the book of Ezekiel is a literary text from which we cannot deduce either the specific circumstances

---

[*] Deborah L. Schneider translated this essay from the original German, including all quotations that were originally in German. An abbreviated version of this essay appeared as "Verlorene Sprache: Das Ezechielbuch als literarische Auseinandersetzung mit dem Trauma des babylonischen Exils," *Pastoraltheologie* 105 (2016): 121–38.

1. See, for example, August Klostermann, "Ezechiel: Ein Beitrag zu besserer Würdigung seiner Person und Schrift," *TSK* 50 (1877): 391–439; Edwin C. Broome, "Ezekiel's Abnormal Personality," *JBL* 65 (1946): 277–92; Karl Jaspers, "Der Prophet Ezechiel: Eine pathographische Studie" [1947], in Jaspers, *Rechenschaft und Ausblick: Reden und Aufsätze* (Munich: Piper, 1951): 95–106.

2. For example, Derek M. Daschke, "Desolate among Them: Loss, Fantasy and Recovery in the Book of Ezekiel," *American Imago* 56 (1999): 105–32; Daniel L. Smith-Christopher, *A Biblical Theology of Exile*, OBT (Minneapolis: Fortress, 2002), 74–104; Nancy R. Bowen, *Ezekiel*, AOTC (Nashville: Abingdon, 2010), xv–xix.

of its production or a specific author.[3] However, we do know that the book took shape in the context of the siege warfare and mass deportation that Judah experienced in the early sixth century BCE. In my view, convergent insights from psycho-traumatology and literary studies into the phenomenon of traumatization facilitate interpretation of the book of Ezekiel as it reflects both individual and collective dimensions of those experiences. Such insights can serve as a key to understanding the violence in Ezekiel.[4]

In the two major sections that follow, I aim to demonstrate how insights from psycho-traumatology and literary studies prove helpful for interpreting specific textual features as well as larger patterns of organization in Ezekiel. My focus is on how certain features may represent or interpret aspects of the traumatic experience, despite the impossibility of fully communicating that experience. The first section (§1) employs psychological categories to explain features of the text that reflect aspects of traumatization and strategies for addressing them. The second (§2) turns to literary theory, identifying Ezekiel as a work of fiction (a trauma narrative) in order to explore again the book's potential to represent trauma and facilitate recovery.

1. TRAUMA AND THE STRUGGLE FOR LANGUAGE

1.1. Ezekiel in a Context of Trauma

Textual, visual, and archeological sources document the great trauma associated with crucial historical events that, according to the book of Ezekiel itself, took place not long before its composition: the siege, fall, and destruction of Jerusalem between 589/588–587/586 BCE; and the deportation of prisoners and life in forced exile from 598/597 BCE on. Those affected by the siege experienced "famine, pestilence, and the sword" (see Ezek 5:12; 7:15), atrocities, torture, forms of sexual or sexualized violence, pillaging, and arson. Deportees had to endure a grueling

---

3. Compare Stephen Garfinkel, "Another Model for Ezekiel's Abnormalities," *JANESCU* 19 (1989): 39–50.

4. Compare David G. Garber, "Traumatizing Ezekiel, the Exilic Prophet," in *Psychology and the Bible: A New Way to Read the Scriptures 2* (*From Genesis to Apocalyptic Vision*), ed. J. Harold Ellens and Wayne G. Rollins (Westport, CT: Praeger, 2004), 215–35; Brad E. Kelle, "Dealing with the Trauma of Defeat: The Rhetoric of the Devastation and Rejuvenation of Nature in Ezekiel," *JBL* 128 (2009): 469–90.

forced march over hundreds of miles. They witnessed the weakening and death of fellow captives. Families were torn apart, and most exiles had no hope of ever returning home. If we take this background as factual and visualize it as a concrete reality, it becomes possible to read the book of Ezekiel in a new light: as a literary confrontation with the violence of war that men, women, and children actually experienced and as a theological example of trauma literature.[5]

In order to discuss Ezekiel as trauma literature, the following definition of trauma provides a starting point:

> [It is the] experience of a fundamental discrepancy between a threatening situation and an individual's possibilities for overcoming it. This experience is accompanied by feelings of helplessness, defenselessness, and abandonment and can permanently disrupt the person's understanding of the self and the world.[6]

Hence *trauma* is not an inherent element of an event or experience as such;[7] not everyone exposed to a potentially traumatizing event develops traumatic symptoms or syndromes. Nevertheless, survivors of war, torture, and sexual violence are affected with particular frequency, as are those who have had to flee or been expelled from their homelands. In general, we can assume that "the traumatizing effect of an event increases according to the size of the role that human beings play in bringing it about and the closeness of the relationship between perpetrator and victim."[8] Other factors include the degree of endangerment of one's own person and involvement in the event, exposure to injury and death, the frequency and duration of traumatic situations, and, last but not least, the resources available for overcoming the threat. Finally, how people in the victim's environment (or society in general) respond can also be decisive.

Traumatic events trigger a great variety of responses, but on closer inspection many of them can be connected with two fundamental, con-

---

5. See Ruth Poser, *Das Ezechielbuch als Trauma-Literatur*, VTSup 154 (Leiden: Brill, 2012), 121–248.

6. Gottfried Fischer and Peter Riedesser, *Lehrbuch der Psychotraumatologie*, 3rd ed. (Munich: Reinhardt, 2003), 82, 375.

7. See ibid., 62.

8. Peter Riedesser, "Belastende Kriegserfahrungen in der Kleinkindzeit," in *Kindheiten im Zweiten Weltkrieg: Kriegserfahrungen und deren Folgen aus psychohistorischer Perspektive*, ed. Hartmut Radebold (Munich: Juventa, 2006), 37.

trary impulses: on the one hand, the violence that victims have suffered preoccupies them and constantly intrudes on their thoughts; on the other hand, victims try as hard as they can to ward off feelings of anxiety, pain, and helplessness and to protect themselves from everything connected with the trauma. The term *intrusion symptoms* is used to describe states in which victims relive the traumatic situation; they include intrusive thoughts, nightmares, and flashbacks. Contrasting *constriction symptoms* may appear as psychological numbing, rigidity, and social withdrawal.[9] This dialectic is closely linked to victims' inability to express what happened to them in symbolic language. They want to tell their stories—indeed, they must in order to grasp the traumatic events as part of their life histories—but they are often unable to do so because they lack words for their experiences. We have no language in which to express senseless violence, and perhaps no such language should exist.[10] In what follows, it will become clear that in Ezekiel the ambiguity of the prophet's voice provides a key to grasping the relationship between trauma symptoms and multiple features of the text.

1.2. The Mute Prophet and the Words of God

Ezekiel's mutism is a phenomenon that continues to puzzle researchers, but it can be plausibly interpreted as generated by trauma.[11] The prophet falls silent (!) after he is forced to eat a scroll covered with words of lamentation and mourning (2:8b–3:3). That it tastes "as sweet as honey" in Ezekiel's mouth is, as Rabbi David Kimchi puts it, perhaps simply a reference to the strange circumstance that it is possible to eat the scroll at all,[12] but it "poisons" not only Ezekiel's "breath" (*rûaḥ*) but also his speech—and leaves him "stunned" (3:14–15).[13] Shortly thereafter YHWH announces that he will make the prophet's tongue cling to the roof of his mouth and

---

9. See Fischer and Riedesser, *Lehrbuch der Psychotraumatologie*, 44–46.

10. See Martina Kopf, *Trauma und Literatur: Das Nicht-Erzählbare erzählen—Assia Djebar und Yvonne Vera* (Frankfurt am Main: Brandes & Apsel, 2005), 9–67.

11. See Poser, *Das Ezechielbuch*, 35–43.

12. For the reference to Rabbi David Kimchi, see Moshe Greenberg, *Ezekiel 1–20: A New Translation with Introduction and Commentary*, AB 22 (New York: Doubleday, 1983), 68.

13. See, on this point, Gregory Y. Glazov, *The Bridling of the Tongue and the Opening of the Mouth in Biblical Prophecy*, JSOTSup 311 (Sheffield: Sheffield Academic, 2001), 222: "It [the scroll] tastes sweet but embitters and inflames, or rather

render him mute (3:25–26; cf. 24:25–27). Ezekiel cannot speak unless YHWH addresses him (3:27).[14] The prophet regains the power of speech only when news of the destruction of Jerusalem reaches him and he has grasped it as a fact (33:21–22). The narrative of Ezekiel presents its protagonist as a traumatized victim of violence who in this respect bears a strong resemblance to David's daughter Tamar (2 Sam 13:20) and Job (Job 2:12–13). As such, he becomes a prophet and embodiment of trauma for the house of Israel and readers of the text.

The fact that so many victims of trauma are unable to tell the story of what happened to them, or find it extremely difficult to do so, leads to (further) symptoms. Trauma researcher Bessel A. van der Kolk sees the cause of this development in the particular nature of traumatic experiences: they cannot be processed symbolically, a necessary step for "classifying them correctly and integrating them into [the individual's] other experiences." Instead of being processed like ordinary information, "they are first registered as feelings or affective states."[15] Van der Kolk accordingly assumes the existence of a "trauma memory" with specific processes for storing such incidents. In many cases, traumatic memories cannot be called up as such; instead, they are largely reexperienced as affective states, in the form of visual images or physical sensations ("embodied memories"). These emotional and sensory states are characterized by their fragmentary nature and are thus difficult to express in words; trauma victims are often unable to translate what they have suffered into a personal narrative. Nevertheless, the passage of time is less likely to distort traumatic memories than ordinary ones,[16] and certain internal and external stimuli can continue to trigger them for the rest of the victim's life. In such cases, traumatic memories may surface (suddenly) or intrude on consciousness. When this happens, victims frequently experience the memories with the

---

poisons, Ezekiel's spirit, throwing him into a seven-day-long state of silent astonishment or stupefaction."

14. For this formulation, see Edgar Conrad, *Reading the Latter Prophets: Toward a New Canonical Criticism*, JSOTSup 376 (New York: T&T Clark, 2003), 173.

15. Bessel A. van der Kolk, "Trauma and Memory," in *Traumatic Stress: The Effects of Overwhelming Experience on Mind, Body, and Society*, ed. Bessel A. van der Kolk, Alexander McFarlane, and Lars Weisaeth (New York: Guilford, 2007), 296. This work offers a good overview of the topic.

16. See Fischer and Riedesser, *Lehrbuch der Psychotraumatologie*, 284–87.

same degree of emotional force and sensory intensity as the original traumatic event.

As the scene in which Ezekiel is told to eat the scroll suggests, the book is one of extreme bodily events. The symbolic actions that YHWH requires Ezekiel to perform get under his skin, so to speak, as when he must live on a starvation diet (4:9–11), shave his head and beard with the blade of a sharp sword (5:1), or "moan with breaking heart and bitter grief" (21:6 NRSV). Nancy R. Bowen, who interprets the book of Ezekiel in terms of trauma, discusses chapters 4 and 5 as follows: "Ezekiel's reenactments of the trauma of the fall of Jerusalem … resemble the acts of victims who continue to live the trauma through various forms of deliberate self-harm…. Such self-destructive behaviors can be understood as symbolic or literal reenactments of the initial abuse."[17]

In the context of trauma theory, the central goal in a recovery process is to reconstruct the traumatic event so that a survivor of trauma can integrate a memory into his or her personal biography. The experience must be relived step by step—often an extremely painful process. The aim is not to "habituate [the patient] to anxiety and stress, as used to be assumed, but rather to 'neutralize' and modify the memory by creating a coherent personal narrative." Those affected should "be able to live with the traumatic memory without being handicapped by unresolved fears and distorted beliefs about themselves or the world."[18]

When victims embed the trauma in the framework of their own history, it acquires meaning for their identity, either explicitly or implicitly, a phenomenon that applies to both individual and collective experiences. They may interpret it as stroke of fate, a catastrophe, a test, punishment, or guilt—but also as a challenge or opportunity for growth.[19] *Rationalizing* a traumatic event in this manner has its problematic side, however, since by making it possible to grasp an occurrence that was originally senseless one can also render it banal.

---

17. Bowen, *Ezekiel*, 28.

18. Martin Sack, "Narrative Arbeit im Kontext 'schonender Traumatherapie,'" in *Narrative Bewältigung von Trauma und Verlust*, ed. Carl Eduard Scheidt et al. (Stuttgart: Schattauer, 2015), 151 and 153.

19. See Carl Eduard Scheidt and Gabriele Lucius-Hoene, "Kategorisierung und narrative Bewältigung bindungsbezogener Traumaerfahrungen im Erwachsenenbindungsinterview," in Scheidt et al., *Narrative Bewältigung*, 27.

In chapters 16, 20, and 23 the book of Ezekiel contains three passages that tell the history of Israel and Jerusalem anew—this time as a story of *degeneration*. It turns the phases of the relationship between Israel's divinity and God's people, which are presented in a positive light in other biblical contexts, into their opposite. These passages depict Israel and Jerusalem as bad from the beginning; the people are unwilling or unable to learn from their mistakes. The early years in Egypt no longer count as a time of innocence, and dark shadows are cast even on the exodus, the gift of the torah, and Israel's experiences of liberation. Rewriting history in this way achieves one positive step, however: it places the contemporaneous catastrophe in a context of cause and effect, thereby offering—however inadequately—a possibility for comprehending the incomprehensible. In this sense, the stories told in the book of Ezekiel can be regarded as creating a form of collective identity in response to the trauma.

Chapters 16 and 23 provide Jerusalem with a metaphorical biography, so to speak. They depict the relationship between the divinity and the city as a kind of marriage, but one in which the wife takes up with other gods and nations. For this *unfaithfulness*, which on another level represents criticism of a failed policy of alliances, the city/wife receives brutal punishment described in a mixture of sexual and martial imagery. Both chapters make use of a strategy employed repeatedly in other passages of Ezekiel: they present Israel and Jerusalem's guilt as massive and by means of this (self-) stigmatization justify YHWH's punishment; YHWH has no choice but to send the people into exile. Despite this pronounced tendency to assign guilt and blame the victim, the text exonerates Jerusalem to some extent: the biography of the city-as-woman in Ezek 16 portrays her as of low birth and the daughter of wicked parents who left their infant in a field to die; she survived only through God's intervention (16:3–14). Such a depiction denigrates Jerusalem but also absolves her of responsibility: if she is incapable of remaining faithful, it is because of the maltreatment she suffered earlier.[20]

As we have seen, whether someone can speak about traumatic experiences to another person at all is connected with the problem that words must be found to express the complete absence of meaning. Yet there is

---

20. For a more detailed discussion of Ezek 16, see Poser, *Das Ezechielbuch*: 371–409; for Ezek 23, 435–45.

more: as Werner Bohleber has pointed out, the question is further related to the processes of interpretation and symbolization.[21]

Massive experiences of violence can also injure the part of the personality that "precedes language, the layer on which language is built and acquires meaning."[22] It can be described as a sense of basic trust in the continuous presence of benevolent object figures and reliable empathy from others.[23] By shattering relationships to others and to oneself, traumatic experience destroys the context in which language functions. Attempts to treat trauma with psychotherapy proceed from the assumption that such an experience must be successfully integrated into a patient's narrative memory, but this requires the renewal of trust: healing can occur only as speech within a relationship based on trust.[24] Establishing a situation in which such communication is possible for both parties—one trying to communicate a traumatic experience and the other taking on the task of listening—is laden with difficulties and profound ambivalence. The former seeks words to describe an event that, despite its overwhelming nature, has not yet become fully real. The victim must try to translate the occurrence into a fundamentally different form, into knowledge that can be recalled. This process exposes the occurrence to the dangers of forgetting and banality. According to Dori Laub, many survivors of violence thus come to see silence as a more appropriate response to what they have suffered. [25]

One reason for remaining silent is the difficulty of finding an empathetic listener "who can hear the anguish of one's memories and thus affirm and recognize their realness."[26] Most outsiders retreat when confronted with trauma. It is challenging to listen to an account of trauma in the necessary manner, to be completely present and not to withdraw out of fear or reluctance to learn of terrible events.[27]

---

21. See Werner Bohleber, "Die Entwicklung der Traumatheorie in der Psychoanalyse," *Psyche* 9/10 (2000): 825–26.

22. Kopf, *Trauma und Literatur*, 42.

23. See Bohleber, "Die Entwicklung der Traumatheorie," 821.

24. See Kopf, *Trauma und Literatur*, 42–43.

25. See Dori Laub, "Bearing Witness or the Vicissitudes of Listening," in *Testimony: Crises of Witnessing in Literature, Psychoanalysis, and History*, ed. Shoshana Felman and Dori Laub (New York: Routledge, 1992), 57–59.

26. Ibid., 68.

27. See Kopf, *Trauma und Literatur*, 46.

If one reads the book of Ezekiel from the perspective of trauma, it emerges as a particular kind of prophecy. It is not a call to the people, especially its political leaders, to repent in the face of imminent catastrophe, nor does it initiate such a process of repentance by citing instructions received from God. Instead, Ezekiel's prophecy recounts a catastrophe that has already occurred, the destruction of Jerusalem by Nebuchadnezzar in 587/586 BCE.[28] With the exception of two introductory verses that legitimate the book from an external vantage point (1:2–3), the book presents itself as Ezekiel's own first-person narrative. Ezekiel tells his story, even though YHWH has rendered him mute. This circumstance runs counter to our fundamental understanding of the role of both a narrator and a prophet.

We gain a sense of a story being told—but not properly, suggesting a situation lacking the interpersonal trust that we have seen is a necessary condition for ordinary personal disclosure. This feeling persists even though the style of Ezekiel's prophecy is elevated and at times even poetic. Many turns of phrase recur as leitmotifs; the narrative structure and levels of discourse are highly complex. The purpose of the latter two features appears to be to transmit every word spoken by YHWH, but the result seems strangely distant and lacking in immediacy. The incapacity of human speech to express unspeakable events becomes evident. An overall impression is created that God alone can still speak—and even that only within limits: if YHWH did not let the divine word be perceived, there would be silence; the catastrophe would go unmentioned; Ezekiel would have nothing to say. In this sense only YHWH bears witness to the trauma, testifying to its truth for the narrator Ezekiel, the house of Israel, and readers of the text. YHWH alone makes it possible to perceive and speak of the suffering that has taken place. Moreover, if one thinks of the forward-looking, hopeful passages of the book, YHWH is also the source

---

28. No consensus exists on the dating of the book of Ezekiel. For the various options or models, see Rainer Albertz, *Israel in Exile: The History and Literature of the Sixth Century B.C.E.*, trans. David Green, SBL Studies in Biblical Literature 3, Biblical Encyclopedia 7 (Atlanta: Society of Biblical Literature, 2003), 345–54; Frank-Lothar Hossfeld, "Das Buch Ezechiel," in *Einleitung in das Alte Testament*, by Erich Zenger et al., 7th ed. (Stuttgart: Kohlhammer, 2008), 500–504. I advocate dating at least considerable portions of the Ezekiel narrative in the period between 570 and 540 BCE, since its traumatic character makes a certain proximity to the terrible events around 587 seem plausible; see Poser, *Das Ezechielbuch*, 668–72.

of information about surviving the catastrophe and developing new strategies for living. Nevertheless, it is Ezekiel who relates all of this, bearing witness to and communicating not only his own survival and that of his people but also the survival of God.

1.3. Making Sense of the Past, Imagining the Future

Thus far we have recognized the capacity of the text to paradoxically articulate both the horrific character of Israel's suffering and the basis for hoping that Israel might maintain a favorable relationship with YHWH. Here insights into two aspects of psychological trauma illuminate the capacity of the text to help trauma survivors make sense of the horrific events of their past, while shaping fragmented images of those horrors into a hopeful vision of the future.

The portrayal of the house of Israel's horrific suffering as violent punishment enacted by God is perhaps one of the most difficult aspects of Ezekiel. Psycho-traumatology reveals that many victims of trauma struggle with shame and guilt; often this adds to the difficulty of talking about what they suffered. If family members and friends have been murdered, some even feel guilty for having survived. Although there is no *objective* reason for them to blame themselves, occasionally survivors will accuse themselves instead of the perpetrator. Such an assumption of guilt after trauma is often connected with the fact "that it can be easier to maintain one's mental balance if one was guilty rather than completely helpless."[29] Frequently victims of trauma feel guilt far out of proportion to their actual responsibility. Nevertheless, it can be important for the healing process to recognize the degree of responsibility that the traumatized person actually bears. This is particularly true when the roles of perpetrator and victim are combined, as in the case of war veterans.

Two aspects are crucial for a discussion of guilt in the book of Ezekiel: the catastrophe occurs because there is no other way to expunge the guilt of the house of Israel, and YHWH is the perpetrator. It is YHWH alone who is responsible for the people's exile, not the Babylonians (cf., however, 24:1–2). The assumption of guilt enables a powerless Israel to take the initiative and act effectively. If Israel follows God's commands in the

---

29. Angela Kühner, *Kollektive Traumata—Annahmen, Argumente, Konzepte: Eine Bestandsaufnahme nach dem 11. September*, Berghof Report 9 (Berlin: Berghof Forschungszentrum für Konstruktive Konfliktbearbeitung, 2002), 32.

future, this will help ensure that no similar catastrophe ever occurs again. Assigning the role of perpetrator to God removes the terrible events from the sphere of human volition and earthly contingency. Above all, however, it preserves the idea of YHWH as a deity of immense power. Ultimately, the fact that God's people take on the burden of guilt makes it possible for God to survive as their deity even after the catastrophe of exile.

This intellectual model is not absolute, however. It is modified, for example, to depict YHWH as also traumatized; it is for this reason that YHWH was "compelled" to strike the people (see 16:42–43). The trauma that YHWH experienced when they abandoned their God reveals YHWH as a deeply human deity, so to speak. It is precisely the depth of divine feeling that enables YHWH to comprehend the depths of human nature. A contradiction—a necessary one—is introduced into the discourse on guilt when the idea finds expression at least once (21:1–12) that there were innocent people among the victims.

In addition to these strategies for coming to terms with the traumatic past, fragments of that past emerge also in Ezekiel's articulation of a vision for a hopeful future. Traumatized people often struggle with powerful, sometimes overwhelming visual images; the terrifying event they have lived through haunts them in the form of nightmares, flashbacks, or hallucinations. Trauma therapy for individuals makes use of this dominance of visual and pictorial elements, employing various techniques with the aim of transforming the traumatic occurrence into an event in the patient's past history that can be consciously recalled. These include exercises that help individuals protect themselves and enable them to view the trauma from a certain distance (e.g., a therapist suggesting that the traumatic event be visualized from the perspective of an outsider or "projected" onto an imaginary screen).[30]

By encouraging victims to return to the trauma, the therapist aims to reduce the subjective burden and to link the memory of the traumatizing event to experiences of competence and mastery; in this process it can also "be very helpful to alter the traumatic narrative and turn it into a story with a positive outcome."[31]

---

30. See Luise Reddemann, *Imagination als heilsame Kraft: Zur Behandlung von Traumafolgen mit ressourcenorientierten Verfahren*, 9th ed. (Stuttgart: Pfeiffer bei Klett-Cotta, 2003), 29–60 and 109–131.

31. Sack, "Narrative Arbeit," 153.

An example of this process can be found in the passage known as the Gog pericope in Ezek 38–39, which can be read as a reimagining and reenactment of Nebuchadnezzar's attack on Jerusalem and the kingdom of Judah; there are persuasive arguments for identifying Gog of Magog as the Babylonian ruler.[32] Several passages in Ezek 38–39 depict different outcomes of the Babylonian siege of Jerusalem: in one YHWH brings about the defeat of the enemy (38:1–8); in another the house of Israel participates in banishing death and war from the world (39:9–20). Finally and importantly, the Israelites do not mete out the same treatment to their enemies as they had received according to 37:1–11; rather, they ensure that the remains of Gog and his people are buried. These alternate outcomes, which can be understood as reflecting increasing integration of the traumatic catastrophe, open a new perspective within Ezekiel's narrative: the vision of a new beginning in the promised land (Ezek 40–48).

2. The Dialectic of Traumatization in Literary Texts

The foregoing has sought to demonstrate the manner in which insights into the psychology of traumatization facilitate interpretation of a range of features in the text of Ezekiel. I now turn to insights from the study of trauma literature in order to identify patterns in Ezekiel that suggest certain capacities of the text to help trauma survivors confront their traumatic experience.

Does telling the story of a traumatic catastrophe inevitably reduce it to a rational and banal event? Are some cultural scholars right when they say that the existence of such a text necessarily represents "the end of the trauma"? Can *trauma literature* exist at all, or is the term an oxymoron? Marisa Siguan Boehmer, who has analyzed texts by Jean Améry, Jorge Semprún, and Herta Müller, observes that the answers to these questions take the form of a paradox; the writings of these authors have muteness at their core. It is the impossibility of communicating that makes it so imperative to tell the story.[33]

---

32. See Julie Galambush, "Necessary Enemies: Nebuchadnezzar, Yhwh, and Gog in Ezekiel 38–39," in *Israel's Prophets and Israel's Past*, ed. Brad E. Kelle and Megan Bishop Moore, LHBOTS 446 (New York: T&T Clark, 2006), 254–67. See also Poser, *Ezechielbuch*: 570–613.

33. Marisa Siguan Boehmer, "Erinnerungsbilder im narrativen Erinnerungsdis-

Anyone who attempts to turn individual or collective traumas into literature unavoidably enters the realm of paradox. On the one hand, massive eruptions of brutality resist expression; there are no words to represent them. On the other hand, it is absolutely necessary to bear witness, to respond so that horror and violence do not have the last word. In recent years scholars have occupied themselves increasingly with the question of how trauma can be portrayed in literary texts and with the kinds of narrative motifs and structures that can appropriately serve this aim.

The following explores two basic dynamics by which literary texts represent trauma. The difficulty that trauma survivors have in processing traumatic memory becomes manifest in repetitions that correspond to fragments of traumatic memory and in gaps in the text that correspond to the inaccessibility of certain aspects of traumatic memory. The difficult task of facing potentially overwhelming memories of trauma becomes bearable through the way in which literature resymbolizes the traumatic experience. I conclude in §2.3 by describing the unique capacity of literature for helping survivors to confront traumatic experience.

2.1. Repetition and Gaps

Stephan Freissmann notes that trauma literature is characterized by certain strategies of repetition and indications of inexpressibility in the form of gaps.[34] The tendency of traumatic events to force themselves into victims' consciousness again and again (intrusive thoughts) can be represented by repetition, while the need to protect the self (emotional constriction) can be represented by breaks at key points in the text.

We observe the same strategies of repetition and omission or gaps in the book of Ezekiel. Chapters 4–24 can be read as recurring reenactment of the destruction of Jerusalem with increasingly violent imagery. At the same time, however, at central points in the narrative Ezekiel turns his gaze away from what is happening. One such instance occurs in Ezek 9–10, when he can no longer bear to watch the massacre of the city's inhabitants; instead, he inspects God's throne with its "wheelwork" and describes it again in detail (cf. ch. 1). Hence the crucial question of whether the "exe-

---

kurs bei Jean Améry und Jorge Semprún," in *Narrative Bewältigung von Trauma und Verlust,* ed. Carl Eduard Scheidt et al. (Stuttgart: Schattauer, 2015), 213, 215.

34. Stephan Freissmann, *Trauma als Erzählstrategie,* master's thesis (University of Konstanz, 2005), 13, http://tinyurl.com/SBLP0686b.

cutioners" (9:1) spare anyone in Jerusalem (9:4–6) remains unanswered. YHWH also suddenly shifts perspective between the end of chapter 24 and the beginning of chapter 25, at the moment when the narrative reaches the siege, conquest, and destruction of the city (24:1–2). God announces the end of the Judean capital one more time with the particularly gruesome image of the rusted cooking pot that will melt together with the meat dish it contains (24:3–13). At just that point YHWH ceases to focus on "God's" city and turns attention to the surrounding peoples (25–32). One could interpret this as a sign that even YHWH cannot endure the sight of the destruction being visited on Jerusalem. Or is it perhaps Ezekiel, who as first-person narrator is responsible for which events are included in the narrative? In any event, the book never presents the annihilation of Jerusalem directly; rather, it is anticipated (Ezek 4–24) or mentioned as an occurrence in the past (33:21–22).

2.2. (Re)symbolization

Ronald Granofsky argues for the existence of a new subgenre, the modern trauma novel, whose defining quality is a concern with catastrophe, either experienced or anxiously anticipated. Its key technique, in his view, involves symbolization.[35] His study reflects two fundamental insights of psycho-traumatology: that the effect of traumatic situations is to destroy "the capacity to symbolize them and grasp their meaning," and that "trauma … can only be assimilated by placing it in a symbolic sequence" (see above).[36] Granofsky observes further that the process of symbolization permits a confrontation with traumatic material with some degree of protection.[37] Since the process may or may not involve a deliberate reworking of prior symbolic representation, it may be considered (re)symbolization.

The process of (re)symbolization is particularly evident in the book of Ezekiel through its use of the motif *rûaḥ* ("air in motion"—wind, breath, spirit), which occurs fifty-two times. From the start, *rûaḥ* appears as a powerful force, activating participants in the narrative and setting changes

---

35. Ronald Granofsky, *The Trauma Novel: Contemporary Symbolic Depictions of Collective Disaster* (New York: Lang, 1995), 7.

36. Bohleber, "Entwicklung der Traumatheorie," 822. Compare also Granofsky, *Trauma Novel*, 6: "The symbolic mode comes into play when new information resists easy assimilation into memory."

37. Granofsky, *Trauma Novel*, 6–7.

in motion. Up to Ezek 20 its nature is ambiguous: it moves the wheels of the throne (1:12, 20; 10:17), but it can also be a windstorm that can bring down walls, signifying God's wrath (13:11, 13). At various points it serves as a metaphor for deportation and captivity (5:10, 12; 12:14; 17:21). Furthermore, it may refer to an individual's spirit that can suffer harm or go astray (11:5; 13:3) but also be renewed (11:19; 18:31). After God proclaims that the news of the coming catastrophe will cause every spirit to grow faint (21:7 [MT: 12]), the term *rûaḥ* does not occur again in a negative context—with one exception. This, however, represents the peak of its destructive potential (27:26). When *rûaḥ* is used after Ezek 36:26, it functions as an unambiguously constructive source of energy that underlies and renews life (37:1–10). It becomes a symbol for the life of Israel in the face of God and in the Torah (37:14; 39:29; 42:20). The images of restoration recall *rûaḥ* as an ambiguous force that contains destructive potential but also is necessary for life. In this sense, *rûaḥ* appears especially suitable as a means of expressing the "secret of surviving" the catastrophe of exile (see §2.3 below) in language close to the victims' experience.

In the context of this literary (re)symbolization process, most of the motifs involve, either directly or indirectly, biological functions or stages of development, such as birth, growth, sexuality, and death. Similarly, as empirical investigations have made clear, trauma narratives in therapeutic settings are dominated by sensorimotor imagery.[38] In particular, as Granofsky notes, the motif of eating occurs frequently in literary treatments of trauma: "The 'perversion' of normal eating patterns, for example, in cannibalism, will often be a symbol for the dislocating effects of trauma both on an individual and a collective scale. In the trauma novel, certain kinds of eating may be symbolic of the necessity to assimilate raw experience, so to speak."[39]

The conversion of "normal," life-supporting consumption of food into symbolic action also occurs in the book of Ezekiel.[40] It extends from God's command that Ezekiel swallow a scroll covered with "words of lamenta-

---

38. See Scheidt and Lucius-Hoene, "Kategorisierung," 28.

39. Granofsky, *Trauma Novel*, 14.

40. See Ruth Poser, "'Das Gericht geht durch den Magen': Die verschlungene Schriftrolle (Ez 2:8b–3:3) und andere Essensszenarien im Ezechielbuch," in *Essen und Trinken in der Bibel: Ein literarisches Festmahl für Rainer Kessler zum 65. Geburtstag*, ed. Michaela Geiger, Christl M. Maier, and Uta Schmidt (Gütersloh: Gütersloher Verlagshaus, 2009), 116–30.

tion and mourning and woe" (2:8b–3:3) to other acts of eating that reflect the food shortage during the siege of Jerusalem (4:9–17). Other passages mention cannibalism (5:10), famine (e.g., 5:16; 7:15), images of "consuming fire" and a land that "devours" its people (36:13–15). Not until Ezek 34 do eating (and drinking) gradually reacquire their role as sustenance for individuals and the community, as when YHWH promises to provide food in abundance (Ezek 34, 36) and gives instructions for ritual sacrifice, that is, food offerings to God and consuming food in the temple (Ezek 42–46). YHWH further instructs Ezekiel regarding how the land, which will then be healed and bountiful, is to be divided among the tribes of Israel (Ezek 47–48). In Ezek 47:1–12, the prophet again comes in contact with edible things; on the banks of the river by the temple he sees marvelous fruit trees that bear fruit every month, and whose leaves can heal. Here we can observe a dual phenomenon: both disaster and redemption (along with healing) are described as events bound up with the human body. At the same time, the trail of food imagery running through the text makes it clear that redemption can emerge only from a long and profound experience of calamity. Not until then do "lamentation and mourning and woe" become "sweet," as Ezekiel described the taste of the scroll.[41]

Granofsky observes that the (re)symbolization process takes place in three interdependent phases that give trauma novels a characteristic structure, which he calls *trauma response*: the element of *fragmentation* (the attempt [or repeated attempts] to depict events that elude comprehension) is followed by *regression* ([unconscious] attempts to ward off the trauma and protect oneself from it), and, finally, by the element of *reunification* (integration of the trauma into the "narrative script").[42]

The Ezekiel narrative as a whole can also be described as trauma response. The component of fragmentation dominates in the first section (1:1–23:49), which is set before the siege of Jerusalem and anticipates the city's destruction in a series of increasingly gruesome images. Regression comes to the fore in the second section (24:1–33:20), which is set during the siege but directs the reader's gaze away from Jerusalem. The third section of the narrative (33:21–48:35) tells of the period after the siege and conquest and is dominated by the element of reunification, although the motif of traumatic fragmentation breaks through at several points and

---

41. Jürgen Ebach, "Ezechiel isst ein Buch—Ezechiel ist ein Buch," in Jürgen Ebach, *Iss dieses Buch!,* Theologische Reden 8 (Wittingen: ErevRav, 2008), 23.

42. Granofsky, *Trauma Novel*, 107–14.

leads to regressive movements (see, e.g., 35:1–15). Overall, this structure reflects the gradual integration of the catastrophic trauma, which nevertheless remains far from complete.

Within this structure one also finds bursts of traumatic imagery. The irrepressible memory of traumatic terror, which forces itself into the survivor's conscious mind without warning, takes the form of "visual images" that lie at "the boundary between speech and speechlessness."[43] In this process the visual element invades the narrative, so to speak: "as a *mémoire involontaire* it shows that the past is an ongoing present and bursts the bounds of language and the possibilities of narrative discourse in order to redefine them."[44]

The book of Ezekiel contains several passages characterized as visions (1–3; 8–11; 37:1–10; 40–48), a quality that indicates a dominance of the visual element. In my view, the phenomenon described by Boehmer is evident in single images of an extreme nature. In the book of Jeremiah the "cup of the wine of wrath" that makes all who drink from it "stagger and go out of their minds" (25:15–16) is still "just" a metaphor, but here a form of "hyper-reality" is introduced (cf., e.g., Ezek 23:31–34 with Jer 25:15–29; 51:7–10).[45] In the book of Ezekiel the city-woman Jerusalem must not only drink "a cup of horror and desolation"; YHWH proclaims further that she must "gnaw its shards" and tear her breasts. Through such "excessive realism" the inexpressible horror of the traumatic catastrophe that occurred at the beginning of the sixth century seeps into the language.[46]

2.3. Imagination, Fictionality, and Bearing Witness to the Truth

Psychotherapeutic and legal measures to deal with traumatic experience for the sake of individual victims and the community (must) ultimately aim to overcome the dialectic of trauma and silence through speaking. Literary depictions, however, can open up and maintain an intermediate space where it is possible to explore both the limits and the transformative possibilities of words and narrative representation. Martina Kopf has observed how the factuality of violence and suffering virtually demands creative treatment; she understands "our imaginative capacities as the

---

43. Ibid., 221.
44. Ibid., 221–22.
45. Also compare Ezek 2:8b–3:3 with Jer 15:16; and Ezek 16 with Jer 3:6–13.
46. See Poser, *Ezechielbuch*, 445–67.

true force working to prevent the possible outcome described by trauma theory, namely, the collapse of a constructive process and the annihilation of form and structure."[47]

For the psychoanalyst Dori Laub, who conducted numerous interviews with Auschwitz survivors for the *Fortunoff Video Archive for Holocaust Testimonies,* it is precisely the imaginative elements of a trauma narrative—elements that transcend the historical truth, as it were—that bear witness to "the very secret of survival and of resistance to extermination."[48] By making what happened more vivid, these components draw viewers and listeners in and connect them with "unspeakable" events. In this sense, fictionalized and imagined scenes actually testify to the emotional and psychological truth of trauma, "the Other" of history.[49] "The very fact of survival seems to carry with it the responsibility of assuming the role of historical witness."[50]

The book of Ezekiel also represents the narrative of a survivor. God renders the prophet mute and stunned (3:15), but God's spirit (*rûaḥ*) sets Ezekiel on his feet again. In both cases the prophet becomes a "sign" (12:6, 11; 24:27), a (fictional) paradigm for his people (23:31–34; 37:1–14). In his extreme contact with YHWH, he embodies the fate of Israel, thereby creating the possibility for the house of Israel to understand itself as a traumatized collective. Paradoxically, the silenced prophet makes language available in a way that enables readers of the text to come to grips with the catastrophe.

3. Summary

Some of the paradoxes with which the book of Ezekiel confronts readers can be approached, and perhaps even grasped, through a hermeneutics of trauma that concentrates on questions of narrative. Against this background, the book of Ezekiel reveals itself as a narrative space where it becomes possible to speak about violence of human origin, and its con-

---

47. Kopf, *Trauma und Literatur*, 53.

48. Laub, "Bearing Witness," 62.

49. See Manfred Weinberg, "Trauma—Geschichte, Gespenst, Literatur—und Gedächtnis," in *Trauma: Zwischen Psychoanalyse und kulturellem Deutungsmuster,* ed. Elisabeth Bronfen, Birgit R. Erdle, and Sigrid Weigel (Cologne: Böhlau, 1999), 173–206.

50. Granofsky, *Trauma Novel*, 14.

sequences with respect to God, and to attempt to grasp their meaning. At the same time, there is room for a "secret of survival." One can understand the Ezekiel narrative, with its extreme and frightening imagery related to the human body, as an indication of the shattering, fragmenting experience of exile in 587–586 BCE. The text's multiple layers and ambiguity give expression to the different fates suffered by members of the house of Israel, putting into words their experiences as individuals and enabling them to perceive their collective trauma. From the latter there emerge steps that perhaps can lead beyond the isolation of traumatic experience and reexperience. The *hyper-reality* of the imagery takes readers to the limits of language and records the *unspeakable* nature of traumatic experiences. The circumstance that for a space of time God alone seems to have the capacity to use words points in a similar direction but at the same time expresses an element of hope: that God can absorb what is unbearable for human beings and respond to experiences about which they cannot speak.[51]

While reflecting on trauma can increase our understanding of the book of Ezekiel (and other books of the Bible), is it also possible that the text can enlarge our reflection about traumatizing catastrophes, particularly in view of current political situations around the world? The fact that the background of this "traumatic" biblical text consists of war and forced migration gives it, in my view, a shocking and painful relevance to current events.

BIBLIOGRAPHY

Albertz, Rainer. *Israel in Exile: The History and Literature of the Sixth Century B.C.E.* Translated by David Green. SBL Studies in Biblical Literature 3, Biblical Encyclopedia 7. Atlanta: Society of Biblical Literature, 2003.

Boehmer, Marisa Siguan. "Erinnerungsbilder im narrativen Erinnerungsdiskurs bei Jean Améry und Jorge Semprún." Pages 212–22 in *Narrative Bewältigung von Trauma und Verlust*. Edited by Carl Eduard Scheidt et al. Stuttgart: Schattauer, 2015.

Bohleber, Werner. "Die Entwicklung der Traumatheorie in der Psychoanalyse." *Psyche* 9/10 (2000): 797–839.

Bowen, Nancy R. *Ezekiel*. AOTC. Nashville: Abingdon, 2010.

---

51. For more on this topic, see Poser, *Ezechielbuch*, 679–86.

Broome, Edwin C. "Ezekiel's Abnormal Personality." *JBL* 65 (1946): 277–92.

Conrad, Edgar. *Reading the Latter Prophets: Toward a New Canonical Criticism.* JSOTSup 376. New York: T&T Clark, 2003.

Daschke, Derek M. "Desolate among Them: Loss, Fantasy and Recovery in the Book of Ezekiel." *American Imago* 56 (1999): 105–32.

Ebach, Jürgen "Ezechiel isst ein Buch—Ezechiel ist ein Buch." Pages 11–24 in Ebach, *Iss dieses Buch!* Theologische Reden 8. Wittingen: ErevRav, 2008.

Fischer, Gottfried, and Peter Riedesser. *Lehrbuch der Psychotraumatologie.* 3rd ed. Munich: Reinhardt, 2003.

Freissmann, Stephan. *Trauma als Erzählstrategie.* Master's thesis. University of Konstanz, 2005. http://tinyurl.com/SBLP0686b.

Galambush, Julie. "Necessary Enemies: Nebuchadnezzar, Yhwh, and Gog in Ezekiel 38–39." Pages 254–67 in *Israel's Prophets and Israel's Past.* Edited by Brad E. Kelle and Megan Bishop Moore. LHBOTS 446. New York: T&T Clark, 2006.

Garber, David G. "Traumatizing Ezekiel, the Exilic Prophet." Pages 215–35 in *Psychology and the Bible: A New Way to Read the Scriptures 2* (*From Genesis to Apocalyptic Vision*). Edited by J. Harold Ellens and Wayne G. Rollins. Westport, CT: Praeger, 2004.

Garfinkel, Stephen. "Another Model for Ezekiel's Abnormalities." *JANESCU* 19 (1989): 39–50.

Glazov, Gregory Y. *The Bridling of the Tongue and the Opening of the Mouth in Biblical Prophecy.* JSOTSup 311. Sheffield: Sheffield Academic, 2001.

Granofsky, Ronald. *The Trauma Novel: Contemporary Symbolic Depictions of Collective Disaster.* New York: Lang, 1995.

Greenberg, Moshe. *Ezekiel 1–20: A New Translation with Introduction and Commentary.* AB 22. New York: Doubleday, 1983.

Hossfeld, Frank-Lothar. "Das Buch Ezechiel." Pages 489–506 in *Einleitung in das Alte Testament.* Edited by Erich Zenger et al. 7th ed. Stuttgart: Kohlhammer, 2008.

Jaspers, Karl. "Der Prophet Ezechiel: Eine pathographische Studie" [1947]. Pages 95–106 in Jaspers, *Rechenschaft und Ausblick: Reden und Aufsätze.* Munich: Piper, 1951.

Kelle, Brad E. "Dealing with the Trauma of Defeat: The Rhetoric of the Devastation and Rejuvenation of Nature in Ezekiel." *JBL* 128 (2009): 469–90.

Klostermann, August. "Ezechiel: Ein Beitrag zu besserer Würdigung seiner Person und Schrift." *TSK* 50 (1877): 391–439.

Kolk, Bessel A. van der. "Trauma and Memory." Pages 279–302 in *Traumatic Stress: The Effects of Overwhelming Experience on Mind, Body, and Society*. Edited by Bessel A. van der Kolk, Alexander McFarlane, and Lars Weisaeth. New York: Guilford, 2007.

Kopf, Martina. *Trauma und Literatur: Das Nicht-Erzählbare erzählen—Assia Djebar und Yvonne Vera*. Frankfurt am Main: Brandes & Apsel, 2005.

Kühner, Angela. *Kollektive Traumata—Annahmen, Argumente, Konzepte: Eine Bestandsaufnahme nach dem 11. September*. Berghof Report 9. Berlin: Berghof Forschungszentrum für Konstruktive Konfliktbearbeitung, 2002.

Laub, Dori. "Bearing Witness or the Vicissitudes of Listening." Pages 57–74 in *Testimony: Crises of Witnessing in Literature, Psychoanalysis, and History*. Edited by Shoshana Felman and Dori Laub. New York: Routledge, 1992.

Poser, Ruth. *Das Ezechielbuch als Trauma-Literatur*. VTSup 154. Leiden: Brill, 2012.

———. "'Das Gericht geht durch den Magen': Die verschlungene Schriftrolle (Ez 2:8b–3:3) und andere Essensszenarien im Ezechielbuch." Pages 116–30 in *Essen und Trinken in der Bibel: Ein literarisches Festmahl für Rainer Kessler zum 65. Geburtstag*. Edited by Michaela Geiger, Christl M. Maier, and Uta Schmidt. Gütersloh: Gütersloher Verlagshaus, 2009.

Reddemann, Luise. *Imagination als heilsame Kraft: Zur Behandlung von Traumafolgen mit ressourcenorientierten Verfahren*. 9th ed. Stuttgart: Pfeiffer bei Klett-Cotta, 2003.

Riedesser, Peter. "Belastende Kriegserfahrungen in der Kleinkindzeit." Pages 37–50 in *Kindheiten im Zweiten Weltkrieg: Kriegserfahrungen und deren Folgen aus psychohistorischer Perspektive*. Edited by Hartmut Radebold. Munich: Juventa, 2006.

Sack, Martin. "Narrative Arbeit im Kontext 'schonender Traumatherapie.'" Pages 150–60 in *Narrative Bewältigung von Trauma und Verlust*. Edited by Carl Eduard Scheidt et al. Stuttgart: Schattauer, 2015.

Scheidt, Carl Eduard, and Gabriele Lucius-Hoene. "Kategorisierung und narrative Bewältigung bindungsbezogener Traumaerfahrungen im Erwachsenenbindungsinterview." Pages 26–38 in *Narrative Bewälti-*

gung von Trauma und Verlust. Edited by Carl Eduard Scheidt et al. Stuttgart: Schattauer, 2015.

Smith-Christopher, Daniel L. *A Biblical Theology of Exile.* OBT. Minneapolis: Fortress, 2002.

Weinberg, Manfred. "Trauma—Geschichte, Gespenst, Literatur—und Gedächtnis." Pages 173–206 in *Trauma: Zwischen Psychoanalyse und kulturellem Deutungsmuster.* Edited by Elisabeth Bronfen, Birgit R. Erdle, and Sigrid Weigel. Cologne: Böhlau, 1999.

Fragmented Voices:
Collective Identity and Traumatization in Lamentations

Elizabeth Boase

"How lonely sits the city…"

So begins the book of Lamentations (1:1), written following the Babylonian destruction of Jerusalem (586 BCE) and arguably one of the clearest expressions of trauma literature in the Hebrew Bible. The image of the isolated and bereaved woman, violated, degraded, lacking anyone to comfort her, represents well the traumatic impact of war and devastation. Metaphorically rich, this personification of the city as woman—Daughter Zion—holds in tension both the personal, individual reality of suffering and a recognition of communal suffering.

This essay explores the interplay between the individual and communal voices in Lamentations through the application of recent sociological theory concerning communal trauma and the role of texts in facilitating collective identity around trauma. Drawing on the work of Jeffrey Alexander, I argue that Lamentations enacts a process that seeks to gather a fragmented community around a shared narrative in order to facilitate collective unity and identity.[1] Through its evocative poetry, its aesthetic artistry, and in the interplay of voices, Lamentations models a movement from the fragmentation of individual suffering and broken narratives to the formation of a collectivity that comes together in unified voice, joined in its recitation of shared trauma. Lamentations facilitates the emergence of a new metanarrative that begins the process of reconstructing meaning for a decimated community.

---

1. Jeffrey C. Alexander, *Trauma: A Social Theory* (Cambridge: Polity, 2012).

Approaches to Trauma

The application of trauma theory to biblical texts is proving to be fruitful in opening up new insights into both the sociological and rhetorical functions of texts so often produced in the wake of events that can be described as traumatic. The range of recent publications points to the efficacious nature of this framework.[2] Through even a cursory reading of this literature, however, it becomes clear that the concepts of *trauma* and *trauma theory* can be applied in a variety of ways and in themselves do not represent a unified theory.

Trauma is a term used across a variety of disciplines, including medicine, psychology, sociology, anthropology, literary studies, and in various fields of religious, theological, and biblical studies. Trauma has been variously defined.[3] With its linguistic origins centered on the wounding of the body, more recent definitions of trauma encompass the lasting injurious effects of violence and terror on the human psyche. A traumatic experience is one that overwhelms and terrifies.[4]

An often-identified feature of a traumatic experience is its disruptive nature. Irene Smith Landsman states:

> Trauma and loss are experiences that push us to our limits. By definition, trauma overwhelms our usual abilities to cope and adjust, calling into question the basic assumptions that organise our experience of ourselves, relationships, the world, and the human condition itself. The crisis of trauma is pervasive, altering emotional, cognitive, and behavioural

---

2. See, for example, David M. Carr, *Holy Resilience: The Bible's Traumatic Origins* (New Haven: Yale University Press, 2014); Kathleen M. O'Connor, *Jeremiah: Pain and Promise* (Minneapolis: Fortress, 2011); Eve-Marie Becker, Jan Dochhorn, and Else Kragelund Holt, eds., *Trauma and Truamatization in Individual and Collective Dimensions: Insights from Biblical Studies and Beyond*, SANt 2 (Göttingen: Vandenhoeck & Ruprecht, 2014); Ruth Poser, *Das Ezechielbuch als Trauma-Literatur*, VTSup 154 (Leiden: Brill, 2012); and David Janzen, *The Violent Gift: Trauma's Subversion of the Deuteronomistic History's Narrative*, LHBOTS 561 (New York: T&T Clark, 2012).

3. See Eve-Marie Becker, "'Trauma Studies' and Exegesis: Challenges, Limits and Prospects," in Becker, Dochhorn, and Holt, 15–29.

4. Judith Herman, *Trauma and Recovery: The Aftermath of Violence—from Domestic Abuse to Political Terror* (New York: Basic Books, 1997), 33; Christopher G. Frechette, "The Old Testament as Controlled Substance: How Insights from Trauma Studies Reveal Healing Capacities in Potentially Harmful Texts," *Int* 69 (2015): 20–34.

experience, and the subjective experience of trauma not infrequently includes a crisis of meaning at a deep level.[5]

These deeper meanings include assumptions about the benevolence of the world, concepts of justice, predictability and control, sense of trust, self and self-worth, and the nature and character of the divine.[6]

Literature on recovery from trauma widely acknowledges the importance of narrative in the process of healing. We can, perhaps, identify two potential levels of narrativization in the wake of trauma. Judith Herman notes that, in the case of individual traumatization, there are three fundamental stages of recovery: establishing safety, reconstructing the trauma story, and restoring the connections between survivors and their community.[7] Recounting the trauma is the first, foundational level of narrativization.[8] Based on the recognition of the collapse of meaning at a deeper level, the construction of a new metanarrative can also be seen as an important task in the wake of trauma.[9] On the one hand, the fundamental narrative represents a process of "cognitive mastery" over the events, an attempt to order the details and to explain what happened.[10] The formation of a new metanarrative, on the other hand, responds to the deeper, existential crises that may arise, and it represents a revised framework of understanding that can "assimilate the reality of trauma."[11]

A range of hermeneutical questions emerge in the application of theories of trauma to biblical studies.[12] Of interest for the current discussion is that of the relationship between individual and communal or collective trauma and how it is that a community might identify itself as one that is defined by trauma. One of the defining features of trauma is its tendency

---

5. Irene Smith Landsman, "Crises of Meaning in Trauma and Loss," in *Loss of the Assumptive World: A Theory of Traumatic Loss*, ed. Jeffrey Kauffman (New York: Brunner-Routledge, 2002), 13.

6. Ibid., 19.

7. Herman, *Trauma and Recovery*, 3, 155.

8. Ibid., 174–95; Landsman, "Crises of Meaning," 26

9. Alexander, *Trauma*, 16–17.

10. Landsman, "Crises of Meaning," 15.

11. Ibid. 19.

12. Questions emerge as to the usefulness of applying what is essentially a contemporary concept to ancient text, given that trauma and the related diagnostic category of post-traumatic stress disorder (PTSD) was not a clinically recognized disorder until 1980. See Frechette, "Old Testament as Controlled Substance," 22–23.

to cause a sense of isolation. Although trauma is most often considered at the level of the individual, there is a growing body of literature on the impact of trauma on communities. At the communal level, Kai Erikson argues, both centripetal and centrifugal forces come into play. Traumatic suffering isolates, in that it draws the sufferer away from the center of a group, yet trauma can lead to the formation of different types of community centered on shared suffering.[13]

Two major frameworks have been applied to the biblical text: those emerging from literary studies, whose theoretical framework has been shaped largely by the seminal work of Cathy Caruth;[14] and studies shaped by concepts of collective trauma developed within the field of sociology and cultural studies. While these two "schools" do share some commonality, they differ significantly in their understanding of the way that a collectivity identifies and expresses itself as one that is traumatized.

The distinction between these two frameworks is centered on the question of representation. Caruth has been described by Ruth Leys as "an exponent of a postmodernist, poststructuralist approach to psychic trauma."[15] Caruth draws on Freudian psychoanalytic theory and the neurobiological insights of Bessel van der Kolk and Judith Herman, arguing that massive trauma so overwhelms the normal mechanisms of consciousness and memory that it is unable to be represented in either memory or language.[16] Trauma is an absence, a gap, unknown yet obsessively replayed in the form of flashbacks, bodily responses, and other associated behaviors. The notion of a failure of language is central: trauma in its essence defies representation in normal discursive language. The presence of trauma may, however, be witnessed in *imaginative* literature, in figurative language.[17] Yet to talk of the literature of trauma is, within this framework, an impossibility because "trauma will resist incorporation into a

---

13. Kai Erikson, "Notes on Trauma and Community," in *Trauma: Explorations in Memory*, ed. Cathy Caruth (Baltimore: Johns Hopkins University Press, 1995), 187.

14. Cathy Caruth, *Unclaimed Experience: Trauma, Narrative and History* (Baltimore: Johns Hopkins University Press, 1996); Caruth, *Trauma: Explorations in Memory* (Baltimore: Johns Hopkins University Press, 1995).

15. Ruth Leys, *Trauma: A Genealogy* (Chicago: University of Chicago Press, 2000), 266.

16. Cathy Caruth, "Trauma and Experience: Introduction," in Caruth, *Trauma: Explorations in Memory*, 4–5.

17. Joshua Pederson, "Speak Trauma: Towards a Revised Understanding of Literary Trauma Theory," *Narrative* 22 (2014): 334.

textual narrative precisely because it resists incorporation into personal narratives."[18] The presence of interruptions and gaps/lacunae in narratives are thus seen as pivotal points where trauma makes itself evident.

Although Caruth's literary theory has been influential, her approach has been critiqued, especially with regard to its application to texts that function at a communal level. Amir Khadem argues that psychoanalytic approaches are "loosely based on a metaphor for individual psychic trauma."[19] There is, Khadem argues, an inherent difficulty in the assumption that insights from the study of individual human psyche can be applied to a collective group. In particular, he notes that for trauma to be communicated in a way that forms a collective identity a process of representation must have occurred. He states: "When the analysis assumes that society at large can be studied like an individual human being, there is no need to explain the mechanisms of social life, nor does it seem important that different bodily aspects of humans may have no parallel in the social sphere."[20] In its application to texts that express a communal understanding of traumatized identity, discussions within this framework operate under what Alexander refers to as a naturalistic fallacy, "an understanding about human nature in the social world, leading to the belief that being culturally traumatized is the only natural reaction of a society to extremely harmful events."[21]

The oft-quoted definition of communal trauma by Kai Erikson highlights this tendency, apparent especially in its biological metaphors:

> By collective trauma ... I mean a blow to the basic tissues of social life that damages the bonds attaching people together and impairs the prevailing sense of community. The collective trauma works its way slowly and even insidiously into the awareness of those who suffer from it, so that it does not have the suddenness normally associated with "trauma." But it is a form of shock all the same, a gradual realisation that the community

---

18. Janzen, *Violent Gift*, 35.

19. Amir Kadhem, "Cultural Trauma as a Social Construct: 9/11 Fiction and the Epistemology of Communal Pain," *Intertexts* 18 (2014): 181; see also Pederson, "Speak Trauma," who critiques Caruth's framework based on its understanding of memory and trauma.

20. Khadem, "Cultural Trauma," 182. Erikson goes so far as to state, "When a community is profoundly affected one can speak of a damaged social organism in almost the same way that one would speak of a damaged body" ("Notes on Trauma," 188).

21. Alexander, *Trauma*, 13.

no longer exists as an effective from of support and that an important
part of the self has disappeared.... "I" continue to exist, though damaged
and maybe even permanently changed. "You" continue to exist, though
distant and hard to relate to. But "we" no longer exist as a connected pair
or as linked cells in a larger communal body.[22]

Erikson's discussion lacks any account of the processes that might occur
within the communal dynamic.

The sociological model of collective trauma developed by Jeffrey Alexander and his associates provides an alternate framework for exploring
the representability of trauma and of the function of representation at the
communal level. Alexander develops a constructivist theory of collective
trauma that seeks to account for the process by which a community might
come to identify itself as traumatized. Important here is the recognition
that the identification of communal trauma is not the automatic outcome
of an event experienced by a group of people. It occurs through a process
of representation that brings about a new collective identity. He argues
that cultural trauma occurs "when members of a collectivity *feel* they have
been subjected to a horrendous event that leaves indelible marks upon
their group *consciousness, marking their memories* forever and *changing
their future identity* in fundamental and irrevocable ways."[23]

While the representation of trauma at the communal level does bear
some resemblance to the importance of reconstructing the trauma story
as identified in Herman's work on recovery from trauma, it is important to
emphasize here that Alexander's focus is on cultural or collective identity
rather than on individual experience.[24] While both function as what I have
referred to as foundational narratives, at the collective level the narrative
functions to shape communal identity. In order for a *collective* identity
to be *defined* by traumatic experience, for a group to cohere and identify itself as traumatized, a process of cultural representation is necessary.

---

22. Erikson, "Notes on Trauma," 187.

23. Alexander, *Trauma*, 6, emphasis added.

24. Jeffrey C. Alexander and Elizabeth Breese argue that the construction of collective trauma is often fueled by individual experiences of suffering, but at stake is
the threat to communal identity ("Introduction," in *Narrating Trauma: On the Impact
of Collective Suffering*, ed. Ron Eyerman, Jeffrey C. Alexander, and Elizabeth Breese
[Boulder, CO: Paradigm, 2014], xii).

Traumas can become collective "only if they are conceived as wounds to social identity."[25]

At the level of collective identity, trauma is socially mediated, woven into communal memory through acts of representation and meaning-making.[26] The formation of group identity involves the representation of a new metanarrative, which reflects the nature of the trauma inflicted and begins the process of redefining cultural meaning in light of the shattering impact of that trauma. This trauma process functions to reconstruct social identity around a shared story, providing an avenue for a new form of social incorporation and the possibility of resolution of social problems.[27]

Alexander argues that representing trauma depends on constructing a framework of cultural classification. Trauma representation constructs a narrative that persuades the audience—the collectivity—that they have been traumatized. Four representations are essential in the creation of this narrative:

- the nature of the pain: what happened and to whom;
- the nature of the victim: who was affected;
- the relation of the trauma victim(s) to the wider audience: the extent to which the trauma narrative prompts a wider audience that has not experienced the victim group's suffering to identify with the immediately victimized group; and
- attribution of responsibility: who caused the trauma.[28]

Through such representation a new plurality is constructed; it is a collective *we* that identifies itself as a traumatized community.[29]

In the discussion that follows, each of these elements will be considered in relation to Lamentations, an aesthetic creation that offers a narrative of suffering and trauma that opens the way for the formation of a new metanarrative. In its interplay of individual and communal voices, Lamentations functions as a form of social reconstruction through which a new communal identity is achieved. In the interplay of voices, there is a movement from individual experiences of suffering to the formation of

---

25. Ibid., xii.
26. Alexander, *Trauma*, 6.
27. Ibid., 27.
28. Ibid., 17–19.
29. Alexander and Breese, "Introduction," xiii.

a group gathered together as a traumatized collectivity. In the shift from third-person gazing at the pain of the personified city in chapter 1, through the speeches of the city, the narrator, and the man of chapter 3, and to the climactic communal lament of chapter 5, we witness the emergence of a new communal identity, one shaped by shared experience.

The Nature of the Pain

In the aftermath of suffering, survivors face the challenge of understanding the event itself. The story needs to be told, an account formed.[30] This is an important first step in the process of representation.[31] Suffering lies at the heart of Lamentations, portrayed using evocative and emotive language. We are confronted with suffering bodies, physical destruction, death, and decay. Language emphasizes the extremity of the experience, asserting that the suffering lies outside the realm of normal experience.[32] The pain encompasses all aspects of life, as is emphasized in the breadth of the images used.

The material destruction of the city. That there was widespread destruction of material aspects of the city is found in both concrete and metaphorical expressions. Direct reference is made to loss of buildings in Lam 2 (dwellings and strongholds, 2:2; palaces and strongholds, 2:5; tabernacle and booth, 2:6; walls of the palaces, 2:7; gates and bars, 2:9), with more metaphorical references further evoking the extent of the destruction (roads mourning and gates desolate, 1:4; ramparts and walls lamenting and languishing, 2:8; references to the wall of Daughter Zion, 2:8, 18; foundations consumed by fire, 4:11). The use of verbs of destruction and warfare reinforce the physical losses with the city: *šlk* "throw down" (2:11); *ngʿ* "bring down" (2:2); *gdʿ* "cut down" (2:3); *šḥt* "lay in ruins" (2:5–6); references to *ʾēš* "fire" (2:3–4). Various references to famine and the need to buy wood point to the decimation of the land (e.g., 1:11; 2:20; 4:4, 8, 10; 5:4).

The collapse of the symbolic and ritual world. A significant component of the suffering experienced speaks clearly to a loss of those institutions and beliefs that framed the meaning world of the community. The collapse of the ritual world is seen in the references to the violated and destroyed

---

30. Landsman, "Crises of Meaning," 15; Herman, *Trauma and Recovery,* 174–95.
31. Herman, *Trauma and Recovery,* 3.
32. This is in line with Landsman's insight of trauma being a limit experience.

temple (1:10; 2:7) and to the abolition of religious festivals (1:4; 2:6). Priests are scorned (4:16), prophets no longer proclaim (2:9), and both are killed (2:20). The king is carried off (4:20). The hope and confidence previously supported by Zion and royal theologies is shattered (2:9, 15; 4:12, 16, 20; 5:18). Meaning has collapsed.

The physical suffering of the people. The presence of wounded and suffering bodies and the piling up of corpses throughout Lamentations leave little doubt as to the reality of physical suffering. Dominant motifs in the description include famine, exile, physical wounding, imprisonment, torture, rape, hard servitude, and death across all ages, gender, and social standing. Particular emphasis is placed on suffering children, who are not only vulnerable but are the hope for the future. All suffer—and suffer grievously.

The emotional distress and anguish. The reality of physical suffering is reinforced and intensified with frequent references to emotions and physical symptoms of distress. Feelings expressed include abandonment, violation, grief, desolation, mourning, humiliation, anguish, weeping, groaning, and feeling faint. Frequent use is made of bodily metaphors of distress, grounding the emotional suffering in the material world, echoing the familiar feelings and sensations of human bodies. Reference is made to hearts (wrung out, 1:20; faint, 1:22), churning stomach/bowels (1:20; 2:11), bones (fire in bones, 1:13) tears (1:2, 16; 2:11, 18; 3:49–51), liver (poured out, 2:11), kidneys (3:13[33]). This embodiment allows individuals, who may have had different experiences, to come together through language that expresses common suffering. The embodied language draws the community into shared understanding of the physical reality of suffering.[34]

THE NATURE OF THE VICTIM

The descriptions of suffering in Lamentations incorporate the whole community. People of all ages, genders, and classes are described. The descriptions are not confined to either those taken into exile or those who remained behind. Chapters 3 and 4 both include references to

---

33. "He shot into my vitals [kidneys] the arrows of his quiver" (3:13 NRSV) can be read either as an example of physical wounding or as a description of a loss of vitality.

34. See Elizabeth Boase, "The Traumatised Body: Communal Trauma and Somatisation in Lamentations," in Becker, Dochhorn, and Holt, 193–209.

deportation, and there is frequent reference to the fate of the elite, the group that most sources suggest were the ones taken into exile.[35] Suffering is not exclusive: it is the whole community that suffers; it is the whole group that is traumatized.

Unifying aspects of the poetry have already been identified in the descriptions of physical and emotional suffering. Beyond this—and of significance for the present argument—changes in point of view made possible by the speaking voices function to evoke a movement from that of a detached individual observer of the suffering to that of a community speaking in one voice.

At least four voices can be identified in the text: the lamenter,[36] Daughter Zion, the man of Lam 3, and the community. The distribution of their speaking voices is as follows:

- Lam 1: lamenter (1:1–9b, 10–11b, 17); Daughter Zion (1:9c, 11c–16, 18–22)
- Lam 2: lamenter (2:1–19); Daughter Zion (2:20–22)
- Lam 3: the man (3:1–39); community (3:40–47); lamenter (3:48–66)
- Lam 4: lamenter (4:1–16, 21–22); community (4:17–20)
- Lam 5: community (5:1–22).

An important progression occurs. Lamentations opens with a third-person description of the personified city (1:1–11), who is given human attributes yet described from a distance—a suffering other. Given that this is the personification of a nonhuman entity, the option exists for hearers to focus on the physical city as object. However, the distancing is not complete; the speaker is empathetic to the plight of the city, as is evident through the attribution of emotion and sentience. That it is the city that is

---

35. Adele Berlin argues that the man in Lam 3 is representative of the exiled community (*Lamentations*, OTL [Louisville: Westminster John Knox, 2002], 84–85).

36. In this designation I follow Miriam Bier, who eschews the traditional designation of this voice as the narrator because such a designation risks suggesting that this voice belongs to an omnipotent observer (*Perhaps There Is Hope: Reading Lamentations as a Polyphony of Pain, Penitence, and Protest*, LHBOTS 603 [New York: T&T Clark, 2015], 42–43). Identifying the voice as the lamenter suggests that the voice belongs to one participating voice among others, and it recognizes that the lamenter is as much a persona within the poems as the other voices.

personified further subverts the distancing achieved through third-person description, as the personification at once incorporates both the physical city and the audience, those who reside in the city. Despite the subversion, the possibility of remaining a detached observer of the suffering remains.

When the city herself speaks (1:11–22), the distance between the sufferer and audience begins to be bridged, facilitated by the content of the speech. Daughter Zion demands that she be noticed (1:12) and comforted (1:16). The use of embodied language (1:13, 14, 16, 20, 21, 22) grounds her suffering in sensations familiar to those who hear. Objectivity and distance begin to break down as the audience is asked to engage with the suffering described.

Chapter 2 draws back again, as the lamenter describes the destruction of the city in third-person speech (2:1–19). The sheer piling up of strong action verbs and adverbs (2:1–9) suggests an intensity of emotion, which finally spills out in 2:11. Here the lamenter, too, breeches a gap as he describes his own response to what he has witnessed, echoing the speech of the woman in chapter 1 (eyes weeping, stomach churning).

A change of voice in chapter 3 foregrounds a different realm of suffering. The descriptions of Daughter Zion in Lam 1 emphasize the interior wounding of rape and violation, while Lam 3 emphasizes the exterior wounding of weapons, imprisonment, and torture (3:1–19). This represents a movement from the domestic to the public, from the citizenry to the military, from predominantly female suffering to male suffering. Suffering is again embodied, with anguish described using culturally powerful metaphors.[37]

Only after these three voices have spoken, each using embodied, personal language, do we hear the voice of the community. In 3:42–47 the community confesses and complains. The confession is brief ("we have transgressed and rebelled") and is followed by an extended complaint about divine absence and silence, echoing the speech of the city in Lam 1.

Chapter 4 includes the voices of both the lamenter and, briefly, the community, describing in more detail the suffering caused by the ongoing conditions within the city. Here there are graphic descriptions of the physical depletion of the entire social group. The extremity of societal collapse is seen in the references to the deprivation of infants (4:4) and to mothers' resorting to cannibalism (4:10). It is clear that the trauma results not only from the past act of war but also from ongoing suffering and deprivation.

---

37. See Boase, "The Traumatised Body."

The continuity of pain and suffering in the text functions to draw the audience further into the representation of trauma.

Finally, in Lam 5, the community speaks. In this extended communal lament, we witness a re-formed community, voicing together its collective identity as a traumatized group, united in suffering. Of the laments in the book, that this is the most pure in terms of genre suggests a unity absent elsewhere in the poems. The community is able to name its suffering together, to express fleeting hope, and to plead to God to bring about change.

That the community speaks together marks a transition from the opening of the book, where suffering is described "from a distance." This trajectory is an important aspect of the trauma process enacted by this poetry, modeling as it does a movement from the fragmentation of individual suffering and broken narratives to the formation of a collectivity speaking in unified voice, joined in its recitation of shared trauma.

The Relation of the Victim to the Wider Audience

In its historical context, Lamentations did not address an audience that had not experienced the suffering of the victim group. Rather, the poetry of Lamentations draws the fragmented victim community together as a unified whole. It is the fragmentation of the victim community that accounts for certain poetic features, such as the narrator's distance and the poetry's appeal to passers-by, that create the impression of an audience separate from the victim group. The primary historical context of the book confirms that such tropes served to address the fragmentation that resulted from the extreme suffering of the victim group, rather than to address an audience that was unaffected by the disastrous events. Lamentations can be seen to represent the trauma to the *carrier group*, to use Alexander's term, in this way forming a new identity centered on the traumatic experience. That this text is subsequently used by future generations, however, does mean that those who use these poems within liturgical contexts are drawn into the dynamic of representation.

Attribution of Responsibility

The attribution of responsibility is identified as one of the critical representations necessary in the creation of a compelling trauma narrative.[38]

---

38. Alexander, *Trauma*, 19.

That process begins in Lamentations, seen through complaints, protests, and confessions, which spread blame around.

- Daughter Zion is described as transgressing, and she confesses rebelliousness and sin (1:5, 8, 14, 18, 20, 22).
- The enemies are accountable for the destruction of the city, the violation of the temple, and the ongoing hardship of daily life (1:1–3, 5–7, 9–10, 17, 21; 2:16; 3:46, 52, 59–66; 4:12, 18–20).
- Priests and prophets are given some responsibility for their failure to lead appropriately (2:14; 4:13).
- Previous generations are identified as sinning, and the current generation is seen as bearing the sins of the past (5:7).
- The present generation confesses their sins (3:42; 5:16).
- Primary responsibility is placed in the hands of God (see especially Lam 2; also 1:5, 12–15; 3:1–33[39]; 4:11, 16). God is described as follows: acting in hot anger, wrath, and with forethought; being like an enemy; abandoning the people; and being merciless. This attribution of responsibility is especially strong in Lam 2, which lacks virtually any confessional language.
- God is described not only as causing the wounding—the trauma—but also as continuing to inflict suffering through failure to see and respond to the people and as refusing to forgive (1:20; 3:40–45, 50; 5:20–22).

Attributing causality is a matter of symbolic and social construction. Alexander notes that, when causality is assigned in the religious arena, it raises issues of theodicy.[40] While the enemies play a significant role in the affliction of suffering, the actions of God are clearly understood to stand behind those of the enemy. There is a tension in Lamentations between human and divine responsibility. A retributive (sin–punishment) model is present in those places where Daughter Zion and the people acknowledge human sinfulness. Divine causality is also strongly named but not always assumed as directly related to human sin (Lam 2).[41] Alongside this, however, stands an antitheodic element that refuses to explain the link

---

39. Note that 3:1 uses a pronominal form and does not name God as perpetrator. It is apparent by 3:18, however, that the man is speaking of God's actions against him.
40. Alexander, *Trauma*, 19.
41. See Elizabeth Boase, "Constructing Meaning in the Face of Suffering: Theod-

between God's actions and sin.[42] The multiple viewpoints emphasize that this is social construction in process, not fixed theological explanation.[43] Landsman notes that the attribution of causality, and especially self-blame and/or blaming the victim, enhances a perception of control.[44] A significant impact of the loss of meaning in the wake of trauma is the loss of confidence in the benevolence and justice of the world. Attribution of responsibility counters this. In the link between sin, suffering, and God's actions—despite that link being questioned and subverted—a modicum of control is reasserted. Even if tentatively, and perhaps problematically, Lamentations asserts a level of personal/communal control. If sin were at the root of the destruction, then the possibility of averting future disaster is present. The role of chance is minimized.[45]

THE REPRESENTATION OF TRAUMA IN LAMENTATIONS

Lamentations can be read as an example of what Alexander calls a trauma process. The story of suffering is told, the victims—in this case the entire community—are identified, and an explanation of causality is offered. In the interplay of voices we see modeled a movement from the fragmentation and isolation of individual suffering to the formation of a new communal identity under the narrative of shared trauma. As a text of representation and social mediation, Lamentations functions to unify and reform the community, creating new meaning out of catastrophic crisis. Alexander and Breese argue, "Trauma scripts are performed as symbolic actions

---

icy in Lamentations," *VT* 58 (2008): 449–86. Note that an educative theodicy (we learn from our suffering) is also present in 3:25–39.

42. F. W. Dobbs-Allsopp, *Lamentations*, IBC (Louisville: Westminster John Knox, 2002), 30.

43. For discussion, see, for example, Elizabeth Boase, *The Fulfilment of Doom: The Dialogic Interaction between the Book of Lamentations and the Pre-exilic/Early Exilic Prophetic Literature*, LHBOTS 437 (New York: T&T Clark, 2006); Kathleen M. O'Connor, *Lamentations and the Tears of the World* (New York: Orbis, 2002); Dobbs-Allsopp, *Lamentations*.

44. See also, Frechette, "Old Testament as Controlled Substance."

45. Landsman, "Crises of Meaning," 16: "Specifically, we tend to attribute causality in ways that allow belief in personal control over future outcomes to be maintained.... An internal locus of control—a belief that events that affect us are consequences of our own actions or attributes—is a generally adaptive attributional style."

in the theatres of everyday collective life."[46] The application of a constructivist model of collective trauma to the text of Lamentations opens up new ways of understanding the rhetorical function of this text. Although the expressive function of Lamentations has long been recognized, its role as representational language that facilitates collective identification as a traumatized group is seldom identified.[47] Lamentations is arguably both discursive and constructive. It provides a discursive space in which the pain and suffering of the community, and the individuals within it, can find expression, giving voice to what may potentially yet be unvoiced. Beyond this, however, it is also constructive, as through its representational language new community identity is formed. The text both makes sense of and shapes collective experience and identity.

The recognition of the representational role of Lamentations, and the rhetorical function it plays, accounts also for the presence of poetry in the midst of crisis. Alexander states that "imagination is intrinsic to the very process of representation. It seizes upon an inchoate experience from life, and forms it, through association, condensation, and aesthetic creation, into some specific shape."[48] Literary form, metaphor, personification, and multiple voices function together to create an aesthetic representation that draws the members of the audience into its world and unites them around a common vision of who they are as a collective.

The power and success of this process become evident when the liturgical use of Lamentations is considered. This text was, and continues to be, used on occasions that commemorate not only the destruction of the temple in 586 BCE but also the destruction in 70 CE and subsequent disasters experienced by the Jewish community. In a poignant reflection on the reading of Lamentations during Tisha B'Av, Eugene Pogany describes his own encounter with the text in the context of mourning his grandmother's death in Auschwitz:

> Finally, on this Tisha B'Av, may the Jews' longing for our holy sanctuary, our sorrow over its destruction, and our pledge by the rivers of Babylon to remember Jerusalem help to bind each and all of us in memory

---

46. Alexander and Breese, "Introduction," xxvii.

47. Tod Linafelt discusses the liturgical role of Lamentations as survival literature (*Surviving Lamentations: Catastrophe, Lament, and Protest in the Afterlife of a Biblical Book* [Chicago: University of Chicago Press, 2000], 35–61).

48. Alexander, *Trauma*, 13–14.

of our suffering and that of others. Of other women and mothers and other babies and other elders and priests and righteous ones whose cries explode even the words of Lamentations—Auschwitz, Hiroshima, Kurdistan, Tibet, Cambodia, Bosnia, Rwanda, Native America, and in thousands of known and unknown cities and villages where people have been subjected to physical and spiritual exile and died longing for home.[49]

As a representational process, Lamentations continues to have an identity-forming role for communities who gather around it.

The application of Alexander's theory to Lamentations provides a hermeneutical frame for a differently nuanced reading of this text. In recognizing an unfolding trauma process, one can argue that Lamentations does more than witness to suffering. It provides a discursive space in which communal experience is narrated, reflecting the emergence of a new meta-narrative shaped by trauma. Lamentations is as a key text that, through its representational power, allows communal coherence to re-form, embedding in story and memory a new sense of identity, shaped and forever marked by unprecedented trauma.

Bibliography

Alexander, Jeffrey C. *Trauma: A Social Theory*. Cambridge: Polity, 2012.
Alexander, Jeffrey C., and Elizabeth Breese. "Introduction". Pages xi–xxxv in *Narrating Trauma: On the Impact of Collective Suffering*. Edited by Ron Eyerman, Jeffrey Alexander, and Elizabeth Breese. Boulder, CO: Paradigm, 2014.
Becker, Eve-Marie. "'Trauma Studies' and Exegesis: Challenges, Limits and Prospects." Pages 15–29 in *Trauma and Truamatization in Individual and Collective Dimensions: Insights from Biblical Studies and Beyond*. Edited by Eve-Marie Becker, Jan Dochhorn, and Else Kragelund Holt. SANt 2. Göttingen: Vandenhoeck & Ruprecht, 2014.
Becker, Eve-Marie, Jan Dochhorn, and Else Kragelund Holt, eds., *Trauma and Truamatization in Individual and Collective Dimensions: Insights from Biblical Studies and Beyond*. SANt 2. Göttingen: Vandenhoeck & Ruprecht, 2014.

---

49. Eugene Pogany, "Exile and Memory: Reflections on Tisha B'Av," *CrossCurrents* 45 (1995): 536.

Berlin, Adele. *Lamentations*. OTL. Louisville: Westminster John Knox, 2002.

Bier, Miriam. *Perhaps There Is Hope: Reading Lamentations as a Polyphony of Pain, Penitence, and Protest*. LHBOTS 603. New York: T&T Clark, 2015.

Boase, Elizabeth. "Constructing Meaning in the Face of Suffering: Theodicy in Lamentations." *VT* 58 (2008): 449–86.

———. *The Fulfilment of Doom: The Dialogic Interaction between the Book of Lamentations and the Pre-exilic/Early Exilic Prophetic Literature*. LHBOTS 437. New York: T&T Clark, 2006.

———. "The Traumatised Body: Communal Trauma and Somatisation in Lamentations." Pages 193–209 in *Trauma and Truamatization in Individual and Collective Dimensions: Insights from Biblical Studies and Beyond*. Edited by Eve-Marie Becker, Jan Dochhorn, and Else Kragelund Holt. SANt 2. Göttingen: Vandenhoeck & Ruprecht, 2014.

Carr, David M. *Holy Resilience: The Bible's Traumatic Origins*. New Haven: Yale University Press, 2014.

Caruth, Cathy. "Trauma and Experience: Introduction." Pages 3–12 in *Trauma: Explorations in Memory*. Edited by Cathy Caruth. Baltimore: Johns Hopkins University Press, 1995.

———. *Unclaimed Experience: Trauma, Narrative and History*. Baltimore: Johns Hopkins University Press, 1996.

———, ed. *Trauma: Explorations in Memory*. Baltimore: Johns Hopkins University Press, 1995 .

Dobbs-Allsopp, F. W. *Lamentations*. IBC. Louisville: Westminster John Knox, 2002.

Erikson, Kai. "Notes on Trauma and Community." Pages 183–99 in *Trauma: Explorations in Memory*. Edited by Cathy Caruth. Baltimore: Johns Hopkins University Press, 1995.

Frechette, Christopher G. "The Old Testament as Controlled Substance: How Insights from Trauma Studies Reveal Healing Capacities in Potentially Harmful Texts." *Int* 69 (2015): 20–34.

Herman, Judith. *Trauma and Recovery: The Aftermath of Violence—From Domestic Abuse to Political Terror*. Rev. ed. New York: Basic Books, 1997.

Janzen, David. *The Violent Gift: Trauma's Subversion of the Deuteronomistic History's Narrative*. LHBOTS 561. New York: T&T Clark, 2012.

Kadhem, Amir. "Cultural Trauma as a Social Construct: 9/11 Fiction and the Epistemology of Communal Pain." *Intertexts* 18 (2014): 181–97.

Landsman, Irene Smith. "Crises of Meaning in Trauma and Loss." Pages 13–30 in *Loss of the Assumptive World: A Theory of Traumatic Loss*. Edited by Jeffrey Kauffman. New York: Brunner-Routledge, 2002.

Leys, Ruth. *Trauma: A Genealogy*. Chicago: University of Chicago Press, 2000.

Linafelt, Tod. *Surviving Lamentations: Catastrophe, Lament, and Protest in the Afterlife of a Biblical Book*. Chicago: University of Chicago Press, 2000.

O'Connor, Kathleen M. *Jeremiah: Pain and Promise*. Minneapolis: Fortress, 2011.

———. *Lamentations and the Tears of the World*. New York: Orbis, 2002.

Pederson, Joshua. "Speak Trauma: Towards a Revised Understanding of Literary Trauma Theory." *Narrative* 22 (2014): 333–53.

Pogany, Eugene. "Exile and Memory: Reflections on Tisha B'Av." *CrossCurrents* 45 (1995): 531–36.

Poser, Ruth. *Das Ezechielbuch als Trauma-Literatur*. VTSup 154. Leiden: Brill, 2012.

Daughter Babylon Raped and Bereaved (Isaiah 47): Symbolic Violence and Meaning-Making in Recovery from Trauma

Christopher G. Frechette

In Isa 47 YHWH declares that violence shall befall Babylon, which is characterized as "virgin Daughter Babylon" and "daughter Chaldea"[1] and referred to in this essay simply as "Daughter Babylon." In the Hebrew Bible, cities are in many cases anthropomorphized as female within discourse that represents interaction between the city and YHWH, and such interaction may be either favorable or unfavorable for the city.[2] In Isa 47:3 YHWH declares to Daughter Babylon, "Your nakedness shall be uncovered, and your shame shall be seen. I will take vengeance"; 47:9 adds, "both these things shall come upon you in a moment, in one day: the loss of children and widowhood shall come upon you in full measure."[3] The agency of YHWH is explicit in verse 3 and implied in verse 9. As argued below, the humiliation described in verse 3 includes rape. The portrayal of Daughter Babylon here in several ways inversely mirrors the portrayal of Jerusalem as Daughter Zion in Isa 49–54.[4]

---

1. *Chaldea* designates the Babylonian dynasty responsible for the devastation of Jerusalem and the exile of Judeans in the early sixth century BCE.

2. See Mark E. Biddle, "The Figure of Lady Jerusalem: Identification, Deification and Personification of Cities in the Ancient Near East," in *The Biblical Canon in Comparative Perspective*, ed. K. Lawson Younger, William W. Hallo, and Bernard F. Batto, Ancient Near Eastern Texts and Studies 11, Scripture in Context 4 (Lewiston, NY: Mellen, 1991), 174–94; and Aloysius Fitzgerald, "Mythological Background for the Presentation of Jerusalem as a Queen and False Worship as Adultery in the OT," *CBQ* 34 (1972): 403–16.

3. All biblical translations are from the NRSV, unless otherwise noted.

4. Cynthia Chapman has observed that in the Hebrew Bible "Daughter Zion" is

Many biblical texts portray God enacting or sanctioning violence, but understanding the effects of such texts is not a simple matter. Interpreters attuned to feminist issues have focused on the capacity of violent imagery such as that in Isa 47 to legitimate violence, and they have emphasized the interpreter's responsibility to resist such appropriation. For instance, in her study of biblical texts that portray rape, Susanne Scholz reads such biblical texts in conversation with contemporary debates about rape, highlighting the texts' capacity to cultivate violent attitudes and behaviors.[5] She advocates interpreting texts about rape in ways that challenge rape-prone attitudes and disturb the pervasive silence about the pain of those who have been raped.[6] In one chapter Scholz focuses on prophetic metaphors that depict God as an agent of rape, emphasizing that such rape metaphors "justify sexual violence as divinely mandated punishment."[7] Scholz warns that the poetics of rape endorses masculine authoritarianism and the "dehumanization of women" and that perhaps this is especially true when the subject is God.[8]

The present essay does not dispute the importance of acknowledging the destructive effects that reception of the violent imagery found in Isa 47 may be understood to have had from antiquity to the present. At the same time, it suggests that we may include among the effects of the violent portrayals of God in Isa 47 a particular capacity to foster healing for the survivors of the traumatic events referred to in the text. The hermeneutic through which these portrayals are interpreted draws upon insights

---

employed exclusively in military contexts (*The Gendered Language of Warfare in the Israelite-Assyrian Encounter*, HSM 62 [Winona Lake, IN: Eisenbrauns, 2004], 92–94). On the personification of Zion and other cities as a daughter, see F. W. Dobbs-Allsopp, "'Daughter Zion'" in *Thus Says the Lord: Essays on the Former and Latter Prophets in Honor of Robert R. Wilson*, ed. John J. Ahn and Stephen L. Cook (New York: T&T Clark, 2009), 125–34; and Julia M. O'Brien, *Challenging Prophetic Metaphor: Theology and Ideology in the Prophets* (Louisville: Westminster John Knox, 2008), 127–34. For a critique of employing *daughter* as a metaphor for Jerusalem, see O'Brien, *Challenging Prophetic Metaphor*, 142–51.

5. Susanne Scholz, *Sacred Witness: Rape in the Hebrew Bible* (Minneapolis: Fortress, 2010), 2.

6. Ibid., 23.

7. Ibid., 181.

8. Ibid., 184. In making this point, Scholz cites Johnny Miles, "Re-reading the Power of Satire: Isaiah's 'Daughters of Zion', Pope's 'Belinda', and the Rhetoric of Rape," *JSOT* 31 (2006): 193–219.

into the psychological effects of traumatic events and the manner in which such effects may persist in subsequent generations. Such insights suggest that it is possible to identify precisely in the dramatically violent dimension of the imagery of Isa 47 a constructive symbolic function within its ancient context.[9] The traumatic events in question are the destruction of Jerusalem and subsequent forced migrations of Judeans to Babylon during the 580s BCE. The audience affected by these events and addressed in Isa 47 includes generations of Judeans living during the latter sixth century BCE whose recent ancestors had experienced those traumatic events. Despite the range of theories concerning the formation of Isa 40–55, most would agree that much of Isa 40–48, including Isa 47, likely originated in the latter years of the Babylonian exile.[10] The functionality discussed here would have continued after the exiles had begun to return to Jerusalem.

THE RATIONALE BEHIND YHWH's "VENGEANCE" AGAINST DAUGHTER BABYLON

The violence enacted against Daughter Babylon is characterized in Isa 47:3 as an act of divine *nāqām*, a nettlesome concept in the Hebrew Bible that is often translated "vengeance," although the adequacy of this translation has been questioned. One promising perspective in the discussion of this concept understands that in the ancient view it represented primarily an activity of restoring justice.[11] In his lucid discussion of the horrific violent

---

9. For discussion, with additional bibliography, of employing insights from trauma studies to identify constructive effects of difficult biblical texts, see Christopher G. Frechette, "The Old Testament as Controlled Substance: How Insights from Trauma Studies Reveal Healing Capacities in Potentially Harmful Texts," *Int* 69 (2015): 20–34.

10. For a recent survey of scholarship on the formation of Isa 40–55, see Rainer Albertz, *Israel in Exile: The History and Literature of the Sixth Century B.C.E.*, trans. David Green, SBLStBL 3 (Atlanta: Society of Biblical Literature, 2003), 377–93. When and in what manner the Judean exiles returned to Jerusalem is disputed. Despite the claim in Ezra 1:1–4 that the Persian king Cyrus allowed the Judean exiles to return in the first year of his reign (538 BCE), Rainer Albertz and others have proposed that the first substantial return of exiles from Babylon to Jerusalem occurred around 521 BCE, not long after the accession of Darius I in 522. See Albertz, *Israel in Exile*, 119–32; and Ulrich Berges, *The Book of Isaiah: Its Composition and Final Form*, trans. Millard C. Lind, Hebrew Bible Monographs 46 (Sheffield: Sheffield Phoenix, 2012), 313–14.

11. See H. G. L. Peels, *The Vengeance of God: The Meaning of the Root NQM and the Function of the NQM-Texts in the Context of Divine Revelation in the Old Testa-*

imagery—likewise directed at Daughter Babylon—that concludes Ps 137,[12] Jon Levenson emphasizes that what may seem like vengeance was understood in the ancient Israelite context as a justice-regulating mechanism embedded within creation.[13] By virtue of this mechanism, evil deeds were believed to have the inherent capacity to bring consequences in the form of proportionate evil upon those who enacted them. Thus, divine or human agents described as enacting proportionate retribution upon evildoers were understood to be acting not independently but, as it were, in harmony with or as extensions of this mechanism embedded in creation. In the Hebrew Bible, of course, in contexts of interpreting evil deeds and their perceived consequences, the metaphor of justice is counterbalanced by the metaphor of mercy, often associated with appeals to the parental compassion of a potential agent of vengeance or justified punishment.

The ancient concept of returning evil upon the evildoer as a means of restoring justice provides a general context for interpreting the vengeance against Daughter Babylon portrayed in Isa 47. Consideration of the manner in which Isa 40–55 is responding to the violations of Jerusalem as portrayed in Lamentations offers a more particular context. It has been demonstrated that Isa 40–55 is responding in various ways to the book of Lamentations, with its expressions of overwhelming pain, devastation, humiliation, and isolation from God.[14] That book emerged as a means for surviving the traumatic effects of the two-year siege and ensuing devasta-

---

ment, OtSt 31 (Leiden: Brill, 1995); and Erich Zenger, *A God of Vengeance? Understanding the Psalms of Divine Wrath,* trans. Linda M. Maloney (Louisville: Westminster John Knox, 1996).

12. "O daughter Babylon, you devastator! Happy shall they be who pay you back what you have done to us! Happy shall they be who take your little ones and dash them against the rock!" (Psa 137:8–9).

13. Jon D. Levenson, "The Horrifying Closing of Psalm 137, or, the Limitations of Ethical Reading," in *Biblical Essays in Honor of Daniel J. Harrington, SJ, and Richard J. Clifford, SJ: Opportunity for No Little Instruction,* ed. Christopher G. Frechette, Christopher M. Matthews, and Thomas D. Stegman (Paulist: New York, 2014), 18–40. In making this argument, Levenson relies upon Klaus Koch, "Is There a Doctrine of Retribution in the Old Testament?" in *Theodicy in the Old Testament,* ed. James L. Crenshaw (Philadelphia: Fortress, 1983), 57–87.

14. See Tod Linafelt, *Surviving Lamentations: Catastrophe, Lament, and Protest in the Afterlife of a Biblical Book* (Chicago: University of Chicago Press, 2000), 62–79; and Patricia Tull Willey, *Remember the Former Things: The Recollection of Previous Texts in Second Isaiah,* SBLDS161 (Atlanta: Scholars Press, 1997), 86–89.

tion of Jerusalem in 587–586 BCE and the assault in 582 BCE. As survival literature, Lamentations provided the Judean survivors a poetic voice for their unspeakable suffering.[15] To this end, one of the book's key rhetorical devices is its depiction of Jerusalem as a woman, Daughter Zion, giving her a voice and also creating the character of the narrator to bear witness to her. Isaiah 49–54 presents the personified Zion in hopeful oracles of Jerusalem's revival, reversing several aspects of Daughter Zion's plight as expressed in Lamentations, most notably her humiliation, loss of spouse, and loss of children. The repopulation of Jerusalem by the Judeans return-ing from Babylon to Jerusalem is, in part, how these chapters imagine the restoration of Daughter Zion's children. A central concern of Isa 40–48 is to convince the Judeans that YHWH is superior to the gods of Babylon, intends for the exiles to return to Jerusalem, and will accomplish this "new exodus" through the agency of Cyrus, the Persian ruler.

Interpreting the function of vengeance specifically in Isa 47, H. G. L. Peels observes, "vengeance removes the obstacle that hindered Israel's lib-eration, and it shames all hubris."[16] In other words, the demise of Daugh-ter Babylon as described here represents the removal of Babylon as an obstacle to the realization of the hopeful message of Isa 40–54 concerning YHWH and Israel. Before considering the dimensions of this obstacle and the manner in which the divine activity described might be understood to remove it, it is worth reviewing the specifics of what that activity entailed.

In Isa 47 vengeance against Daughter Babylon is grounded in two con-demnations, both of which can be seen as responses to the complaints of Daughter Zion in Lamentations. First, Daughter Babylon overstepped her divinely appointed authority to punish Judah. In one of the few refer-ences to the destruction of Jerusalem in Isa 40–55, YHWH first admits, "I was angry with my people, I profaned my heritage," but then condemns Daughter Babylon for her actions against Judah: "I gave them into your hand, but you showed them no mercy. Even on the aged you made your yoke exceedingly heavy" (Isa 47:6, NRSV modified). This specific condem-nation leads to the broader one, that Daughter Babylon failed to recognize the superiority of YHWH, claiming for herself what Isaiah attributes to YHWH alone: "I am, and there is no one besides me" (Isa 47:8, 10; cf. Isa 45:5–6, 18).

---

15. See Linafelt, *Surviving*, 20–25, 35–61; and Kathleen M. O'Connor, *Lamenta-tions and the Tears of the World* (Maryknoll, NY: Orbis, 2002).

16. Peels, *The Vengeance of God*, 163.

The divine actions against Daughter Babylon in Isa 47 mirror several of the violations suffered by Daughter Jerusalem at the hands of the Babylonians in Lamentations, including severe humiliation (47:1–3, 5) and loss of both spouse and children (47:8–9).[17] Multiple expressions convey humiliation by creating contrast with Babylon's former royal status: the loss of throne paired with commands to come down and sit in the dust (47:1), the loss of the regard of others as being tender and delicate (47:1), the loss of fine clothing and the imposition of manual labor (47:2), and the command to be silent and enter darkness (47:5). Although scholars do not agree on whether the imagery of nakedness and shame in Isa 47:3 refers clearly to rape, the relationship of Isa 40–55 to Lamentations strongly suggests that it does. The expressions *tiggāl 'erwātēk* ("your nakedness shall be uncovered") and *tērā'eh ḥerpātēk* ("your shame shall be seen") allow for several possible levels of meaning, including sexual abuse, rape, public humiliation, and shaming or reproach by enemies.[18] Nevertheless, taking *'erwātēk* in this case as an explicit reference to "pudenda," Joseph Blenkinsopp argues that the combination of the phrase "your nakedness shall be uncovered" with images of the removing of veil and skirt in the prior verse make clear that the activity described involves rape.[19]

Beyond this argument, however, the relationship of Isa 40–55 to Lamentations strongly suggests that rape is an intended meaning here. Within the program of reversal apparent in Isa 40–55, there is no question that Daughter Babylon in Isa 47 is shamed, widowed, and bereaved of children, all conditions of which Daughter Zion complained in Lamentations and from which in Isa 49–54 she is being declared free. Yet it is clear that the images expressing Daughter Zion's shame in Lamentations include rape. F. W. Dobbs-Allsopp and Tod Linafelt have argued convincingly that several images employed in Lamentations to express what has befallen Daughter Zion constitute images of rape; these images include: *rā'û 'erwātāh* "they have seen her nakedness" (Lam 1:8); *bā'û miqdāšāh* "they entered her sanctuary" (1:10); and *nətānanî šōmēmâ* "he has made

---

17. Even though Babylon is never mentioned in Lamentations, the horrific disasters reflected in the book were enacted by the Babylonians.

18. Chris Franke, *Isaiah 46, 47, and 48: A New Literary-Critical Reading*, Biblical and Judaic Studies 3 (Winona Lake, IN: Eisenbrauns, 1994), 115–16.

19. Joseph Blenkinsopp, *Isaiah 40–55: A New Translation with Introduction and Commentary*, AB 19A (New York: Doubleday, 2002), 280.

me desolate" (1:13).[20] The imagery of Isa 47:3 echoes the idiom from Lam 1:8, "seeing her nakedness." Recognizing the purposeful way in which Isa 40–55 responds to the complaints in Lamentations allows the imagery of Isa 47:3 to be understood as referring to rape.

Thus far we have seen that the "vengeance" declared against Daughter Babylon in Isa 47 would have been understood by the ancient Judean audience to be the justified consequence of Babylon's violations against YHWH and Judah. It has been suggested that this vengeance functioned to remove Babylon as an obstacle to the message of Isa 40–55. While one could identify a variety of ways in which Babylon might be considered such an obstacle, I focus here on the manner in which Daughter Babylon symbolically represents lingering psychological effects of the traumatic events involved in the destruction of Jerusalem and the Babylonian exile. For the violent imagery of Isa 47, insights into the effects of trauma suggest a specific psychological functionality that is capable of, if not removing, at least eroding such an obstacle. In the following section I explore this functionality in relationship to three phenomena: the deep psychological effects of trauma, the ways in which survivors of massive traumatic disasters pass on those effects to their children, and certain mechanisms that can facilitate recovery from those effects.

A HEALING FUNCTION FOR THE VIOLENT IMAGERY OF ISAIAH 47

The Judean experience of the Babylonian assaults and forced deportation to Babylon would have constituted a massive trauma with both individual and collective dimensions. Psychological categories developed in recent decades for understanding trauma have emerged largely in the context of research conducted in Western cultures. Nevertheless, psychology promises to illuminate patterns in human responses to trauma that are immediate (sometimes with lasting effects) and largely unconscious. As such, these patterns are less culturally conditioned, and recognizing them can provide a basis from which to assess across cultures strategies—which are more culturally specific—for recovering from the effects of such traumatic responses.[21] For the present purpose, particularly suggestive is the way in

---

20. F. W. Dobbs-Allsopp and Tod Linafelt, "The Rape of Zion in Thr 1,10," *ZAW* 113 (2001): 77–81.

21. See Marten W. deVries, "Trauma in Cultural Perspective," in *Traumatic Stress: The Effects of Overwhelming Experience on Mind, Body, and Society*, ed. Bessel A. van

which traumatic experience tends to impact adversely the processes that shape fundamental assumptions about the value of the self and the safety of the world.[22]

Lamentations attests to the manner in which the Judean population was overwhelmed, terrified, and violated such that solidarity and collective identity were shattered. Individuals would have sustained injurious psychological effects that were fundamental and lasting, including diminished sense of dignity and capacity to feel safe and to trust others or YHWH. These effects would have compromised the ability of the collective to reconstruct solidarity and identity. Moreover, studies of intergenerational trauma suggest that these effects to some extent would have been passed on to subsequent generations. In light of this understanding of the lasting effects of the trauma experienced by the Judeans, I propose a healing function for the violent portrayal of YHWH in Isa 47. This function involved addressing a psychological malformation with the capacity to diminish both a sense of dignity and a capacity to feel safe and to trust.

The Injurious "Core Beliefs" Resulting from Trauma and Their Persistence across Generations

Judith Herman describes trauma in terms of being rendered helpless in ways that arouse intense fear, loss of control, and threat of annihilation: "Traumatic events produce profound and lasting changes in physiological arousal, emotion, cognition, and memory."[23] These events also prompt interpretations that produce equally profound and lasting changes in perceptions of self and world: "Traumatic events destroy the victim's fundamental assumptions about the safety of the world, the positive value of the self, and the meaningful order of creation."[24] One may experience confusion regarding one's internal sense of right and wrong, one's moral compass. Long after the events of the trauma, feelings of fear, anxiety, helplessness, and shame may occur in connection with beliefs about the self as utterly

---

der Kolk, Alexander C. McFarlane, and Lars Weisaeth (New York: Guilford, 2007), 398–413.

22. See Judith Lewis Herman, *Trauma and Recovery: The Aftermath of Violence—From Domestic Abuse to Political Terror*, rev. ed. (New York: Basic Books, 1997), esp. 51–114.

23. Ibid., 33–34.

24. Ibid., 51.

abandoned, worthless, and somehow even deserving of being violated by the perpetrator. Such beliefs, which some psychologists call "core beliefs" or "schemas," are embedded deeply within the survivors, remaining largely unconscious.[25] Their injurious power derives from the manner in which they continually operate as interpretive frames that generate thoughts and feelings by filtering the subject's experiences. Because such injurious core beliefs are intimately linked to the memory of the perpetrator of the trauma, I refer to them as an "internalized perpetrator."[26] A situation of captivity typically results in complex trauma, which is characterized by much more complex and intractable symptoms than is a single traumatic event.[27] In cases of complex trauma, in which the victim has repeatedly experienced the perpetrator as omnipotent, the survivor's capacity to trust is severely damaged.[28]

These effects of trauma resonate with Lamentations and other biblical literature that reflects the Judeans' experience of Babylonian aggression during the 580s BCE, but there is reason to believe that these effects would have persisted in succeeding generations. In recent decades studies of the effects of massive communal disaster across cultures have demonstrated that the traumatic experience of one generation affects their children.

Concerning offspring of survivors of a range of massive communal traumas of the twentieth century, Yael Danieli has observed: "Massive trauma shapes the internal representation of reality of several generations, becoming an unconscious organizing principle passed on by parents and internalized by their children."[29] This observation suggests that, if survivors of the massive Judean traumas of the 580s BCE internalized

---

25. The idea that core beliefs or schemas give rise to thoughts and emotions is foundational for the influential form of psychotherapy initially developed independently by Aaron T. Beck and Albert Ellis, which later became known as cognitive behavioral therapy (CBT) (Stefan G. Hofmann, *An Introduction to Modern CBT: Psychological Solutions to Mental Health Problems* [Malden, MA: Wiley-Blackwell, 2012], 1–4).

26. Christopher G. Frechette, "Destroying the Internalized Perpetrator: A Healing Function of the Violent Language against Enemies in the Psalms," in *Trauma and Traumatization in Individual and Collective Dimensions: Insights from Biblical Studies and Beyond*, ed. Eve-Marie Becker, Jan Dochhorn, and Else Holt, SANt 2 (Göttingen: Vandenhoeck & Ruprecht, 2014), 71–84.

27. Herman, *Trauma and Recovery*, 86–87.

28. Ibid., 51–56, 93–94.

29. Yael Danieli, "Conclusions and Future Directions," in *International Handbook*

core beliefs about lacking dignity of self and lacking safety in relationships with others and with YHWH, these core beliefs were likely passed on to their children.

One cultural feature of ancient Israel greatly strengthens the likelihood that internalized core beliefs about self would have passed from survivors to succeeding generations. Personal identity in ancient Israel was constructed with much more emphasis on the individual's being part of the collective than is the case in the modern West.[30] Especially significant for the present discussion is the way in which parents and their children were regarded as actually sharing an identity; children were construed as continuing the identity of the parents into the future. Such close identification between children and parents would have strengthened the transfer of internalized core beliefs about the self from parents to children. The ways in which memories of the horrific Babylonian violations of the 580s BCE were interpreted in subsequent generations would have affected those beliefs.

The Role of Symbolized Rage in Reinterpreting Traumatic Memories and Resulting Core Beliefs

Herman proposes three fundamental tasks in the process of recovery from trauma: establishment of safety, remembering and grieving the trauma, and reconnecting with ordinary life.[31] The capacity of the violent imagery of Isa 47 to diffuse injurious core beliefs linked to the memory of the perpetrator relates principally to the second task; it facilitates *affective engagement* and *reinterpretation of the traumatic events*, two necessary aspects of remembering and grieving.

As already noted, traumatic events often give rise to core beliefs regarding the self that, although largely out of consciousness, diminish the

---

of Multigenerational Legacies of Trauma, ed. Yael Danieli, Plenum Series on Stress and Coping (New York: Plenum, 1998), 670.

30. Robert A. Di Vito, "Old Testament Anthropology and the Construction of Personal Identity," *CBQ* 61 (1999): 217–38; Jon D. Levenson, "The Resurrection of the Dead and the Construction of Personal Identity in Ancient Israel," in *Congress Volume: Basel, 2001*, ed. André Lemaire, VTSup 92 (Leiden: Brill, 2002), 305–22; and Levenson, "Individual Mortality and Familial Resurrection," in *Resurrection and the Restoration of Israel: The Ultimate Victory of the God of Life* (New Haven: Yale University Press, 2006), 109–22.

31. Herman, *Trauma and Recovery*, 155.

survivor's sense of dignity and safety. Such core beliefs are not easily dislodged. Altering them requires engaging the traumatic memories so that those memories can be interpreted differently. However, the intensity of feelings accompanying the traumatic events makes the core beliefs arising from those events resistant to confrontation. Their reinterpretation most often requires support from outside the subject to assist in engaging the intense feelings associated with the events in a safe way. This reinterpretation must allow for a retelling of the traumatic events that integrates the safe processing of emotions, including feelings of rage. Studies of intergenerational trauma confirm the importance for trauma survivors' children and grandchildren of constructing a narrative of the communal traumas experienced by their parents.[32] When the trauma results from violent human action, it is important for successive generations not only to retain the memory of it but also to interpret the violation as wrong.[33]

Interpretation of the traumatic events typically must integrate coming to terms with feelings of rage associated with those events. Put simply, latent rage results when a threatening situation so overwhelms a person that the normal response of anger cannot be expressed. The intensity of the threat prompts a correspondingly intense degree of pent-up anger that is best described as rage. Survivors of trauma, and especially complex trauma, often carry intense feelings of justifiable rage within themselves. They are likely to direct those feelings not only at the perpetrators but also at those whom they perceive to have had the power to help them but did not, especially at God.[34] This rage requires expression within the process of reinterpretation, but contemporary psychology emphasizes that expressing rage is best done in ways that are safe for everyone involved. Consequently, any expression of violent rage should be directed toward not the actual perpetrator but a symbolic representation. For the survivor, the psychological benefit of expressing the rage has nothing at all to do with harming the actual perpetrator. Rather, in a therapeutic process it is intended as a dramatic exercise to diminish the survivor's internal barriers to accepting the interpretation that the violations of dignity and safety experienced by the survivor were wrong.

---

32. Danieli, "Conclusions and Future Directions," 673.

33. Diane Kupelian, Anie Sanentz Kalayjian, and Alice S. Kassabian, "The Turkish Genocide of the Armenians: Continuing Effects on Survivors and Their Families Eight Decades after Massive Trauma," in Danieli, *International Handbook*, 203.

34. Herman, *Trauma and Recovery*, 94–95.

It is helpful to distinguish in psychological terms between a revenge fantasy and a safe, controlled, expression of rage. Herman explains that a revenge fantasy occurs when survivors become fixated on imagining that they will feel better only if they can do to the perpetrator what was done to them; however, clinging to such a fixation allows them to avoid remembering the trauma and facing its associated intense and painful feelings.[35] Not only is failure to address such feelings problematic; research reveals that those who enact such fantasies do not succeed in getting rid of post-traumatic symptoms but rather suffer the most severe and intractable disturbances. Unlike a revenge fantasy, a safe, controlled expression of rage is characterized by the following: it is directed at the perpetrator *symbolically* and does not intend actual harm; it engages the emotions and the reinterpretation of the traumatic events; it does not violate the survivor's value system and is best witnessed by others who can be trusted to serve as a moral compass; a representation of God or other supreme moral authority may also be invoked; finally, it does not become a fixation but occurs as a phase in a recovery process that does not circumvent but rather affectively engages in remembering and reinterpreting the trauma.[36]

It is important for the present argument to distinguish between the general notion of envisioning revenge and Herman's psychological explanation of a revenge fantasy.[37] Many biblical texts imagine God engaging in violent retribution against those who have violated God's people, and offended ancient readers of such texts may well have delighted in envisioning their enemies being harmed. However, the violent imagery in Isa 47—as in many other biblical texts, especially prayers—differs from Herman's psychological explanation of a revenge fantasy in two ways: such texts do not envision the human agents enacting the violence, nor do larger literary contexts in which those images occur promote the fantasy that relief

---

35. This discussion of revenge fantasy relies on ibid., 189.

36. The descriptions draw largely from Amanda Curtin, "Childhood Reparenting and Grief Groups: For Adults Who Want to Heal from Childhood Experiences That Are Still Affecting Them," forthcoming.

37. For further discussion of how the biblical motif of divine violence as a consequence enacted upon those who violate God's people differs from Herman's psychological explanation of a revenge fantasy, see Frechette, "Destroying the Internalized Perpetrator," 79–83; and Frechette, "Two Biblical Motifs of Divine Violence as Resources for Meaning-Making in Engaging Self-Blame and Rage after Traumatization," *Journal of Pastoral Psychology*, forthcoming.

can be obtained without processing the painful feelings associated with the violation.

Confronting the Obstacle That Daughter Babylon Posed to Receiving the Message of Isaiah 40–55

The Judeans who received Isa 47 may well have derived great satisfaction from imagining the Babylonians being humiliated and violated. Nevertheless, the present discussion up to this point supports the argument that the violent imagery in this text would have functioned as a symbolic drama in which rage was enacted on behalf of the survivors and their children by an agent regarded as the universal arbiter of right and wrong. Read in response to Lamentations, this drama would have served to validate the latent pain and anger associated with the memory of the traumatic events. With respect to healing, it is most important that the imagery would have served to support a reinterpretation of those events along the following lines: the Babylonians' actions were morally wrong to the extent that they left the survivors with a diminished sense of dignity, safety, and ability to trust YHWH. It is the manner in which the violent imagery in Isa 47 promotes reinterpretation of the past traumatic events that serves a healing function.

Within the larger program of Isa 40–55, chapter 47 emerges as both a response and a corrective to the interpretations of the traumatic events of the 580s BCE contained in Lamentations. Those interpretations offered various poetic means of surviving the catastrophe, including protest over divine abandonment and self-blame linked to affirmations that the brutal violations constituted justified punishment enacted by YHWH. Self-blame in response to trauma can serve as a survival strategy by asserting an explanation for inexplicable and overwhelming experiences and so prevent psychic collapse. However, self-blame can also fuel toxic core beliefs about the self as lacking dignity and safety. Decades after Lamentations was written, Isa 40–55 proclaimed a new message, one in which YHWH indeed desired to comfort Daughter Zion and to renew a relationship with her, affirming both her dignity and her safety.

Considered in light of insights into the psychological effects of traumatization, however, the traumatic quality of the Judeans' experience allows us to posit the existence of a deeply rooted and resistant barrier to accepting such a message in their experience. The lingering effects of traumatization by the Babylonians would have become an obstacle to accepting the message, operating as an "internalized perpetrator," an authoritative inner arbiter of toxic meaning. This internalized obstacle had to be delegitimized before belief in renewed dignity and safety in relationship to YHWH could be appropriated. We may imagine that, as a result of their collective trauma, the Judeans felt themselves deeply incapable or unworthy of relationship with YHWH or of the safety, comfort, and dignity that YHWH might bestow on them. To the extent that this was the case, it is hard to imagine that simple words to the contrary would have been sufficient to persuade them otherwise. Because of the intensity of the traumatic experience, such core beliefs would have been resistant to reinterpretation.

The horrific, violent imagery of Isa 47 may be read as a rhetorical means of disempowering the internalized image of the Babylonian perpetrators that was linked to such toxic beliefs. For this purpose, several elements of the imagery are important. The violence imagined is carried out not by the Judeans themselves but by YHWH, the acknowledged arbiter of justice and meaning. This violence is directed at the symbolic representation of the Babylonian perpetrators in a way that confronts them with the same behaviors by which they had violated the Judeans: humiliation, rape, and bereavement. The violence is imagined not as blind rage but in conjunction with the new interpretation that the violations experienced by the Judeans at the hands of the Babylonians were wrong. Such intensely dramatic imagery has a capacity to reach largely unconscious core beliefs in a way that propositional discourse simply does not.

While not disagreeing with traditions that YHWH intended the destruction of Jerusalem in order to punish Israel, Isa 47 nevertheless condemns the human agents, symbolized by Daughter Babylon, for the manner in which they enacted that destruction: "You showed them no mercy. Even on the aged you made your yoke exceedingly heavy" (Isa 47:6, my trans.). At issue here is the meaning of the catastrophe for the Judeans' identity and for their relationship with YHWH. Isaiah 47 is not concerned with distinguishing what sort of military behavior by the Babylonians might have counted as morally acceptable. Rather, the text is concerned with how the Judean survivors' experience of what actually occurred should be interpreted. When YHWH condemns the Babylonians for their merciless behavior, doing so effectively distances YHWH from the memory of those violations and the toxic meaning derived from them that would have eroded the Judeans' sense of dignity and capacity to trust. In this way, the text asserts with the authority of YHWH that the Judeans should not have been so treated. The violent symbolic drama of Isa 47 had the capacity to confront the Judeans' internalized obstacle to receiving the message of Isa 40–55 that affirmed their dignity and sought to cultivate their capacity to trust in YHWH.

Bibliography

Albertz, Rainer. *Israel in Exile: The History and Literature of the Sixth Century B.C.E.* Translated by David Green. SBLStBL 3. Atlanta: Society of Biblical Literature, 2003.

Berges, Ulrich. *The Book of Isaiah: Its Composition and Final Form.* Translated by Millard C. Lind. Hebrew Bible Monographs 46. Sheffield: Sheffield Phoenix, 2012.

Biddle, Mark E. "The Figure of Lady Jerusalem: Identification, Deification and Personification of Cities in the Ancient Near East." Pages 174–94 in *The Biblical Canon in Comparative Perspective.* Edited by K. Lawson Younger, William W. Hallo, and Bernard F. Batto. Ancient Near Eastern Texts and Studies 11, Scripture in Context 4. Lewiston, NY: Mellen, 1991.

Blenkinsopp, Joseph. *Isaiah 40–55: A New Translation with Introduction and Commentary.* AB 19A. New York: Doubleday, 2002.

Chapman, Cynthia. *The Gendered Language of Warfare in the Israelite-Assyrian Encounter.* HSM 62. Winona Lake, IN: Eisenbrauns, 2004.

Curtin, Amanda. "Childhood Reparenting and Grief Groups: For Adults Who Want to Heal from Childhood Experiences That Are Still Affecting Them." Forthcoming.

Danieli, Yael. "Conclusions and Future Directions." Pages 669–89 in *International Handbook of Multigenerational Legacies of Trauma.* Edited by Yael Danieli. Plenum Series on Stress and Coping. New York: Plenum, 1998.

deVries, Marten W. "Trauma in Cultural Perspective." Pages 398–413 in *Traumatic Stress: The Effects of Overwhelming Experience on Mind, Body, and Society.* Edited by Bessel A. van der Kolk, Alexander C. McFarlane, and Lars Weisaeth. New York: Guilford, 2007.

Di Vito, Robert A. "Old Testament Anthropology and the Construction of Personal Identity." *CBQ* 61 (1999): 217–38.

Dobbs-Allsopp, F. W. " 'Daughter Zion.' " Pages 125–34 in *Thus Says the Lord: Essays on the Former and Latter Prophets in Honor of Robert R.*

Wilson. Edited by John J. Ahn and Stephen L. Cook. New York: T&T Clark, 2009.

Dobbs-Allsopp, F. W., and Tod Linafelt. "The Rape of Zion in Thr 1,10." *ZAW* 113 (2001): 77–81.

Fitzgerald, Aloysius. "Mythological Background for the Presentation of Jerusalem as a Queen and False Worship as Adultery in the OT." *CBQ* 34 (1972): 403–16.

Franke, Chris. *Isaiah 46, 47, and 48: A New Literary-Critical Reading.* Biblical and Judaic Studies 3. Winona Lake, IN: Eisenbrauns, 1994.

Frechette, Christopher G. "Destroying the Internalized Perpetrator: A Healing Function of the Violent Language against Enemies in the Psalms." Pages 71–84 in *Trauma and Traumatization in Individual and Collective Dimensions: Insights from Biblical Studies and Beyond.* Edited by Eve-Marie Becker, Jan Dochhorn, and Else Holt. SANt 2. Göttingen: Vandenhoeck & Ruprecht, 2014.

———. "The Old Testament as Controlled Substance: How Insights from Trauma Studies Reveal Healing Capacities in Potentially Harmful Texts." *Int* 69 (2015): 20–34.

———. "Two Biblical Motifs of Divine Violence as Resources for Meaning-Making in Engaging Self-Blame and Rage after Traumatization." *Journal of Pastoral Psychology.* Forthcoming.

Herman, Judith Lewis. *Trauma and Recovery: The Aftermath of Violence— From Domestic Abuse to Political Terror.* Rev. ed. New York: Basic Books, 1997.

Hofmann, Stefan G. *An Introduction to Modern CBT: Psychological Solutions to Mental Health Problems.* Malden, MA: Wiley-Blackwell, 2012.

Koch, Klaus. "Is There a Doctrine of Retribution in the Old Testament?" Pages 57–87 in *Theodicy in the Old Testament.* Edited by James L. Crenshaw. Philadelphia: Fortress, 1983.

Kupelian, Diane, Anie Sanentz Kalayjian, and Alice S. Kassabian. "The Turkish Genocide of the Armenians: Continuing Effects on Survivors and Their Families Eight Decades after Massive Trauma." Pages 191–210 in *International Handbook of Multigenerational Legacies of Trauma.* Edited by Yael Danieli. Plenum Series on Stress and Coping. New York: Plenum, 1998.

Levenson, Jon D. "The Horrifying Closing of Psalm 137, or, the Limitations of Ethical Reading." Pages 18–40 in *Biblical Essays in Honor of Daniel J. Harrington, SJ, and Richard J. Clifford, SJ: Opportunity for No*

Little Instruction. Edited by Christopher G. Frechette, Christopher M. Matthews, and Thomas D. Stegman. New York: Paulist, 2014.

———. *Resurrection and the Restoration of Israel: The Ultimate Victory of the God of Life*. New Haven: Yale University Press, 2006.

———. "The Resurrection of the Dead and the Construction of Personal Identity in Ancient Israel." Pages 305–22 in *Congress Volume: Basel, 2001*. Edited by André Lemaire VTSup 92. Leiden: Brill, 2002.

Linafelt, Tod. *Surviving Lamentations: Catastrophe, Lament, and Protest in the Afterlife of a Biblical Book*. Chicago: University of Chicago Press, 2000.

Miles, Johnny. "Re-reading the Power of Satire: Isaiah's 'Daughters of Zion', Pope's 'Belinda', and the Rhetoric of Rape." *JSOT* 31 (2006): 193–219.

O'Brien, Julia M. *Challenging Prophetic Metaphor: Theology and Ideology in the Prophets*. Louisville: Westminster John Knox, 2008.

O'Connor, Kathleen M. *Lamentations and the Tears of the World*. Maryknoll, NY: Orbis, 2002.

Peels, H. G. L. *The Vengeance of God: The Meaning of the Root NQM and the Function of the NQM-Texts in the Context of Divine Revelation in the Old Testament*. OtSt 31. Leiden: Brill, 1995.

Scholz, Susanne. *Sacred Witness: Rape in the Hebrew Bible*. Minneapolis: Fortress, 2010.

Willey, Patricia Tull. *Remember the Former Things: The Recollection of Previous Texts in Second Isaiah*. SBLDS161. Atlanta: Scholars Press, 1997.

Zenger, Erich. *A God of Vengeance? Understanding the Psalms of Divine Wrath*. Translated by Linda M. Maloney. Louisville: Westminster John Knox, 1996.

SHARED PLEASURE TO SOOTHE THE BROKEN SPIRIT: COLLECTIVE TRAUMA AND QOHELETH

Philip Browning Helsel

Modern sociologist Kai Erikson studied human-caused disasters as a witness for plaintiffs in disaster lawsuits. He maintained that communal responses to disaster share some common features. He noted that the symptoms of collective trauma coalesce into a form of syndrome that is more than the injury to each of the individuals combined.[1] He also indicated that there is a spiritual or existential component to such harm, what we might call a collective sense of "broken-spiritedness," to borrow a term from the psychologist John Wilson, who works with refugees.[2] Broken-spiritedness refers to massive disruption that interferes with sources of meaning and the sacred, challenging the power of religion. Recent collective-trauma theorists influenced by postcolonial thought have maintained that massive trauma is more chronic than discrete, lacking a fixed beginning point or ending point, and thus cannot be grieved easily.[3] Broken-spiritedness, rather than leading to a rapid resolution of trauma, is more like being in "mid-mourning." Mid-mourning is the response to a situation of chronic oppression in which the source of trauma is continually present so that the trauma cannot be grieved and left behind.[4]

---

1. Kai Erikson, *Everything in Its Path: Destruction of Community in the Buffalo Creek Flood* (New York: Simon & Schuster, 1978).

2. John P. Wilson and Boris Droždek, eds., *Broken Spirits: The Treatment of Traumatized Asylum Seekers, Refugees, and War and Torture Victims* (New York: Brunner-Routledge, 2005).

3. Stef Craps, *Postcolonial Witnessing: Trauma out of Bounds* (New York: Palgrave McMillan, 2012); Mary Watkins and Helene Shulman, *Toward Psychologies of Liberation* (New York: Palgrave McMillan, 2008).

4. Craps, *Postcolonial Witnessing*, 34.

I maintain that the book of Qoheleth, since it was written in a situation of colonial oppression, is both a reflection of, and a response to, collective trauma.[5] It seems to be written in a condition resembling "mid-mourning," and this suggests that it might bear the marks of broken-spiritedness, such as an inability to make sense of the world or direct one's voice to God in complaint. Nevertheless, in its injunctions to shared pleasure Qoheleth goes some way toward treating the erosion of community that can take place in collective trauma.[6] The framework I propose here cannot explain everything about this inscrutable book, but it does shed some light on difficult concepts such as the notion of *ḥebel*, the gap between deeds and retribution, and the significance of shared pleasure.

Collective Trauma

Kai Erikson analyzed the collective trauma of exploited groups who have faced environmental disasters in *Everything in Its Path* and *A New Species of Trouble*.[7] Hired as an expert witness on behalf of Appalachian miners and Ojibwa First Nations people in Canada, he documented the symptoms of collective trauma. He discussed both the individual effects of trauma and its social effects. Individual symptoms of trauma have been described as fear, aversion, and nightmares, resulting in an evaluation that the world was untrustworthy. Erikson's distinctive contribution was diagnosing the collective trauma, that is, the impact of massive trauma on communities. People would stop visiting one another, cease religious activities, and no longer be able to care for their neighbors in the same way. Individual trauma symptoms fed into collective trauma—a phenomenon I describe in this essay—but Erikson maintained that collective trauma constituted a distinctive form of suffering.

In *Everything in Its Path*, Erikson describes how a mining company placed its refuse in a large pile above the town of Buffalo Creek. This pile eventually collapsed and released floodwaters that swept the town away. After the disaster the government resettled families in trailers far apart

---

5. Jennifer Barbour [now Grillo], *The Story of Israel in the Book of Qohelet: Ecclesiastes as Cultural Memory* (Oxford: Oxford University Press, 2012).

6. Eunny P. Lee, *The Vitality of Enjoyment in Qoheleth's Theological Rhetoric*, BZAW 353 (Berlin: de Gruyter, 2005).

7. Kai T. Erikson, *A New Species of Trouble: Explorations in Disaster, Trauma, and Community* (New York: Norton, 1994).

from one another, a choice that proved to be severely disruptive. Erikson depicted a vicious cycle in which the miners appraised the world as a less trustworthy place, leading them to reach out less often to their new neighbors. This, in turn, led to a shared conviction that their new community was less trustworthy.

Previously, people in the town would help themselves to a cup of coffee in each other's homes or bring meals to their neighbors during a difficult time. Erikson defines this shared "communality" as consisting in "a cluster of people acting in concert and moving to the same collective rhythms."[8] As a result of the disaster, people were distanced from the land, which was almost unrecognizable after the flood. The misrecognition of the geography also led to a misrecognition of community: they did not see their neighbors because they were split up in the resettlement.

The fact that miners appraised their neighbors as less trustworthy seems to have diminished social bonds. Miners now described their new environment as a place where neighbors were more likely to be delinquent. Erikson depicts what might be called a vicious cycle of disconnection in which individual trauma and the erosion of communality went hand in hand.

Even the individual symptoms of trauma had a social component. Miners and their families lived in constant fear of water, often dressing their children before bed so they could escape quickly. One man dreamed that he was being buried alive, surrounded by his old neighbors, but that no one could see him. The dream suggests both the fear of the traumatic stressor and also the lack of empathic witnesses after the resettlement of neighbors. In addition to individual trauma symptoms, there was also trauma to the social body, which, since it moved as a collective, could also be damaged at a quite basic level. In summing up the impact of the environmental disasters on communities, Erikson argues that communal trauma is something more than many individuals' trauma put together:

> By individual trauma I mean a blow to the psyche that breaks through one's defenses so suddenly and with such brutal force that one cannot react to it effectively.... By collective trauma, on the other hand, I mean a blow to the basic tissues of social life that damages the bonds attaching people together and impairs the prevailing sense of community. The collective trauma works its way slowly and even insidiously into the

8. Erikson, *A New Species*, 234.

awareness of those who suffer from it, so it does not have the quality of suddenness normally associated with "trauma." But it is a form of shock all the same, a gradual realization that the community no longer exists as an effective source of support and that an important part of the self has disappeared. "We" no longer exist as a connected pair or as linked cells in a communal body.[9]

Erikson suggests that we should no longer try to evaluate something as a disaster by scientific measures, such as the magnitude of an earthquake, but that we should evaluate it retrospectively on the basis of whether it seemed to cause the kind of collective trauma he describes.

As with individual trauma, in cases where prior trauma exists the vulnerability created by the prior trauma exacerbates the harm experienced in the present. Groups that are oppressed often have long histories of traumatization. In each of the studies that Erikson undertakes, the victims of disaster had been exploited beforehand. Decades before the flood, the miners lost the rights to their land and the ability to unionize. The Ojibwa Indians in northern Ontario who were affected by a chemical spill had previously faced the erosion of their traditional way of life. This happened as their children were sent to white schools, as their medicine men could not heal a flu pandemic, and as a money economy replaced hunting and gathering in the course of one generation. Erikson calls the Appalachian miners "among the most truly exploited people to be found anywhere."[10] In each of these scenarios there was both a defining disaster and also pre-existing structural disempowerment. Nevertheless, collective trauma does not by definition imply previous oppression, since it is possible for a single-blow collective trauma to occur among the privileged as well.[11]

Erikson also notes that the effects of trauma persisted long after a discrete event. While a rush of communal support and cheer is seen after some disasters, it was notably absent after the Buffalo Creek flood. Entering a room of miners, Erikson remarked on the "gray" lifelessness of the scene.[12] This led him to conclude that such disasters, despite the fact that they included a specific stressor, should be considered chronic rather than

---

9. Erikson, *Everything in Its Path*, 153–54.

10. Ibid., 68.

11. Jon Allen, *Coping with Trauma: Hope through Understanding*, 2nd ed. (Washington, DC: American Psychiatric Publishing, 2004), 26.

12. Erikson, *Everything in Its Path*, 11.

acute. We might say that there was a reconfigured relationship to body, communality, and land after each disaster and that this reconfigured relationship is reflected in disruption to the tissues of the social body.

Such disruption preceded a discrete stressor and continued long after a traumatic event. When collective trauma comes after prolonged oppression, this tends to worsen its effects.[13]

The collective traumas Erikson studied also interfered with religious expression. On the one hand, there was a material violation as Bibles and other sacred objects were swept away in the Buffalo Creek flood. On the other hand, there were existential wounds as people blamed God or simply stopped attending religious celebrations after the dam collapsed. The Ojibwa First Nations group experienced a range of religious changes. There was a progressive weakening of religious ties as their community leaders were unable to stem the tide of converts to Christianity. The cumulative effect of this spiritual malaise could be called broken-spiritedness, since it touched on central questions of meaning.[14]

Psychologist John Wilson coined the term *broken spirit* in his work with refugees. He defined "spirit" as "a sense of connection to self, others, and nature; to the vision and hopes for the future; to God and sources of meaning in life; and to the sacred."[15] By eroding human bonds, collective trauma foreshortens hope for the future and faith in God. I argue that we can expand Wilson's individual definition of a broken spirit to include collectivities, especially those facing massive disruptions. We may even be able to trace the symptoms of broken-spiritedness in the collective body.

In this section I have maintained that oppressed communities struck by disasters share a collective trauma syndrome.[16] A particularly difficult

---

13. Boris Droždek and John P Wilson, "Uncovering: Trauma-Focused Treatment Techniques with Asylum Seekers," in Wilson and Droždek, *Broken Spirits*, 261.

14. John P. Wilson, "The Broken Spirit: Posttraumatic Damage to the Self," in Wilson and Droždek, *Broken Spirits*, 112.

15. Ibid., 110.

16. Throughout this essay I have focused more on the immediate psychological shock and dislocation of collective trauma and so have favored the collective trauma syndrome theory articulated by Kai Erikson. Another important recent approach posits that collective trauma is a social construction in which, through a *trauma process*, people are able to claim that they were harmed and gain restitution. This approach is not incompatible with my thesis but does not fully explore that psychological harm stemming from collective trauma. See Jeffrey C. Alexander, *Trauma: A Social Theory* (Cambridge: Polity, 2012).

manifestation of this syndrome is the erosion of communal life. A key claim I make here is that collective trauma syndrome and the resulting destruction of communality can also take place in more chronic forms of collective oppression. In this erosion of communality, collective trauma builds on individual stress reactions. Personal appraisals of terror can make it harder for people to connect with each other, and relocation far from one another makes it difficult to visit neighbors. People facing collective trauma often are broken-spirited, which means that religious life rings hollow and fails to bring comfort. Rather than experiencing an uptick of community support, these groups, some of which had been exploited long before the disaster, suffer from broken-spiritedness.

Qoheleth and Collective Trauma

The plight of those living under colonial powers is similar in some ways to the struggles faced by Erikson's postdisaster communities. The book of Qoheleth, an ancient wisdom text, speaks of a world in which oppression seems omnipresent and greed an all-consuming reality.[17] Perhaps because of its unconventional themes and structure, the book is the subject of much scholarly debate. Scholars disagree about several factors, including the coherence of the work, whether to date the book in the Persian or Hellenistic periods, and whether *ḥebel* means that everything is ultimately futile.[18] I treat the book as a seamless whole and do not attend to tensions among the voices in the book or to what some have considered the growth of the book over time.[19] For the present purpose, it is sufficient to

---

17. Several postcolonial biblical scholars have interpreted Ecclesiastes, although somewhat reductionistically: R. S. Sugirtharajah, *Postcolonial Criticism and Biblical Interpretation* (Oxford: Oxford University Press, 2002); and Elsa Tamez and Margaret Wilde, *When Horizons Close: Rereading Ecclesiastes* (Eugene, OR: Wipf & Stock, 2002).

18. C. L. Seow, *Ecclesiastes: A New Translation with Introduction and Commentary*, AB 18C (New York: Doubleday, 1997); Richard J. Clifford, *The Wisdom Literature*, Interpreting Biblical Texts (Abingdon: Nashville, 1998); James L. Crenshaw, *Ecclesiastes* (Westminster: Philadelphia, 1987); Michael Fox, *Qoheleth and His Contradictions*, JSOTSup 71 (Sheffield: Almond, 1989); Ronald E. Murphy, *Ecclesiastes*, WBC 23 (Dallas: Word, 1992); R. N. Whybray, *Ecclesiastes*, NCB (Grand Rapids: Eerdmans, 1989); Eric S. Christiansen, *Ecclesiastes through the Centuries* (San Francisco: Wiley Blackwell, 2007); and Craig G. Bartholomew, *Ecclesiastes* (Grand Rapids: Baker Academic, 2014).

19. Some have argued that the book as a whole intentionally holds tension and

recognize that the book was written long after the Babylonian exile in a situation of ongoing subjugation to empire as the Israelite people sought to understand their relationships to God, to one another, and to the land. For this reason, some of the key themes of the book can be grasped more effectively through the lens of collective trauma.

The following review of the social situations reflected in Qoheleth suggests that they contributed to shattering traditional assumptions so that even the fundamental notion that the wise shall prosper seemed no longer valid. Qoheleth echoes the wisdom tradition's concern for the foolish and the wise, but it challenges the standard wisdom teaching that the just are rewarded and the foolish are not. On the contrary, the foolish do not receive retribution for their foolishness (Eccl 2:14). Even in institutions that are supposed to represent justice, wickedness is present. The book asks what it all adds up to, attempting to discern what benefit people gain for their diligent labor (3:22). If the wicked and the righteous are treated the same and wickedness is almost universally present, what does wisdom mean?

---

contradiction together rather than relieving it and thus see the book as a unified whole. See Michael Fox, "Frame-Narrative and Composition in the Book of Qohelet," *HUCA* 48 (1977): 83–106. More recently, some have pointed to ambiguity and irony as critical for understanding the book. Doug Ingram has argued that the text of Qoheleth represents deliberate ambiguity (*Ambiguity in Ecclesiastes*, LHBOTS 431 [New York: T&T Clark, 2006]). Carolyn J. Sharp has argued that the entire book is shaped by irony, such that the view voiced by Qoheleth is intended to be rejected by the reader ("'How Long Will You Love Being Simple?' Irony in Wisdom Traditions," in her *Irony and Meaning in the Hebrew Bible* [Bloomington: Indiana University Press, 2009], 187–239). Sharp and other postmodern interpreters helpfully display the literary ambiguity of the text, but my approach, while not solidifying a single meaning for the text, strengthens its plurivocity by rooting it in the social world of the community and its ritual life. Deconstructive theory helps explore ambiguity but does not as richly describe the social-scientific contributions that come from an analysis of collective historical trauma. While Qoheleth is certainly a complex text, it is still a meaningful one, and its meaning reflected the social world in which it was written. Over a century ago, Carl von Siegfried argued that the text is made up of many parts that each represent different authors (*Prediger und Hoheslied*, HKAT 3.2 [Göttingen: Vandenhoeck & Ruprecht, 1898]), and Alan McNeile argued that later redactors added to the text to sort out its contradictions or provide a more traditional perspective (*An Introduction to Ecclesiastes* [Cambridge: Cambridge University Press, 1904]). Whether or not such additions were made, however, the contradictions of the book have not been resolved.

In one attempt at describing the purpose of human life, Qoheleth suggests that each person has a portion in life, but the considerable labor required to work one's portion should be shared with others in order to make it more pleasurable (Eccl 4:9–12). Qoheleth is concerned that a person might spend an entire life laboring alone and have his or her wealth taken by strangers, implying that there would be little enjoyment from the work done. This lack of enjoyment is a concern of existential proportions, equivalent to not having a burial.[20]

While it may be the case the isolation can be a coping strategy used briefly, it seems that a permanent disruption of the social bond is so problematic that alienated persons lack the support of others who might witness what they are going through and help them. "Further, I saw all the oppressions that are being done under the sun: lo, the tears of the oppressed, but there is none to comfort them; power comes from the hand of the oppressors, but there is none to comfort them" (Eccl 4:1).[21] As a member of the scribal class, Qoheleth is positioned as witness to the lack of comfort in oppression.[22] It seems that, when people can work in pairs or groups, they are less likely to suffer alone and are more likely to experience enjoyment in their work. Among the greatest tragedies for Qoheleth is a life full of ambition and hard work that is lonely, lived apart from the comforts of enjoyment. The interpersonal dimension seems essential to enjoyment for Qoheleth.

In the social context of Qoheleth's time, it seems that a money economy was rapidly replacing an agrarian one and that persons were forced off their land.[23] Economic themes pervade the book, which includes vocabulary such as:

> money, riches, rich, private possession, salary, reward, compensation, inheritance, success, accomplishment, surplus, advantage, deficit/what's

---

20. Benjamin W. Porter and Alexis T. Boutin, "Introduction," in *Remembering the Dead in the Ancient Near East: Recent Contributions from Bioarchaeology and Mortuary Archaeology*, ed. Benjamin W. Porter and Alexis T. Boutin (Boulder: University Press of Colorado, 2014), 15.

21. Translation from Seow, *Ecclesiastes*, 176.

22. Mark R. Sneed, *The Politics of Pessimism: A Social-Science Perspective*, AIL 12 (Atlanta: Society of Biblical Literature, 2012), 63.

23. Seow, *Ecclesiastes*, 33.

lacking, account, assets, yield, abundance/wealth, preoccupation, venture, business, toil, fruit of toil, consumer, worker, lot ... and portion.[24]

This vocabulary indicates that in the postexilic context money was highly significant.[25] The appropriate image of the time seems to be one of vast uncertainty and quick change. A few were able to benefit from these changes and rapidly accumulate wealth for themselves.[26] Under the Persian land-grant system, Seow argues, the land was divided up and given to overlords who could then give it away to favored persons. It is likely that disconnection from the land led to disconnection in interpersonal relationships in Qoheleth's community. Seow notes that under the land-grant system people had to be authorized to use the land that had been returned to them but that this authorization did not always happen (Eccl 6:2).[27]

Seow maintains that Qoheleth's main audience is the "dependent classes," the commoners or small landholders who lived with the recent memory of "extreme poverty."[28] People tried to work harder to secure their futures, but because of the arbitrary nature of the system there was no way to ensure that their hard work would be rewarded.[29]

Understanding the social situation of Qoheleth's time helps interpreters to grasp its key themes. Seow glosses the term *hebel* as "confoundingly unknowable and unpredictable ... beyond human ability to grasp" and thus highlights the meaning-making aspects of the word.[30] He clarifies that this term is decidedly negative in the text. Moreover, in the context of a land-grant system that separated people from the earth and made it more difficult to pass on a legacy to their children, this community faced a collective trauma that was similar in some ways to broken-spiritedness.

In broken-spiritedness a person loses a sense of connection to self, others, and nature and thereby one's hope, meaning, and faith in God. When a group has faced a collective trauma, this broken-spiritedness extends beyond individuals to impact the tissue of the social body. In the context of capricious land grants, it is reasonable that Qoheleth questioned

---

24. Translation from Seow, *Ecclesiastes*, 22.
25. Ibid.
26. Ibid., 32.
27. Lee, *Vitality of Enjoyment*, 46.
28. Ibid., 32.
29. Ibid., 23.
30. Ibid., 102.

whether toil was meaningful. Qoheleth's use of the term *ḥebel* suggests that the social bonds of his time were being broken: behind the feeling of frustrating unknowability (*ḥebel*) is the reality that an increasing number of persons could no longer rely on the community as a resource.

In his analysis of traumatic disaster events, Erikson noted that collective trauma can be worsened by previous oppression. In some cases, it builds on previous forms of oppression, such as the mining company signing away family land and disrupting union organizing in Appalachia. Likewise, the Ojibwa faced a structural degradation of their culture by Euro-Canadians. In these circumstances disaster builds upon preexisting stress, leading to cumulative damage. Qoheleth's context seems to be postexilic—meaning that the Israelite land was occupied by foreign powers. This experience might best be described as something like "postcolonial syndrome" or "postcolonial traumatic stress disorder."[31] Paradoxically, such conditions are hardly "post" for the occupied because the oppression continues in the present.[32]

As the Israelites resettled after exile, they faced the domination of the Persian Empire that wrenched their land away. In such a context, the relationship to land can be reconfigured, making returning home a kind of exile in itself. Cultural psychoanalyst Vamik Volkan describes how, in the 1990s, the Serbians set up a concentration camp within a Kosovar village and killed many of its citizens. "Their village had become a 'foreign' land to them because it no longer induced a sense of home in the inhabitants."[33] This seems to have contributed to collective trauma by transforming their experience of the homeland into something strange. If memories of the exile had a traumatically intrusive character, this reconfiguration of the land through occupation may have worsened collective trauma.

Qoheleth may reflect some of these themes in the notion of *ḥebel* and the gap between deed and retribution. His skepticism is likely a reflection of communal realities as much as an individual disposition.[34] Likewise, the emphasis on the dangers of the isolated life may be an attempt to address postexilic broken-spiritedness. With great economic insecurity and the

---

31. Craps, *Postcolonial Witnessing*, 25.

32. Ibid., 63.

33. Vamik Volkan, "From Hope for a Better Life to Broken Spirits: An Introduction," in Wilson and Drożdek, *Broken Spirits*, 11.

34. Lee, *Vitality of Enjoyment*, 33; for a contrasting argument, see Frank Zimmerman, *The Inner World of Qoheleth* (New York: Ktav, 1973).

turn to a money economy, Qoheleth reflects on his own culture's preoccupation with money, but this preoccupation is a form of "mid-mourning," reflecting the loss of tradition and meaning.[35]

Shared Pleasure as One Potential Treatment
for Broken-Spiritedness

Seen within the context of the collective trauma of Qoheleth's time, the book's recommendation of enjoyment may be understood as more than "a narcotic of sorts that dulls the pain of existence."[36] Indeed, enjoyment may address some of the key symptoms of broken-spiritedness at a collective level. It may provide an important step toward restoring a feeling of home when one's own land seems foreign.

Qoheleth belongs to the wisdom tradition where the plight of humankind prompts reflection on what is good. The repeated injunctions to enjoy life in Qoheleth lead some interpreters to conclude that enjoyment is the primary theme of the text.[37] Enjoyment for Qoheleth, however, is not private but rather interpersonal, having to do with shared pleasure and reflecting a ritual context. In this section I argue that the injunctions to shared pleasure may go some distance to redeeming the collective broken-spiritedness of the Israelite people after the Babylonian exile.

Qoheleth seems to have thought of human life as similar to a land grant that a person had to work. Each person's portion could be worked with enjoyment:

> Here is what I have observed is good: that it is appropriate (for people) to eat, drink, and enjoy good in all their toil which they toil under the sun, during the few days of their lives, which God has given them, for this is their portion. Indeed, to all people, God has given wealth and assets, and he authorized them to partake of them, to take up their portion, and to have pleasure in their toil. This is the gift of God. Indeed, they should not much call to mind the days of their lives, for God gives a preoccupation [ma'ăneh] through the joy in their hearts! (Eccl 5:18–20)[38]

---

35. Craps, *Postcolonial Witnessing,* 61.
36. Lee, *The Vitality of Enjoyment,* 33.
37. Ibid., 4.
38. Translation from Seow, *Ecclesiastes,* 202.

The passage that recommends shared pleasure is a crucial transition from a philosophical (Eccl 1:1–5:20) to a more ethical section of the book (6:10–12:14).

In her work *The Vitality of Joy in Qoheleth's Rhetoric*, Eunny Lee argues that these repeated calls to enjoyment can be understood as redeeming the inner space of one's life, constituting both a call from God and a duty. The early rabbinic interpreters Rashbam and Ibn Ezra noted that the term *ma'ăneh*, translated "preoccupation" in 5:20 could mean "answer."[39] Previously Qoheleth described people as "preoccupied" with *hebel*, but now it seems possible to be preoccupied or to find an answer with enjoyment.[40] This focal text suggests that the author has in mind more than simply an unfulfilled existence that is always beyond our grasp but that there are meaningful possibilities for shared pleasure.

Making a case that these are interpersonal pleasures, Lee links them to the festal history of Israel. She notes that God authorizes people to enjoy their lives (Eccl 6:2), and she claims that this is part of the ethical slant within the text.[41]

Given Lee's emphasis on their interpersonal dimensions, I argue that shared pleasures are especially pertinent in times of collective trauma. These pleasures may even begin to address rifts in the social body that come from a sense of isolation and collective broken-spiritedness. Lee argues that human relationships have ritual elements, and she links religious feasts to the injunctions to enjoyment, maintaining that, by extension, these passages call Israel to reclaim its sacred history. Since a key theme in the text is isolation, and since the injunctions to enjoyment focus on interpersonal events such as conjugal union and meals, it is possible that enjoyment could begin to redeem this isolation, without, of course, remediating the entire injustice of such traumas.[42]

Lee depicts the injunctions to eat and drink within the Purim festival that celebrates the salvation of the Jewish people (Esth 9:22).[43] Moreover, Qoheleth is read in the synagogue during the Feast of Sukkoth, purposely reinforcing the centrality of enjoyment:

---

39. Ibid., 210.
40. Lee, *Vitality of Enjoyment*, 49.
41. Ibid., 138.
42. Ibid., 65.
43. Ibid., 64.

Go, eat your food in pleasure and drink your wine with a merry heart, for God has already favored what you have done. Always let your garments be white, and let not oil be lacking upon your head. Enjoy life with your beloved spouse all the days of your vain [hebel] life which has been given to you under the sun, for that is your portion in life and in your toil which you are toiling under the sun. (Eccl 9:7–9)[44]

Lee places this discussion of pleasure in a larger ritual setting in which interpersonal relationships are at the fore. Citing Gary Anderson, Lee notes, "In ancient Israel and its cognate cultures, there is a behavioral dimension to joy that is specialized and ritualized.... eating and drinking, anointing with oil, donning festal garments, and conjugal relations" all reinforce community.[45] She notes other places in which faithfulness to torah requires festal engagement with one's neighbors, including passages from Deuteronomy and Nehemiah. In the postexilic context, being faithful meant cultivating times to be with one another in person and to see each other face to face.

The one who lives in isolation from others reflects the greatest tragedy possible in his or her life (Eccl 4:7). Being with others is essential to enjoying life, and Qoheleth maintains that one who cannot enjoy life is worse off than one who has not been buried. The text seems to reflect what Erikson analyzed in Appalachia, that collective trauma has the potential to disrupt the tissues of the social body, making it more difficult for us to see and hear one another, but he also indicates that the social body might heal such trauma.

As one important part of the treatment for broken-spiritedness, Qoheleth recommends interpersonal vitality, noting that the ability to be "in the good" and enjoy one's life is like a gift from God.[46] The injunction to work with all one's strength means living "in contrast with the dead" and thus affirming one's close companionship with one another.[47] It is possible that the Judeans may have had difficulty observing the Sabbath because they worked in the Persian mercantile system, yet perhaps they were able to bring the Sabbath into everyday life by "concentrating on the

---

44. Translation from Seow, *Ecclesiastes*, 296.

45. Lee, *Vitality of Enjoyment*, 65, citing Gary A. Anderson, *A Time to Mourn, a Time to Dance: The Expression of Grief and Joy in Israelite Religion* (University Park: Pennsylvania State University Press, 1991), 74–77.

46. Lee, *Vitality of Enjoyment*, 62.

47. Ibid., 65.

responsibility of what is at hand, and engaging joyously in the ordinary activities of daily life with gratitude and contentment."[48] To the degree that they had ritual and sacred overtones, these injunctions to pleasure may have gone some way toward treating not only individual trauma but also collective broken-spiritedness by linking persons in relationship.

Critics may wonder if this answer is adequate and may ask if Qoheleth is simply conceding to oppression by advocating enjoyment rather than addressing social change. This line of argument might suggest that advocating pleasure is an inadequate solution to the multiple traumas of collective broken-spiritedness. In the context of my argument, however, when a chief symptom of collective trauma is a disruption of communality, the kinds of enjoyment that Qoheleth proposes seem well-suited to the concern. As we have seen, communal bonds that link the social body are disrupted in collective trauma. Feasts, shared meals, and conjugal relations all contribute to soothing the pain of *hebel,* that collective violation of justice that creates the feeling that nothing adds up. Such celebrations are not shallow evasions of reality; they address important conditions of what it means to be an organic social body threatened by despair due to injustice. While collective trauma can feel like mid-mourning, Lee suggests that collective celebration is more like "the termination of the mourning cycle."[49] Given how collective trauma can give rise to profound grief, it is important to note that this is not simply turning one's head from suffering to avoid it but can be the fulfillment of a particular kind of joy that does not neglect the fact that past harm existed.

Conclusion

The human species shares much in common with our evolutionary ancestors in that we organize our lives to share pleasurable activities (e.g., meals) that bind us together as a social body.[50] Communal trauma has the power to disrupt such connection, and when it does it can challenge the core of what is means to be human. When the Appalachian miners were resettled among new neighbors in government trailers, they lacked the ability to

---

48. Ibid., 129.

49. Ibid., 65.

50. Raymond L. Neubauer, *Evolution and the Emergent Self: The Rise of Complexity and Behavioral Versatility in Nature* (New York: Columbia University Press, 2012), 73.

care for one another any longer. The challenge they faced was not simply that the old neighbors were not around but that the capacity for care was somehow eroded. Indeed, Erikson's analysis indicated that the resettlement was as painful for the tight-knit community as the disaster itself. This adjustment suggests that what is most at stake in collective trauma is *communality*, or the ways that a group has of seeing one another, celebrating with each other, and engaging shared grief and joy.

This essay has described collective trauma as a disruption to the tissues of the social body. This is something more than a collection of individuals suffering from post-traumatic stress disorder. When individuals suffer sudden harm, they often interpret the world as a less trustworthy place. Collectively, a social body suffers when its members can no longer see one another, care for one another, or care for the land that was a central part of their existence. Collective trauma is the name for the syndrome that disrupts communal harmony by breaking bonds. It tends to be chronic rather than acute, it builds on previous oppression, and it reconfigures relationship to the physical body, communality, and land.

One of the marked consequences of communal trauma is collective broken-spiritedness. As we have seen, broken-spiritedness interferes with the capacity to hope, to believe in God, and to see a future. Collective broken-spiritedness is reflected in the material loss as people's religious spaces and sacred objects are destroyed. It can also be seen in losses in the existential spirit, whether a community rages against God or finds worship not to be meaningful any longer. In the context of Qoheleth, the pervasive sense of life being beyond one's grasp—and the decidedly negative tone of this evaluation—seems to be related to the collective trauma of living in postexilic times. Under the Persian land system, money replaced other forms of meaning, and people were denied the ability to pass on wealth for their children. In an unpredictable world, there was a smaller share for those at the bottom than ever before, and the arbitrary power of rulers made life difficult for increasing numbers of persons.

The distance between the world of the ancient Near East and modern times is vast, and the gap between these worlds can strain our attempt to make meaning of the ancient texts. In this essay I have used sociological analyses of collective trauma to help understand some key themes of a postexilic text. Recent analyses of social theory have claimed that colonial oppression's collective trauma can be chronic rather than acute, radically disrupting relationships over time. Theorists of ethnic violence have shown that, when people face hardship in their homeland, their relationship to the place they called home can change radically. I have claimed in this chapter that the cumulative violence of exile and resettlement under foreign rule bears some similarities to current contexts where ethnic violence, colonization, and refugee status can cause a pervasive broken-spiritedness. In applying specific insights from present social-science theories to the interpretation of ancient contexts, I have sought to demonstrate lines of continuity between present and ancient contexts sufficient to warrant such application.

This essay has laid a conceptual groundwork for further practical explorations. Later explorations might place more stress on chronic rather than acute trauma, on the interval after disastrous events as communities are rebuilt instead of the disaster event as a discrete occurrence. Throughout, the theoretical basis of the present chapter suggests that the emphasis should be laid on the importance of human relationships in restoring communality after collective trauma. Seow calls Qoheleth a highly theological text but insists that this is "theology from below."[51] In this instance, by focusing on the powers of interpersonal pleasure in community to begin to heal collective broken-spiritedness, I argue that shared enjoyment is a kind of theology from below that redeems social relationship.

As David Carr has argued in Holy Resilience: The Bible's Traumatic Origins, ongoing efforts in biblical studies informed by trauma theory should foreground the impact of communal trauma on social bonds, highlighting the chronic nature of these traumas.[52] In this essay I have attempted to contribute to this broader research agenda by arguing that collective trauma is a disruption to the relational fabric of the community that can lead to a sense of broken-spiritedness. By interpreting Qoheleth through the lens of collective trauma, I have shown how isolation from community is one of the key themes of the book and how the repeated calls to shared enjoyment have the potential to transform this isolation. Sharing pleasures such as conjugal relations and meals may also evoke the broader festal context of Israel's life, thereby addressing the symptom of God-forsakenness that is so prevalent in broken-spiritedness. In this light, some of the key themes of Qoheleth seem to refer to collective suffering rather than the trauma of an individual. Future work in the discipline of pastoral theology can use the lens of collective trauma to help frame what interventions are

---

51. Seow, Ecclesiastes, 55.

52. David Carr, Holy Resilience: The Bible's Traumatic Origins (New Haven: Yale University Press, 2014), 269.

needed at a communal level to restore broken social bonds. This can be especially important in a time such as ours, not unlike the world in which Qoheleth lived, where money has an important place in how people evaluate themselves in relationship to one another.

Bibliography

Alexander, Jeffrey C. *Trauma: A Social Theory*. Cambridge: Polity, 2012.

Allen, Jon. *Coping with Trauma: Hope through Understanding*. 2nd ed. Washington, DC: American Psychiatric Publishing, 2004.

Anderson, Gary A. *A Time to Mourn, a Time to Dance: The Expression of Grief and Joy in Israelite Religion*. University Park: Pennsylvania State University Press, 1991.

Barbour [now Grillo], Jennifer. *The Story of Israel in the Book of Qohelet: Ecclesiastes as Cultural Memory*. Oxford: Oxford University Press, 2012.

Bartholomew, Craig G. *Ecclesiastes*. Grand Rapids: Baker Academic, 2014.

Carr, David. *Holy Resilience: The Bible's Traumatic Origins*. New Haven: Yale University Press, 2014.

Christiansen, Eric S. *Ecclesiastes through the Centuries*. San Francisco: Wiley Blackwell, 2007.

Clifford, Richard J. *The Wisdom Literature*. Interpreting Biblical Texts. Abingdon: Nashville, 1998.

Craps, Stef. *Postcolonial Witnessing: Trauma out of Bounds*. New York: Palgrave McMillan, 2012.

Crenshaw, James L. *Ecclesiastes*.Westminster: Philadelphia, 1987.

Droždek, Boris, and John P Wilson. "Uncovering: Trauma-Focused Treatment Techniques with Asylum Seekers." Pages 243–76 in *Broken Spirits: The Treatment of Traumatized Asylum Seekers, Refugees, and War and Torture Victims*. Edited by John P. Wilson and Boris Droždek. New York: Brunner-Routledge, 2005.

Erikson, Kai. *Everything in Its Path: Destruction of Community in the Buffalo Creek Flood*. New York: Simon & Schuster, 1978.

———. *A New Species of Trouble: Explorations in Disaster, Trauma, and Community*. New York: Norton, 1994.

Fox, Michael. "Frame-Narrative and Composition in the Book of Qohelet." *HUCA* 48 (1977): 83–106.

———. *Qoheleth and His Contradictions*. JSOTSup 71. Sheffield: Almond, 1989.

Ingram, Doug. *Ambiguity in Ecclesiastes*. LHBOTS 431. New York: T&T Clark, 2006.

Lee, Eunny P. *The Vitality of Enjoyment in Qoheleth's Theological Rhetoric*. BZAW 353. Berlin: de Gruyter, 2005.

McNeile, Alan. *An Introduction to Ecclesiastes*. Cambridge: Cambridge University Press, 1904.

Murphy, Ronald E. *Ecclesiastes*. WBC 23. Dallas: Word, 1992.

Neubauer, Raymond L. *Evolution and the Emergent Self: The Rise of Complexity and Behavioral Versatility in Nature*. New York: Columbia University Press, 2012.

Porter, Benjamin W., and Alexis T. Boutin. "Introduction." Pages 1–25 in *Remembering the Dead in the Ancient Near East: Recent Contributions from Bioarchaeology and Mortuary Archaeology*. Edited by Benjamin W. Porter and Alexis T. Boutin. Boulder: University Press of Colorado, 2014.

Seow, C. L. *Ecclesiastes: A New Translation with Introduction and Commentary*. AB 18C. New York: Doubleday, 1997.

Sharp, Carolyn J. *Irony and Meaning in the Hebrew Bible*. Bloomington: Indiana University Press, 2009.

Siegfried, Carl von. *Prediger und Hoheslied*. HKAT 3.2. Göttingen: Vandenhoeck & Ruprecht, 1898.

Sneed, Mark R. *The Politics of Pessimism: A Social-Science Perspective*. AIL 12. Atlanta: Society of Biblical Literature, 2012.

Sugirtharajah, R. S. *Postcolonial Criticism and Biblical Interpretation*. Oxford: Oxford University Press, 2002.

Tamez, Elsa, and Margaret Wilde. *When Horizons Close: Rereading Ecclesiastes*. Eugene, OR: Wipf & Stock, 2002.

Volkan, Vamik. "From Hope for a Better Life to Broken Spirits: An Introduction." Pages 7–12 in *Broken Spirits: The Treatment of Traumatized Asylum Seekers, Refugees, and War and Torture Victims*. Edited by John P. Wilson and Boris Droždek. New York: Brunner-Routledge, 2005.

Watkins, Mary, and Helene Shulman. *Toward Psychologies of Liberation*. New York: Palgrave McMillan, 2008.

Whybray, R. N. *Ecclesiastes*. NCB. Grand Rapids: Eerdmans, 1989.

Wilson, John P. "The Broken Spirit: Posttraumatic Damage to the Self." Pages 109–58 in *Broken Spirits: The Treatment of Traumatized Asylum Seekers, Refugees, and War and Torture Victims*. Edited by John P. Wilson and Boris Droždek. New York: Brunner-Routledge, 2005.

Wilson, John P., and Boris Droždek, eds. *Broken Spirits: The Treatment of Traumatized Asylum Seekers, Refugees, and War and Torture Victims.* New York: Brunner-Routledge, 2005.
Zimmerman, Frank. *The Inner World of Qoheleth.* New York: Ktav, 1973.

2
NEW INSIGHTS INTO OLD QUESTIONS

Fragments of Traumatic Memory: Ṣalmê zākār and Child Sacrifice in Ezekiel 16:15–22

Margaret S. Odell

Ezekiel 16, the problematic narrative of Jerusalem as YHWH's adopted daughter and faithless wife, has been richly illuminated for contemporary readers by way of postcolonial theory and postmodern literary approaches to metaphor and gender.[1] These interpretations have helped modern

---

1. For initial work on the use of metaphor in Ezek 16, see Julie Galambush, *Jerusalem in the Book of Ezekiel: The City as Yahweh's Wife*, SBLDS 130 (Atlanta: Scholars Press, 1992); and Peggy L. Day, "Adulterous Jerusalem's Imagined Demise: Death of a Metaphor in Ezekiel xvi," *VT* 50 (2000): 285–309; Day, "The Bitch Had It Coming to Her: Rhetoric and Interpretation in Ezekiel 16," *BibInt* 8 (2000): 231–54. Subsequent studies build on this initial work by combining feminist criticism with other postmodern approaches to interpretation. For gender analysis, see especially Cynthia R. Chapman, *The Gendered Language of Warfare in the Israelite Assyrian Encounter*, HSM 62 (Winona Lake, IN: Eisenbrauns, 2004), ch. 4; Chapman, "Sculpted Warriors: Sexuality and the Sacred in the Assyrian Palace Reliefs and in Ezekiel 23:14–17," in *The Aesthetics of Violence in the Prophets*, ed. Julia M. O'Brien and Chris Franke, LHBOTS 517 (New York: T&T Clark, 2010), 1–17; and Christl M. Maier, *Daughter Zion, Mother Zion: Gender, Space, and the Sacred in Ancient Israel* (Minneapolis: Fortress, 2008), 117–33. For postcolonial theory combined with trauma theory, see Gale A. Yee, *Poor Banished Children of Eve: Woman as Evil in the Hebrew Bible* (Minneapolis: Fortress, 2003), 111–34; and Corrine L. Patton, "'Should Our Sister Be Treated Like a Whore?' A Response to Feminist Critiques of Ezekiel 23," in *The Book of Ezekiel: Theological and Anthropological Perspectives*, ed. Margaret S. Odell and John T. Strong, SBLSymS 9 (Atlanta: Society of Biblical Literature, 2000), 221–38. For studies focusing primarily on trauma themes, see David G. Garber, "Traumatizing Ezekiel, the Exilic Prophet," in *From Genesis to Apocalyptic Vision*, vol. 2 of *Psychology and the Bible: A New Way to Read the Scriptures*, ed. J. Harold Ellens and Wayne G. Rollins (Westport, CT: Praeger, 2004), 215–35; Garber, "Trauma, History and Survival in Ezekiel 1–24" (PhD diss., Emory University, 2005); Daniel Smith-Christopher, "Ezekiel in Abu Ghraib: Reread-

readers move from initial feelings of revulsion and shock at this tale of YHWH's violent punishment of daughter/wife Jerusalem to a more complex assessment of its symbolic treatment of the city's destruction. To be sure, nothing can dispel the tale's unsettling violence; nevertheless, it has become possible to appreciate how the narrative's use of metaphor and gender allowed its ancient readers to work through the real violence of the destruction of Jerusalem, and modern readers have been reminded that the figure of YHWH's wife is not to be read literally but metaphorically, that the text derives its emotional power precisely from the association of siege warfare with the brutality of gang rape, and, finally, that the narrative is not about private morality but public theopolitical concerns. Particularly through the use of gender analysis and postcolonial theory, what is problematic for modern readers can be explained as an ancient attempt to address the real and ultimately fatal imbalance of power between Judah and its allies.

For reasons that remain difficult to discern, Ezek 16:15–22 have eluded this sophisticated analysis. In this unit, the newly married Jerusalem embarks on her career of marital infidelity. For the sake of every passerby (*kol-ʿôbēr*), Jerusalem takes her wedding gifts and constructs shrines (*bāmôt*) and male images (*ṣalmê zākār*), which she then clothes and feeds with gifts YHWH had given to her. Even more outrageously, she offers her children in sacrifice to them, never once remembering the day of her birth, when she was left to die by the same nations for whom she now squanders her identity and lifeblood.

Although these passersby are subsequently identified as Jerusalem's political allies, the Assyrians, Babylonians, and Egyptians (16:25–28), the scholarly consensus regards these earlier verses as an account of Jerusalem's prior *religious* apostasy. Referential difficulties abound. For example, the explicit reference to "male images" does not square with the abundance of female figurines in the archaeological record. In order to work around this problem, it is frequently suggested that the expression *ṣalmê zākār*, "male images," is a creative invention consistent with the metaphorical requirements of the narrative that can nevertheless be taken to refer "truthfully" to a variety of nonnormative practices, including the manufacture of

---

ing Ezekiel 16:37–39 in the Context of Imperial Conquest," in *Ezekiel's Hierarchical World: Wrestling with a Tiered Reality*, ed. Stephen L. Cook and Corrine L. Patton, SBLSymS 31 (Atlanta: Society of Biblical Literature, 2004), 141–57; and Ruth Poser, *Das Ezechielbuch als Trauma-Literatur*, VTSup 154 (Leiden: Brill, 2012).

female figurines.[2] However, this is not the only problem. The clothing of cult statues is otherwise unknown in Israel, and the food offered to them is not known as food offered to the gods.[3] Finally, it remains difficult to equate the sacrifice of children as described in 16:20–21 with any known practice. In his own review of this material, Daniel Block concedes, "Ezekiel provides few clues about the nature of child sacrifice in Israel."[4] Yet the lack of clues does not prevent Block or others from positing that the reference to child sacrifice alludes to the Molech cult—itself a problematic reconstruction based on scant biblical evidence. Despite these difficulties, the scholarly consensus holds: even if it is not possible to verify that the ritual practices described in this unit were actually practiced in ancient Israel and Judah, it nevertheless *must* be an account of nonnormative religious practice.[5]

In my view, this approach to 16:15–22 fails because there is no evidence to support it. Worse, it generates a degree of incoherence in the interpretation of Ezek 16 as a whole. These verses introduce the theme of Jerusalem's rejection of YHWH, yet in the announcement of judgment what must come to an end is not the construction of images or the sacrifice of children but the "payments" to the lovers, Jerusalem's political allies, who are not introduced until verses 23–29 (16:41; see also 16:33–34). Peggy Day does suggest that child sacrifice appears in 16:38, where it is metaphorized as murder and linked to Jerusalem's political infidelity, which, in turn, is metaphorized as adultery: "I will judge you as adulterers and murderers are judged."[6] However, even if this reading is correct, it does not account for the way in which a prior religious offense has been subordinated to, if not equated with, a later political offense.

---

2. Leslie Allen, *Ezekiel 1–19,* WBC 28 (Dallas: Word, 1994), 239; Moshe Greenberg, *Ezekiel 1–20: A New Translation with Introduction and Commentary,* AB 22 (New York: Doubleday, 1983), 280.

3. Greenberg, *Ezekiel 1–20,* 280.

4. Daniel I. Block, *The Book of Ezekiel, Chapters 1–24,* NICOT (Grand Rapids: Eerdmans, 1997), 491.

5. For the persistence of this claim, see, most recently, Poser, *Das Ezechielbuch als Trauma-Literatur,* 382. In the interest of disclosure, I note that her source for this claim is my own earlier work on this chapter, which also reflects the scholarly consensus I now challenge. See Margaret S. Odell, *Ezekiel,* SHBC (Macon, GA: Smyth & Helwys, 2005), 191.

6. Day, "Adulterous Jerusalem's Imagined Demise," 295 n. 30; the translation is Day's.

This study seeks to resolve the above difficulties by treating 16:15–22 as an emblematic introduction to the ensuing account of Jerusalem's political infidelity. Crucial to this interpretation is the reference in 16:17 to *ṣalmê zākār*, "male images," an expression that has otherwise defied explanation as a reference to idols. In my opinion, the expression is more readily explained in light of the widespread Assyrian practice of setting up royal images (*ṣalmu*) in conquered territories. In order to show how this term becomes the basis for symbolic development in Ezek 16, I draw on trauma theory to suggest that *ṣalmê zākār* persisted in the exilic imagination as fragments associated with both the landscape of Jerusalem and the experience of political subjugation. As such, they were a fruitful image for the development of Ezekiel's extended metaphorical narrative of Jerusalem's whoring with political powers. Rather than describing religious practices, then, this unit creatively appropriates fragments of visual memory in order to launch an extended theopolitical critique. As far as child sacrifice is concerned, the vignette of 16:15–22 presents in starkest possible terms the alternatives of service to YHWH, on the one hand, and subjection to the nations, on the other. Where YHWH had invested Jerusalem with abundance and vitality in the form of many children, the empires have not only drained Jerusalem of its resources but will not be satisfied until they have exacted sacrifices of the worst kind.

Memory and Trauma

The basic understanding of trauma as buried or missed experience—an experience or event so deeply wounding that it cannot be assimilated into consciousness—is a starting point for theorizing about the impact of trauma on meaning-making. It is not so much that the experience is repressed but that it is never fully experienced. This is the case even if the initial trauma continues to haunt the sufferer through uninvited repetitions.[7] While one might infer that subsequent repetitions and hauntings eventually lead to understanding, Cathy Caruth maintains that they simply recapitulate the incomprehensibility of the initial experience. According to Caruth, it is this very elusiveness of meaning that gives trauma its significance. As she observes, traumatic repetitions suggest "a larger relation to

---

7. Cathy Caruth, "Introduction," in *Trauma: Explorations in Memory*, ed. Cathy Caruth (Baltimore: Johns Hopkins University Press, 1995), 4.

the event that extends beyond what can simply be seen or what can be known, and is inextricably tied up with the belatedness and incomprehensibility that remain at the heart of this repetitive seeing."[8]

The concept of the "missed event" raises important questions for interpretation because it paradoxically requires the recovery of an event that, by definition, is no longer accessible. In the case of Ezek 16, what can be recovered is not the event itself but its traces, those repetitions that may indicate an earlier traumatic event, and Ezek 16 is nothing if not a series of repetitions in which Jerusalem's initial betrayal of her marriage bond plays itself out over and over again, as she proves unfaithful not only to her "husband" YHWH but also to her lovers, whom she plays off against one another with deadly consequences. Moshe Greenberg draws attention to the historical precision underlying the harlotry metaphor in 16:27–29, pointing out that the enumeration of Jerusalem's allies corresponds to the order in which Judah/Jerusalem initiated alliances with them in the eighth century.[9]

It is the narrator who explicitly connects these repetitions with a forgotten trauma: "And in all your abominations and your whorings you did not remember the days of your youth, when you were naked and bare, flailing about in your blood" (16:22 NRSV). What is important to note here is that it is the narrative that posits the connection between a primal traumatic event and Jerusalem's historical experience of mistreatment by the nations. But this connection is a fictional one, in the sense that it is a metaphorical representation of the city as an abandoned girl-child. Despised and left for dead by the nations at the beginning of her life, Jerusalem becomes trapped in a series of deadly repetitions that will leave the city ravaged and its population destroyed. By locating Jerusalem's trauma in a natal event that is by definition unrecoverable to memory, the narrative implicitly suggests that Jerusalem is caught up in political practices that elude conscious understanding—even as it condemns it for this failure. For this reason, it may be useful to seek other approaches to the relationship between trauma and meaning-making.

Other theorists define the problem of meaning not as a missed experience but as epistemic failure, a fundamental inability to understand the

---

8. Cathy Caruth, "Traumatic Awakenings (Freud, Lacan, and the Ethics of Memory)," in her *Unclaimed Experience: Trauma, Narrative, and History* (Baltimore: Johns Hopkins University Press, 1996), 91–92.

9. Greenberg, *Ezekiel 1–20*, 282–83.

complexity of the traumatic event. Writing about the testimonies of Holocaust survivors, Dori Laub observes that memory cannot help but distort reality: "The horror is, indeed, compelling not only in its reality but even more so, in its flagrant distortion and subversion of reality."[10] The actual event has already defied reality, while its "horror … is maintained in the testimony only as an elusive memory that feels as if it no longer resembles any reality."[11] What this suggests to Laub is that the heart of the traumatic experience is epistemic failure; among those survivors of the Holocaust whose testimonies he had recorded, what was missing was the human "cognitive capacity to perceive and to assimilate the totality of what was really happening at the time."[12]

It is into this sense of epistemic failure that Shoshana Felman introduces the concept of fragments of memory, "overwhelmed by occurrences that have not settled into understanding or remembrance, acts that cannot be construed as knowledge nor assimilated into full cognition, events in excess of our frames of reference."[13] Felman's conception of fragments is particularly helpful to my elucidation of the ṣalmê zākār in Ezek 16, since it suggests, on the one hand, that they may have a forgotten significance quite apart from their role in the present narrative, and, on the other, that meaningful discourse and narrative come into existence only by way of reflection on them.

Bringing one's fragmented experience into narrative form is not simply a transfer of information or an establishment of the facts of the matter; rather, narration allows one to assimilate and come to terms with loss. Testimony is therefore itself "a form of action, of change, which one has to actually pass through, in order to continue and complete the process of survival."[14] By way of illustration, Laub tells the story of a child who escapes the camps with a photograph of his mother and with the parents' promise that they will find him. He survives, and the parents do find him, but his mother no longer looks like the woman in the picture; since the parents have been changed, they are no longer the people they once were.

---

10. Dori Laub, "Truth and Testimony," in Caruth, *Trauma*, 62.

11. Ibid.

12. Ibid., 69.

13. Shoshana Felman, "Education and Crisis: Or, the Vicissitudes of Teaching," in Caruth, *Trauma*, 13–60 (16).

14. Laub, "Truth and Testimony," 70.

The son thus experiences the reunion as a broken promise. Only through telling the story can he accept that things will never be as they once were.[15]

In situations in which entire communities have experienced catastrophe, the relation between trauma, memory, and narrative is even more complex. Perpetrators, victims, and bystanders all relate to the catastrophe in different ways. Not all victims experience catastrophe as trauma, nor do all wish to remember or relive those horrific events by calling them back to mind. Commenting on the fragility of memory under ordinary circumstances, Primo Levi has sought to understand just how the traumatic experiences of the concentration camps deformed, even obliterated, the memories of both victims and oppressors,[16] while Alexander and Margarete Mitscherlich have examined the extent to which denial served as a coping mechanism for Germans to move on after World War II.[17] A life made possible through denial and forgetting may initially appear healthy and resilient; however, trauma theorists maintain that it is only through a painful process of coming to terms with loss that there can be any genuine healing.

Narrative can aid in that process by representing to the readers what has not yet been adequately understood and remembered.[18] In his own work on the trauma novel, Ronald Granofsky describes a number of genres that have played a role in working through trauma[19] and further suggests that symbolic expression becomes important especially when an experience is not easily integrated into memory. Just as human memory achieves distance temporally, the symbol in fiction achieves it spatially by imposing itself between the reader and the thing symbolized. The symbol functions analogously to memory in other ways as well, drawing together

---

15. Ibid., 73.

16. Primo Levi, "The Memory of the Offense," in his *The Drowned and the Saved,* trans. Raymond Rosenthal (New York: Random House, 1989), 23–35.

17. Alexander and Margarete Mitscherlich, *The Inability to Mourn: Principles of Collective Behavior,* trans. Beverley R. Placzek (New York: Grove, 1975).

18. For the social forces at work in these processes, see Jeffrey C. Alexander, "Cultural Trauma: A Social Theory," in his *Trauma: A Social Theory* (Cambridge: Polity, 2012), 6–30.

19. Ronald Granofsky, *The Trauma Novel: Contemporary Symbolic Depictions of Collective Disaster* (New York: Lang, 1995), 5. To these fictional genres one may also add historical narrative; see Michael S. Roth, "Trauma, Representation, and Historical Consciousness," in his *Memory, Trauma, and History: Essays on Living with the Past* (New York: Columbia University Press, 2012), 77–86.

two or more distinct phenomena so that only certain aspects of the experience are foregrounded.[20]

Taken together, the perspectives of Felman and Granofsky facilitate interpretation of Ezek 16:15–22. Felman's concept of memory fragments provides a useful framework for thinking about the reference to the male images in 16:17. Granofsky's principles of selection in the construction of a literary symbol encourage reflection on how this unit brings together the male images, on the one hand, with child sacrifice, on the other, all in order to bring the exiles to a greater understanding of what Jerusalem has forgotten or failed to understand about its place among the nations.

ṢALMÊ ZĀKĀR AS FRAGMENTS OF MEMORY

If current treatments of Ezek 16:15–22 rest on the assumption of a more or less direct relationship between the text's references to cult practice and an underlying Judean context, trauma theory allows for a different kind of relationship between literary reference and historical reality. It does so in part by accounting for the myriad ways in which memory is distorted but also by explaining how narrative confronts its audience with the "truth" of the past in ways that are not simply referential. As such, trauma theory allows for a reappraisal of the way in which one particular reference, the mention of ṣalmê zākār, or male images, forms the nucleus of a symbolic representation of Jerusalem as a city tragically colluding with intruders in draining its resources and immolating its population. By treating the expression as a fragment of memory, it will be possible to show how it functions as a symbol of Jerusalem's long experience of political subjugation.

If the expression ṣalmê zākār cannot be explained in light of Judean religious practices, it is perfectly intelligible in the ancient Near Eastern context as a reference to human, more specifically royal, images. In a series of articles Irene Winter has written extensively on the meaning and significance of ṣalmu in Akkadian royal ideology and iconography.[21] Observing

---

20. Granofsky, *The Trauma Novel*, 6–7.

21. Irene J. Winter, "Art *in* Empire: The Royal Image and the Visual Dimensions of Assyrian Ideology," in *Assyria 1995: Proceedings of the 10th Anniversary Symposium of the Neo-Assyrian Text Corpus Project, Helsinki, Sep 7–11, 1995*, ed. Simo Parpola and Robert M. Whiting (Helsinki: Neo-Assyrian Text Corpus Project, 1997), 359–81; Winter, "The Body of the Able Ruler: Toward an Understanding of the Statues of Gudea," in *DUMU-E₂-DUB-BA: Studies in Honor of Åke Sjöberg*, ed. Hermann Beh-

that the term *ṣalmu* is far more widely attested for royal images than for divine ones,[22] Winter has demonstrated that the royal image functioned in a variety of ways to extend the king's presence and legitimate his rule, as well as to represent iconographically the entire theopolitical program of Assyrian kingship.[23] Royal images were to be found everywhere in a variety of media. They appear as three-dimensional statues as well as on stelae and reliefs, in the architectural and iconographic programs of Assyrian palaces as well as throughout the Assyrian imperium, where "free-standing stone stelae … seem to have been liberally distributed throughout the realm."[24]

It may even be possible to suggest that city and royal image go hand in hand in the landscape of the Assyrian imperium. In one relief, for example, a royal stela is prominently featured outside a city wall,[25] and the positioning of these stelae in relation to cities may be one feature of visual memory reflected in Ezek 16:17. Stela fragments commemorating Assyrian conquests have been found in Samaria and along the borders of the Judean highlands,[26] and Christl Maier posits that royal stelae may well have constituted the basis for Ezekiel's fantastic account of Jerusalem's "whoring" in Ezek 16:23–34:

> The only installation in relation to political power one would expect in a city square or at the gate is a pedestal for a stele that either depicts an image of the foreign overlord or an inscription or both. Assyrian rulers are known for erecting victory stelae in conquered territories with inscriptions that testify to their political power. To pay reverence to such a stele while passing the gate or the square would be "whoring

---

rens, Darlene Loding, and Martha T. Roth, Occasional Publications of the Samuel Noah Kramer Fund 11 (Philadelphia: Samuel Noah Kramer Fund, 1989), 573–83; Winter, "Idols of the King: Royal Images as Recipients of Ritual Action in Ancient Mesopotamia," *Journal of Ritual Studies* 6 (1992): 13–42; and Winter, "What/When Is a Portrait? Royal Images of the Ancient Near East," *Proceedings of the American Philosophical Society* 153 (2009): 254–70.

22. Winter, "Idols of the King," 15, 36 n.1.

23. Winter, "Art *in* Empire," 367, 376; Winter, "Idols of the King," 34.

24. Winter, "Art *in* Empire," 363–64; see also Mordechai Cogan, *Imperialism and Religion in Assyria, Judah, and Israel in the 8th and 7th Centuries B.C.E.*, SBLMS 19 (Missoula, MT: Scholars Press, 1974), 56.

25. Winter, "Art *in* Empire," 375 fig. 13.

26. Wayne Horowitz and Takayoshi Oshima, with Seth Sanders, *Cuneiform in Canaan: Cuneiform Sources from the Land of Israel in Ancient Times* (Jerusalem: Israel Exploration Society; Hebrew University of Jerusalem, 2006), 19–22.

with foreign powers" in the eyes of Ezekiel since the stele symbolizes that
Jerusalem is a vassal city.[27]

Since Ezekiel employs the exact term for such an image in 16:17, there
is no reason to assume that the ṣalmê zākār of 16:15–22 and the objects
of Jerusalem's desires in 16:23–29 are different entities. In fact, the ritual
activities associated with the ṣalmê zākār in 16:17–19 are intelligible as
the animation and veneration of royal images. Here again, Winter draws
attention to the way in which royal images went through rituals of animation analogous to that of divine images—all in order to function within
sacred space as the living manifestation of the king. Winter's evidence
is clearest for the Gudea statues (ca. 2100 BCE); however, she notes that
the practice of providing royal images with regular offerings of food is
also attested for the Neo-Babylonian period.[28] What is presented in Ezek
16:17–19 looks like Mesopotamian practice because it *is* Mesopotamian
practice, that of venerating the royal image by situating it within sacred
space and providing it with offerings of food and clothing. However, it
reflects the custom of venerating the image of a human king, not a deity.
The expression so closely reflects Akkadian terminology that it can hardly
be a creative invention to fit the needs of the narrative. Rather, it suggests
a memory of imperial practice.

Winter also draws attention to the way in which kingship was iconographically coded with traits associated with masculinity. The exposed,
hyper-developed muscular right arm on the numerous statues of Gudea
of Lagash signified that king's capacity to rule, while his broad face and
even gaze signified other qualifications of the just and able ruler.[29] As early
as the Stela of Naram-Sin, the king's full beard and upright bearing signified his power and capacity to establish order as the rightful king; these
features persisted well into the Neo-Assyrian period as idealized traits signifying the king's capacity and right to rule.[30]

Textual elements underscored these visual aspects of the iconographic
program. Drawing on Winter's work and further subjecting the Assyr-

---

27. Maier, *Daughter Zion, Mother Zion,* 119.
28. Winter, "Idols of the King"; cf. Paul-Alain Beaulieu, *The Reign of Nabonidus,
King of Babylon 556–539 BC,* YNER 10 (New Haven: Yale University Press, 1989),
135–36.
29. Winter, "Body of the Able Ruler," 586–83, summarized in "Art *in* Empire," 370.
30. Winter, "Art *in* Empire," 371.

ian iconographic program to gender analysis, Cynthia Chapman points out that these traits of masculinity were characterized by the term *zikru*, masculinity, a preeminent royal attribute included in royal titularies from Ashurnasirpal to Ashurbanipal.[31] From the Assyrian perspective, then, ideological conceptions of kingship and characteristic traits of masculinity would have been interchangeable, and an Assyrian king would have described his highly masculine representation as an "image of my kingship" (*ṣalam šarrūtiya*). The Assyrian parallels suggest that what is emphasized in the expression *ṣalmê zākār* is not maleness but masculinity, those gendered traits associated with the political ideology of Assyrian kingship. The expression clearly reflects a visual memory of images whose characteristically masculine traits signified domination and power.

ṢALMÊ ZĀKĀR IN TRAUMA NARRATIVE

If Ezekiel's reference to the male images—or, rather, masculine images—becomes intelligible within this larger ancient Near Eastern context, it must be admitted that their role in Ezek 16 does not immediately invite comparison with Assyrian iconography. Assyrians do not set them up; Jerusalem does. For that matter, the images are not stone stelae but crafted of gold and silver. One way to explain this variation is to see Ezek 16 as a selective reframing of Jerusalem's past in order to accentuate its culpability. Even so, traces of the images' association with domination and power remain, as they are the means whereby Jerusalem comes under the control of the intruders who first prompted her turn from YHWH.

Interestingly, the narrative also engages in ideology critique. As Chapman has demonstrated, the Assyrian ideal of masculinity included claims to care for the vulnerable,[32] yet Jerusalem's lovers do nothing of the kind; indeed, one can hardly see how these passersby (16:15, 25) would have any other claim to rule Jerusalem than what Jerusalem hands over to them on her own terms. They systematically drain Jerusalem of all that YHWH has bestowed on her in the way of life and material abundance. Verses 23–33 parody this damage to Jerusalem as the reversal of the ordinary transactions of prostitution: "no one solicited you to play the whore; and you gave payment, while no payment was given to you; you were different" (16:34

---

31. Cynthia Chapman, *Gendered Language of Warfare*, 29.
32. Ibid., 29–32.

NRSV). Quite in contrast with YHWH's role as "husband," the political allies represented by the male images have done little to care for Jerusalem but have only drained her dry.

They also demand loyalty on threat of further loss. Moreover, it is this threat of loss that explains how the ṣalmê zākār came to be associated with child sacrifice. As I have noted above, Ezek 16 does not single out child sacrifice as a separate crime but subordinates it to Jerusalem's political infidelities. The hendiadys of 16:38, in which Jerusalem is judged as an adulteress and murderer, establishes this connection, and the relationship is more fully developed in the announcement of judgment in 16:35–36. The accusation is relatively complex; however, the grammatical parallelism discloses a relationship between Jerusalem's lovers and gillûlîm, on the one hand, and what Jerusalem does to her children, on the other:

> Because you remained in a constant state of arousal,
> you revealed your nakedness in your whoring
>> against ['al] your lovers
>> and against ['al] all your abominable gillûlîm,
> and so you gave them your sons' blood. (16:36 my translation)

The indictment is based on the preceding narrative account of Jerusalem's infidelities (16:30–34). Not satisfied with the Assyrians or the Chaldeans, Jerusalem has sent for other lovers as well. As a result, she has committed adultery against, or to the disadvantage of, her lovers, as indicated by the preposition 'al.[33] Moreover, the close parallelism of the two prepositional phrases "against your lovers and against all your abominable gillûlîm" closely identifies the lovers and the gillûlîm as corresponding, if not identical, entities. Although this latter term is commonly understood to be Ezekiel's favorite term for idols,[34] it is better understood as a pejorative twist

---

33. Although BHS suggests reading this preposition as 'el, the adversative connotation of MT 'al makes perfect sense in this context of multiple betrayals. For the use of znh 'al in this sense, see Judg 19:2.

34. See, for example, H. D. Preuss, "גלולים gillûlîm," TDOT 3:1–5; and Daniel Bodi, "Les gillûlîm chez Ézéchiel et dans l'ancien Testament, et les différentes pratiques cultuelles associées à ce terme," RB 100 (1993): 481–510. For the extent to which this position influences Ezekiel studies, see, e.g., Andrew Mein, Ezekiel and the Ethics of Exile, Oxford Theological Monographs (Oxford: Oxford University Press, 2001), 136; and John F. Kutsko, Between Heaven and Earth: Divine Presence and Absence in the Book of Ezekiel, Biblical and Judaic Studies 7 (Winona Lake, IN: Eisenbrauns, 2000),

on an Akkadian term for the stone employed in the construction of stelae (galālu).[35] As such, the term gillûlîm would constitute yet another memory of the Assyrian practice of setting up royal stelae. If the reference to ṣalmê zākār in 16:15–22 obscures this Assyrian background, the equation of the gillûlîm with the lovers brings it back into focus and, not coincidentally, preserves the Assyrian understanding of the function of images as onto-logical extensions of the royal presence. In effect, Jerusalem's betrayal of the lovers *is* a betrayal of the gillûlîm/ṣalmê zākār and vice versa.

The final clause of the indictment indicates that the fate of Jerusalem's children is tied to these betrayals. Introduced by the preposition k, this clause hints at an equivalence between Jerusalem's infidelity, on the one hand, and Jerusalem's handing over of her sons, on the other. At its most basic, the clause suggests that Jerusalem's breach of covenant was so great that she was even willing to spill her children's blood. However, the indict-ment may reflect a closer connection. Since her whoring is to her lovers' disadvantage, the clause may specify a penalty: she must hand over her children as a penalty for breaking faith. The connection between political infidelity and bloodshed is reiterated in 16:38 when it is announced that she will be judged as "women who commit adultery and shed blood are judged" (NRSV). The bloodshed of which she is accused, then, is not child sacrifice but the reckless endangerment of her population through breach of covenant.

Jerusalem's culpability thus lies more in the realm of treaty violation than in ritual practice. Indeed, the verb employed in 16:35 (√ntn) is not restricted in its usage to ritual killing but is also used in accounts of treaty penalties (see Deut 28:32). Treaty curses involving threats against chil-dren are attested in Near Eastern futility curses and were well known in

---

25. Although this position has enjoyed a strong consensus in recent years, Johan Lust has drawn attention to the wide range of Septuagint translations of the term and has called for a reconsideration of the meaning of Hebrew gillûlîm; see Johan Lust, "Idols? גלולים and εἴδωλα in Ezekiel," in *Florilegium lovaniense: Studies in Septuagint and Tex-tual Criticism in Honor of Florentino García Martínez*, ed. Hans Ausloos, Bénédicte Lemmelijn, and Marc Vervenne (Leuven: Peeters, 2008), 317–33. I hope to revisit this issue in a future study.

35. See W. W. Baudissin, "Die alttestamentliche Bezeichnung der Göttzen mit gillūlīm," *ZDMG* 58 (1904): 395–425, esp. 418–21; R. A. Bowman, "גלל אבן—*aban galalu* (Ezra 5:8; 6:4)," in *Dōrōn: Hebraic Studies*, ed. Israel T. Naamani and David Rudarsky (New York: National Association of Professors of Hebrew in American Insti-tutions of Higher Learning, 1965), 64–74; see also citations under *galālu, CAD* 5:11.

the biblical tradition (again, Deut 28:32).[36] The seizure of children was a historical reality: Nebuchadnezzar had Zedekiah's sons slaughtered in his presence before he himself was blinded and taken prisoner (2 Kgs 25:7; cf. Ezek 16:21). In Ezek 23:10, Oholah's children are seized by the Assyrians in retaliation for her breach of covenant, and all but one of the other references to children in Ezekiel reflect the treaty curse of being bereaved of children.[37]

This historical reality has come to be represented as child sacrifice in 16:15–22 by way of a creative reworking of fragments of historical memory. Elsewhere in the exilic literature the trope of mother and children is employed to speak of Jerusalem and its *inhabitants*, not literal children. It remains an open question why readers revert to literal and referential readings of these verses as accounts of child sacrifice, especially when they are embedded in an obviously metaphorical narrative. What the trope of mother and children conveys here is a city not only colluding in the destruction of its population but inaugurating the conditions that will lead to its demise. Jerusalem does not acquiesce as hapless victim to the intrusion of the passersby; rather, she actively encourages them to take up residence by building *bāmôt* and *ṣalmê zākār*. The imagery accurately reflects the circumstances of the eighth century, when Judean kings initiated alliances with neighboring empires. Far from alluding to religious apostasy, Ezek 16:15–22 reflects a keen understanding of Jerusalem's historical *political* entanglements. The circumstances leading to Jerusalem's destruction have old and deep roots, but they do not begin with religious apostasy, as if ritual aberrations constituted the gateway drug to Jerusalem's more recent and more deadly political disloyalty.

Now living among the nations, the survivors of Jerusalem's destruction are invited to consider their own experience of having been brutalized by the nations. By presenting the slaughter of Jerusalem's children as a sacrifice to *ṣalmê zākār*, Ezek 16:15–22 calls attention to the ironic cost of Jerusalem's desperate search for political security. It also brings to consciousness that which remains hidden in all claims to political domina-

---

36. For the destruction of a city's inhabitants, see Paul Bentley Kern, *Ancient Siege Warfare* (Bloomington: Indiana University Press, 1999), 24, 70, 72, 76.

37. Ezek 5:17; 14:16, 18, 20, 22; 36:12, 13, 14; cf. Lev 26:22; the exception is Ezek 24:21, which refers to the exiles' abandonment of their sons and daughters to Jerusalem.

tion. If there is a promise of deliverance and security, that promise rests on the power to decree who lives and who dies.[38] Jerusalem had already fallen prey to that power when her Hittite and Amorite parents abandoned her to die; its long history of engagement with the nations was nothing but a series of epistemic failures, lost opportunities to learn that bitter lesson. By associating the male images with the sacrifice of Jerusalem's children, Ezek 16 exposes the lie inherent in the empires' offer of security, and it clearly establishes the alternatives between Jerusalem's so-called life among the nations and life with YHWH. It is only YHWH who gives life; the nations can only take it away. By coming to understand what Jerusalem had failed to grasp in its own experience of the nations, the survivors just might be able to break the cycle of trauma that Jerusalem has endured throughout its all too brief history.

BIBLIOGRAPHY

Agamben, Giorgio. *Sovereign Power and Bare Life*. Translated by Daniel Heller-Roazen. Homo Sacer 1. Stanford, CA: Stanford University Press, 1998.

Alexander, Jeffrey C. *Trauma: A Social Theory*. Cambridge: Polity, 2012.

Allen, Leslie. *Ezekiel 1–19*. WBC 28. Dallas: Word, 1994.

Bahrani, Zainab. *Rituals of War: The Body and Violence in Mesopotamia*. New York: Zone Books, 2008.

Baudissin, W. W. "Die alttestamentliche Bezeichnung der Göttzen mit *gillūlīm*." *ZDMG* 58 (1904): 395–425.

Beaulieu, Paul-Alain. *The Reign of Nabonidus, King of Babylon 556–539 BC*. YNER 10. New Haven: Yale University Press, 1989.

Block, Daniel I. *The Book of Ezekiel, Chapters 1–24*. NICOT. Grand Rapids: Eerdmans, 1997.

Bodi, Daniel. "Les *gillûlîm* chez Ézéchiel et dans l'ancien Testament, et les différentes pratiques cultuelles associées à ce terme." *RB* 100 (1993): 481–510.

Bowman, R. A. "גלל אבן—*aban galalu* (Ezra 5:8; 6:4)." Pages 64–74 in *Dōrōn: Hebraic Studies*. Edited by Israel T. Naamani and David Rudar-

---

38. Giorgio Agamben, *Sovereign Power and Bare Life*, trans. Daniel Heller-Roazen, Homo Sacer 1 (Stanford, CA: Stanford University Press, 1998), 6; cf. Zainab Bahrani, *Rituals of War: The Body and Violence in Mesopotamia* (New York: Zone Books, 2008), 102–12.

sky. New York: National Association of Professors of Hebrew in American Institutions of Higher Learning, 1965.

Caruth, Cathy. "Introduction." Pages 3–12 in *Trauma: Explorations in Memory*. Edited by Cathy Caruth. Baltimore: Johns Hopkins University Press, 1995.

———. *Unclaimed Experience: Trauma, Narrative, and History*. Baltimore: Johns Hopkins University Press, 1996.

Chapman, Cynthia R. *The Gendered Language of Warfare in the Israelite Assyrian Encounter*. HSM 62. Winona Lake, IN: Eisenbrauns, 2004.

———. "Sculpted Warriors: Sexuality and the Sacred in the Assyrian Palace Reliefs and in Ezekiel 23:14–17." Pages 1–17 in *The Aesthetics of Violence in the Prophets*. Edited by Julia M. O'Brien and Chris Franke. LHBOTS 517. New York: T&T Clark, 2010.

Cogan, Mordechai. *Imperialism and Religion in Assyria, Judah, and Israel in the 8th and 7th Centuries B.C.E.*, SBLMS 19. Missoula, MT: Scholars Press, 1974.

Day, Peggy L. "Adulterous Jerusalem's Imagined Demise: Death of a Metaphor in Ezekiel xvi." *VT* 50 (2000): 285–309.

———. "The Bitch Had It Coming to Her: Rhetoric and Interpretation in Ezekiel 16." *BibInt* 8 (2000): 231–54.

Felman, Shoshana. "Education and Crisis: Or, the Vicissitudes of Teaching." Pages 13–60 in *Trauma: Explorations in Memory*. Edited by Cathy Caruth. Baltimore: Johns Hopkins University Press, 1995.

Galambush, Julie. *Jerusalem in the Book of Ezekiel: The City as Yahweh's Wife*. SBLDS 130. Atlanta: Scholars Press, 1992.

Garber, David G. "Trauma, History and Survival in Ezekiel 1–24." PhD diss., Emory University, 2005.

———. "Traumatizing Ezekiel, the Exilic Prophet." Pages 215–35 in *From Genesis to Apocalyptic Vision. Vol. 2 of Psychology and the Bible: A New Way to Read the Scriptures*. Edited by J. Harold Ellens and Wayne G. Rollins. Westport, CT: Praeger, 2004.

Granofsky, Ronald. *The Trauma Novel: Contemporary Symbolic Depictions of Collective Disaster*. New York: Lang, 1995.

Greenberg, Moshe *Ezekiel 1–20: A New Translation with Introduction and Commentary*. AB 22. New York: Doubleday, 1983.

Horowitz, Wayne, and Takayoshi Oshima, with Seth Sanders. *Cuneiform in Canaan: Cuneiform Sources from the Land of Israel in Ancient Times*. Jerusalem: Israel Exploration Society; Hebrew University of Jerusalem, 2006.

Kern, Paul Bentley. *Ancient Siege Warfare*. Bloomington: Indiana University Press, 1999.

Kutsko, John F. *Between Heaven and Earth: Divine Presence and Absence in the Book of Ezekiel*. Biblical and Judaic Studies 7. Winona Lake, IN: Eisenbrauns, 2000.

Laub, Dori. "Truth and Testimony." Pages 61–75 in *Trauma: Explorations in Memory*. Edited by Cathy Caruth. Baltimore: Johns Hopkins University Press, 1995.

Levi, Primo. *The Drowned and the Saved*. Translated by Raymond Rosenthal. New York: Random House, 1989.

Lust, Johan. "Idols? גלולים and εἴδωλα in Ezekiel." Pages 317–33 in *Florilegium lovaniense: Studies in Septuagint and Textual Criticism in Honor of Florentino García Martínez*. Edited by Hans Ausloos, Bénédicte Lemmelijn, and Marc Vervenne. Leuven: Peeters, 2008.

Maier, Christl M. *Daughter Zion, Mother Zion: Gender, Space, and the Sacred in Ancient Israel*. Minneapolis: Fortress, 2008.

Mein, Andrew. *Ezekiel and the Ethics of Exile*. Oxford Theological Monographs. Oxford: Oxford University Press, 2001.

Mitscherlich, Alexander, and Margarete Mitscherlich. *The Inability to Mourn: Principles of Collective Behavior*. Translated by Beverley R. Placzek. New York: Grove, 1975.

Odell, Margaret S. *Ezekiel*. SHBC. Macon, GA: Smyth & Helwys, 2005.

Patton, Corrine L. " 'Should Our Sister Be Treated Like a Whore?' A Response to Feminist Critiques of Ezekiel 23." Pages 221–38 in *The Book of Ezekiel: Theological and Anthropological Perspectives*. Edited by Margaret S. Odell and John T. Strong. SBLSymS 9. Atlanta: Society of Biblical Literature, 2000.

Poser, Ruth. *Das Ezechielbuch als Trauma-Literatur*. VTSup 154. Leiden: Brill, 2012.

Preuss, H. D. "גלולים *gillûlîm*." *TDOT* 3:1–5.

Roth, Michael S. *Memory, Trauma, and History: Essays on Living with the Past*. New York: Columbia University Press, 2012.

Smith-Christopher, Daniel. "Ezekiel in Abu Ghraib: Rereading Ezekiel 16:37–39 in the Context of Imperial Conquest." Pages 141–57 in *Ezekiel's Hierarchical World: Wrestling with a Tiered Reality*. Edited by Stephen L. Cook and Corrine L. Patton. SBLSymS 31. Atlanta: Society of Biblical Literature, 2004.

Winter, Irene J. "Art *in* Empire: The Royal Image and the Visual Dimensions of Assyrian Ideology." Pages 359–81 in *Assyria 1995: Proceedings of the 10th Anniversary Symposium of the Neo-Assyrian Text Corpus Project, Helsinki, Sep 7–11, 1995.* Edited by Simo Parpola and Robert M. Whiting. Helskinki: Neo-Assyrian Text Corpus Project, 1997.

———. "The Body of the Able Ruler: Toward an Understanding of the Statues of Gudea." Pages 573–83 in 2 *DUMU-E₂-DUB-BA: Studies in Honor of Åke Sjöberg.* Edited by Hermann Behrens, Darlene Loding, and Martha T. Roth. Occasional Publications of the Samuel Noah Kramer Fund 11. Philadelphia: Samuel Noah Kramer Fund, 1989.

———. "Idols of the King: Royal Images as Recipients of Ritual Action in Ancient Mesopotamia." *Journal of Ritual Studies* 6 (1992): 13–42.

———. "What/When Is a Portrait? Royal Images of the Ancient Near East." *Proceedings of the American Philosophical Society* 153 (2009): 254–70.

Yee, Gale A. *Poor Banished Children of Eve: Woman as Evil in the Hebrew Bible.* Minneapolis: Fortress, 2003.

Reflections on the Prose Sermons in the Book of Jeremiah: Duhm's and Mowinckel's Contributions to Contemporary Trauma Readings

Louis Stulman

The study of trauma has taken center stage in fields as varied as film and orthopedics, psychotherapy and education, aesthetics and international politics. This diversity speaks to the influence of trauma studies across disciplines.[1] Notwithstanding this interdisciplinary reach, biblical studies is actually a latecomer to trauma studies. Although a number of fine works have recently appeared that explore the intersection of trauma and the Bible,[2] until November 2013 the Society of Biblical Literature had not devoted a program unit to the hermeneutics of trauma.

---

1. See Cathy Caruth, *Unclaimed Experience: Trauma, Narrative, and History* (Baltimore: Johns Hopkins University Press, 1996); Cathy Caruth, ed., *Trauma: Explorations of Memory* (Baltimore: Johns Hopkins University Press, 1995); Judith Herman, *Trauma and Recovery* (New York: Basic Books, 1992); Elaine Scarry, *The Body in Pain* (Oxford: Oxford University Press, 1985); Ibrahim Aref Kira, "Taxonomy of Trauma and Trauma Assessment," *Traumatology* 7.2 (2001): 73–86; Jean-Marie Lemaire, "Disconcerting Humanitarian Interventions, and the Resources for Collective Healing," in *Psychosocial and Trauma Response in War-Torn Societies: The Case of Kosovo*, ed. Natale Losi, Psychosocial Notebook 1 (Geneva: International Organization for Migration, 2000), 71–77; Elzbieta M. Gozdziak, "Refugee Women's Psychological Response to Forced Migration: Limitations of the Trauma Concept," http://tinyurl.com/SBL0689c. See also Ruth Leys, *From Guilt to Shame: Auschwitz and After* (Princeton: Princeton University Press, 2007); Leys, *Trauma: A Genealogy* (Chicago: University of Chicago Press, 2000).

2. E.g., Daniel L. Smith-Christopher, *A Biblical Theology of Exile*, OBT (Minneapolis: Fortress, 2002); Kathleen M. O'Connor, *Jeremiah: Pain and Promise* (Minneapolis: Fortress, 2011); Brad E. Kelle, Frank Ritchel Ames, and Jacob L. Wright, eds., *Interpreting Exile: Displacement and Deportation in Biblical and Modern Contexts*, AIL 10

At the same time, biblical scholars have long studied literary artifacts riddled with intimate and collective pain. The Tanak itself is arguably disaster and survival literature. The Torah tells the story of a displaced and marginalized people who survive against all odds, a story that is in part anachronistic. That is to say, it reflects the concerns of exilic and postexilic communities that had suffered massive disruptions of life: the destruction of Jerusalem and its temple, the wreckage of war, the collapse of national theologies, and the trauma of displacement and captivity. The Nevi'im is war literature, or, as Paul Kim and I have suggested, "a meditation on the horror of war."[3] Its multiplicity of voices is not only set against the background of war, but it reenacts the ravages of war in poetry and artistic prose.[4] The residual Ketuvim grapples with a range of concerns, including the traumatized body, displacement, loss of cultural memory, and prolonged life in diaspora. It is difficult to find in the Tanak a text that has not been refracted by its ancient writers and/or readers through the lens of traumatic violence.

The book of Jeremiah is a case in point. Anyone who broaches Jeremiah enters a world that bristles with pain and trauma. The manner in which this complex ancient writing represents trauma can be characterized in various ways. These texts represent on multiple levels "an affiliation of the powerless." They are texts beset with events that "overwhelm the ordinary human adaptations of life," events that involve "threats to life or bodily integrity, or a close personal [or communal] encounter with violence and death," events that "confront human beings with the extremities of helplessness and terror, and evoke the responses of catastrophe."[5] No other prophetic text pulsates with as much raw pain, not even the exilic book of Ezekiel. Often with atonal expressions and savage imagery, Jer-

---

(Atlanta: Society of Biblical Literature, 2011); Eve-Marie Becker, Jan Dochhorn, and Else K. Holt, eds., *Trauma and Traumatization in Individual and Collective Dimensions: Insights from Biblical Studies and Beyond*, SANt 2 (Vandenhoeck & Ruprecht, Göttingen, 2014). See also David M. Carr, *Holy Resilience: The Bible's Traumatic Origins* (New Haven: Yale University Press, 2014). For a broader treatment of trauma and theological studies, see Serene Jones, *Trauma and Grace: Theology in a Ruptured World* (Louisville: Westminster John Knox, 2009).

3. Louis Stulman and Hyun Chul Paul Kim, *You Are My People: An Introduction to Prophetic Literature* (Nashville: Abingdon, 2010), 6.

4. See Louis Stulman, "Reading the Bible through the Lens of Trauma and Art," in Becker, Dochhorn, and Holt, *Trauma and Traumatization*, 177–92.

5. Judith Herman, *Trauma and Recovery*, 33.

emiah reenacts the breakdown of cherished beliefs and cultural arrangements. Specifically, it "re-presents" the devastating realities of war for the historical losers, that is, for the broken and dispossessed whose experience of upheaval has caused them to entertain doubts about the moral order of the universe. Jeremiah's communal struggle to find meaning in disaster, order amid chaos, defies singular expression. Instead, it emerges in a rich polyphony, as Mark Biddle has described it, or even a cacophony, as others have said.[6] In some respects, John Bright was exactly correct when he labeled Jeremiah's complexity "a hopeless hodgepodge."[7] At the same time, he failed to discern in this literary din the unwieldy character of trauma.

Unlike most postwar literary artifacts preserved by the losers, the book of Jeremiah refuses to deny the atrocities of war.[8] Its multiplicity of voices—poetic and prose, female and male, individual and communal— moves beyond cognitive numbness and emotional shock to narrate the collapse of long-standing social and symbolic worlds. Most extraordinarily, this penetrating text, this concentrate of pain often embodied in the persona of Jeremiah, leads to the survival of the defeated and disenfranchised.

This essay focuses primarily on one voice in this montage, the prose sermons of Jer 1–25 (7:1–8:3; 11:1–17; 18:1–12; 21:1–10; and 25:1–14),

---

6. Mark Biddle, *Polyphony and Symphony in Prophetic Literature: Rereading Jeremiah 7–20*, Studies in Old Testament Interpretation 2 (Macon, GA: Mercer University Press, 1996); Robert P. Carroll, *The Book of Jeremiah*, OTL (Philadelphia: Westminster, 1986).

7. John Bright, *Jeremiah: Introduction, Translation, and Notes*, AB 21 (Garden City, NY: Doubleday, 1965), lvi.

8. Winfried G. Sebald describes the uncanny ability of the population of postwar Germany "to carry on as if nothing had happened" (*On the Natural History of Destruction* [New York: Random House, 2003], 41). Bessel van der Kolk notes, "nobody wants to remember trauma. In this regard, society is no different from the victims themselves. We all want to live in a world that is safe, manageable, and predictable, and victims remind us that this is not always the case" (*The Body Keeps the Score: Brain, Mind, and Body in the Healing of Trauma* [New York: Penguin Books, 2015], 194). Of people who deal with pain and spirituality, Henri Nouwen observes, "Our first and most spontaneous response to our undesirable memories is to forget them.… We want to forget the pains of the past—our personal, communal, and national traumas—and live as if they did not really happen. But by not remembering them we allow the forgotten memories to become independent forces that can exert a crippling effect on our functioning as human beings.… Forgetting the past is like turning our most intimate teacher against us" (*The Living Reminder: Service and Prayer in Memory of Jesus Christ* [New York: HarperCollins, 1977], 21–22).

arguably the most denigrated part of the book. I suggest that these prose discourses function as literature of trauma and healing no less than the Jeremianic poetry. As a point of departure, I employ a number of observations from Bernhard Duhm's 1901 Jeremiah commentary and Sigmund Mowinckel's 1914 work on the composition of the book.[9] I begin with Duhm and Mowinckel for two reasons: their early twentieth-century studies serve as the point of departure for modern Jeremiah scholarship, and the disparagement of the prose sermons in Jeremiah began essentially, as best I can determine, with the critiques posed by these two scholars. Although their work has been subject to incisive, sometimes scathing, criticism in recent years, any reexamination of the prose in Jeremiah must begin with their seminal contributions.[10]

Duhm and Mowinckel devoted much time to the differentiation of prose and poetry in Jeremiah. In his commentary, Duhm demarcated three primary types of writing in Jeremiah: poetic sayings, narrative prose, and a residual category characterized by diffuse language and conventional diction.[11] Mowinckel refined Duhm's categories and proposed a more nuanced scheme. He employed the following nomenclature: A for authentic Jeremianic poetry and for a few prose pieces; B for narrative prose; and C for Deuteronomistic prose.[12] Mowinckel's categories left an indelible mark on twentieth-century Jeremiah scholarship. Although most scholars today reject both Duhm's and Mowinckel's understandings of the origin and development of the book, few dispute the broad outlines

---

9. Bernhard Duhm, *Das Buch Jeremiah* (Tübingen: Mohr, 1901), x–xvii, 106–11; Sigmund Mowinckel, *Zur Komposition des Buches Jeremia* (Kristiania: Dywad, 1914).

10. For an assessment of Duhm, see Joseph Michael Henderson, "Jeremiah under the Shadow of Duhm: An Argument from the History of Criticism against the Use of Poetic Form as a Criterion of Authenticity" (PhD diss., Fuller Theological Seminary, 2010). See also Henderson, "Duhm and Skinner's Invention of Jeremiah," in *Jeremiah Invented: Constructions and Deconstructions of Jeremiah*, ed. Carolyn J. Sharp and Else K. Holt, LHBOTS 595 (New York: Bloomsbury T&T Clark, 2015), 1–15.

11. For a brief critique of Duhm and Mowinckel on Jeremiah, see Louis Stulman, *The Prose Sermons of Jeremiah: A Redescription of the Correspondences with Deuteronomistic Literature in Light of Recent Text-Critical Research*, SBLDS 83 (Atlanta: Scholars Press, 1986), 7–13.

12. Later Mowinckel referred to these blocks of material as traditions rather than strata. See his *Prophecy and Tradition: The Prophetic Books in the Light of the Study of the Growth and History of the Tradition* (Oslo: Dybwad, 1946).

of their literary demarcation into poetry, narrative prose, and discursive prose, or *Kunstprosa*.[13]

Central to Duhm's and Mowinckel's exegesis of Jeremiah was the destruction of Jerusalem in 587/586 BCE, which was the definitive event in their understanding of virtually every layer/stratum/tradition of the prophetic book. For instance, in a quest for the historical Jeremiah, Duhm discerned the authentic voice of the prophet in sixty or so poems that were principally lamentations in the 3:2 meter, that is, the typical dirge form.[14] Robert R. Wilson noted, "like many scholars of his era, [Duhm] assumed that prophetic inspiration and poetic inspiration were closely related, and he therefore located the authentic words of Jeremiah within the relatively brief, lyrical poetic oracles now found in chaps 1–25."[15] While Wilson is no doubt correct, it is germane to contemporary trauma studies of Jeremiah that Duhm specifically identifies the dirge, the literary expression of despair, as the defining mark of Jeremianic authenticity.

Equally important, both Duhm and Mowinckel argued that the later prose, Mowinckel's C, is characterized not only by a particular style and lexical relationship to the Deuteronomistic literature but also by a preoccupation with the national catastrophe, which it views as a consequence of Judah's transgressions of God's laws, particularly the Deuteronomic law. Consequently, Duhm and Mowinckel read the poetry *and* the prose of Jeremiah as a "treatise" on tragedy, although the poetry and prose could not be more different in the ways they approach it.

The poetry of Jeremiah, they argued, is rich in imagery, complex in thought, intense in emotion, and palpable in distress, as chiefly evident in the prophet's warnings of impending doom. In contrast, the Deuteronomistic prose is, in their terms, repetitive, inflexible, stereotypical, and

---

13. Michael J. Williams employs these categories even though he argues for more nuanced distinctions for the prose material. See "An Investigation of the Legitimacy of Source Distinctions for the Prose Material in Jeremiah," *JBL* 112 (1993): 193–210.

14. Karl Budde, "Das hebräische Klagelied," *ZAW* 2 (1882): 1–52. Since Karl Budde's analysis, this 3:2 *qînâ*-line has almost universally been accepted "as a typical dirge-pattern." See Erhard S. Gerstenberger, "Elusive Lamentations: What Are They About?" *Int* 67 (2013): 125.

15. See Robert R. Wilson, "Poetry and Prose in the Book of Jeremiah," in *Ki Baruch Hu: Ancient Near Eastern Studies in Honor of Baruch A. Levine*, ed. Robert Chazan, William W. Hallo, and Lawrence H. Schiffman (Winona Lake, IN: Eisenbrauns, 1999), 414.

moralistic.[16] It lacks originality, depends on older materials, and is legalistic, specifically Deuteronomistic, in orientation. Duhm caricatured the writers of the residual prose materials as follows: "Their theology is that of legalism, the torah is their be-all and end-all."[17] Similarly, for Mowinckel, the C material transforms a dynamic Jeremiah into a *Schattfigur* (a "shadowy figure") who preaches a dogmatic theology.[18]

Despite obvious shortcomings, the pioneering work of Duhm and Mowinckel is instructive to current trauma readings of Jeremiah in several respects. First, it recognizes the deeply rooted character of pain throughout the book. The observation that the sixth-century Judean catastrophe is crucial to virtually every facet of the book anticipates the argument that traumatic violence holds together this unreadable text, indeed that the text is unreadable because it is essentially reading impenetrable traumatic violence. Also instructive in this regard is Duhm's attention to the dirge as the defining index of the Jeremianic tradition. Second, the separation of prose and poetry is still an efficient way to mark catastrophic moments, as Samuel E. Balentine has maintained in a recent article and as Kathleen M. O'Connor has demonstrated in *Jeremiah: Pain and Promise*.[19] O'Connor, and most other Jeremiah scholars, accept the broad parameters of Duhm and Mowinckel's prose and poetry demarcation, even though they are not particularly interested in their diachronic conclusions. Third, the contention that the poetry and nonnarrative prose of Jeremiah represent distinctive theological interpretations of the sixth-century disaster paves the way

---

16. Duhm, *Das Buch Jeremiah*, x–xvii, 106–11; Mowinckel, *Zur Komposition des Buches Jeremia*, 39.

17. Duhm, *Das Buch Jeremiah*, xviii. This and subsequent translations of the German are mine.

18. Mowinckel, *Zur Komposition des Buches Jeremia*, 39. Duhm and Mowinckel were on a quest for the historical Jeremiah and the redaction history of the book. They were concerned, fundamentally, with which texts in the book are Jeremianic and Deuteronomistic: Which are authentic and which inauthentic? Which are early and which late? Which texts hold value and which are expendable, or, put differently, which are dynamic and spiritual, and which are legalistic and harmful? It is hard not to hear supersessionist currents in their work, especially when insisting that the earlier poetry bristles with spiritual genius while the Deuteronomistic prose reflects the "legalistic piety" of late Judaism. Tragically, these interpretive perspectives reflect a significant stream of nineteenth-century and early twentieth-century European scholarship.

19. Samuel E. Balentine, "The Prose and Poetry of Exile," in Kelle, Ames, and Wright, *Interpreting Exile*, 345–63; and O'Connor, *Jeremiah*, esp. 93–102.

for reading the two as (conflicting and often competing) renderings of the horror of war.

Also noteworthy, and related to my latter point, is the characterization of the Deuteronomistic prose of Jer 1–25 by Duhm and Mowinckel as inflexible, retributive, and conservative (in that it employs earlier values as crucial to the present and the future). They were mistaken, however, to disparage this literature on account of this ideological bent. They failed to recognize that the Deuteronomistic prose of Jeremiah merely inhabits a different symbolic and literary terrain than that of the Jeremianic poetry. Whereas the poetry of Jer 1–25 is wild and unwieldy, layered and lyrical, eliciting "a multiplicity of meaning,"[20] the prose delights in singularity, clarity, predictability, and stability. The poetry convulses with pain and regret as well as despair and rage, while the prose is far more controlled, methodical, and coherent. In the Jeremianic poetry, we encounter the raw anguish of victims of war whose cries inundate the ever-present now, or "empty time."[21] The prose, in contrast, is more measured, exacting, and teleological with "progression of thought [that] is linear, sequential, and contextually embedded in historical contingencies."[22]

The poetry in Jeremiah resists such coherent arrangements. Under the weight of traumatic violence, it obscures, at times deconstructs, conventional spatial and temporal markers as well as distinctions between the individual and nation. We cannot always tell, for instance, whose cries of anguish inundate the poetry of the first twenty-five chapters of Jeremiah. Are they the tears of the people, the prophet, the mourning women, disconsolate Zion, or God?[23] We cannot tell what time it is either. Are we reading predisaster, disaster, or postdisaster vignettes (i.e., preexilic, exilic, or postexilic)? Where does the suffering take place: in the north or the south, in the land or the earth, in the streets of Jerusalem or among the invading

---

20. Balentine ("Prose and Poetry of Exile," 345–46) notes, "Prose narratives are generally offered as normative and factual accounts of events that happened, their cause and their effect. The progression of thought is linear, sequential, and contextually embedded in historical contingencies. Poetry is generically terse, figurative, and decontextualized. Its paratactic and elliptical style typically omits conjunctions; the connections between juxtaposed lines (or cola) are left open, unexplained, inviting a *multiplicity of meaning*" (emphasis added).

21. See ibid., 346.

22. Ibid.

23. For an incisive discussion of the tears of God, see David A. Bosworth, "The Tears of God in the Book of Jeremiah," *Bib* 94 (2013): 24–46.

troops in Dan? Who is actually under siege: faithless Israel, blind and deaf Jacob (e.g., 5:20–31), or an embattled prophet? Are we reading Jeremiah the individual or Jeremiah the embodiment of a people, as Reventlow and others have argued?[24] This poetry of trauma clearly defies either-or categories or anything resembling Aristotelian logic. It is too ruptured and dangerous, too wounded and devastated, for binary classifications.

The prose, however, also throbs with pain, although in all likelihood at a greater historical distance.[25] It offers answers, asserts control, and does not resist binary categories. This literary expression constructs moral order amid chaos. The prose in Jer 1–25 organizes the dissociated poetry[26] and historicizes poetic time. Even more strikingly, it creates a master narrative in which readers can broach the otherwise unimaginable poetry. This master narrative serves a function analogous to the narrative in Thornton Wilder's *The Bridge of San Luis Rey*, which begins, "On Friday noon, July the twentieth, 1714, the finest bridge in all Peru broke and precipitated five travelers into the gulf below. This bridge was on the highroad between Lima and Cuzco and hundreds of persons passed over it every day.... The bridge seemed to be among the things that last forever; it was unthinkable that it should break."[27]

The exilic or postexilic prose literature invites audiences to revisit the unthinkable: the destruction of the grand temple (7:1–8:3), the end of the covenant (11:1–17), the election tradition turned on its head (18:1–12), the enduring Davidic dynasty under assault and reconfiguration (21:1–10), and the inversion of the promise of land, that is, the normalization of life in diaspora (25:1–14).[28] This prose discourse reenacts the dismantling

---

24. Henning Graf Reventlow, *Liturgie und prophetisches Ich bei Jeremia* (Gütersloh: Gütersloher Verlagshaus, 1966).

25. See Louis Stulman, *Jeremiah*, AOTC (Nashville: Abingdon, 2005), 1–18; See also O'Connor, *Jeremiah*, 93–95.

26. Louis Stulman, *Order amid Chaos: Jeremiah as Symbolic Tapestry*, BibSem 57 (Sheffield: Sheffield Academic, 1998), 23–55.

27. Thornton Wilder, *The Bridge of San Luis Rey*, Perennial Classics (New York: HarperCollins, 2003), 5.

28. Prose speeches or sermons in other biblical books often provide clues for understanding the focal concerns and distinctive theological character of the literature. I have argued that the prose sermons of Jeremiah play a meaningful role in the overall architecture of the book. The sermons operate as structural guides that mark important transitions. They reenact the dismantling of Judah's most treasured institutions and preexilic tenets of faith, including the temple and its systems of worship,

of Judah's sure and certain cultural and sacred world, its "bridge of San Luis Rey." In other words, the prose no less than the poetry shifts the worst of circumstances to a bearable distance. It removes the trauma of war from ground zero to the symbolic world of language, thus making it not only manageable but also intelligible for individuals and the nation (categories that are blurred in the text). As social scientists have long observed, victims of violence yearn for viable explanations of their crisis, or, as survivor Viktor Frankl put it, "to find meaning in … suffering."[29]

When the prose sermons speak of Judah's sacred world under divine judgment, for instance, they are not only shifting the nation's unbearable pain to the symbolic world of language; they are also placing the wreckage of war within a context of meaning. Jeremiah, the Deuteronomic preacher, garners an array of tropes to harness gratuitous suffering, including accusations, indictments, and scathing homilies, all to create order and meaning out of inexplicable chaos. More precisely, the prophet contours a morally exacting universe in which military defeat and national humiliation neither impugn the character of God nor destroy faith in life. With the aid of Deuteronomic categories, Jeremiah makes sense of the national disaster by drawing a clear correlation between Judah's conduct and condition, acts and consequences:

> [1] The word that came to Jeremiah from YHWH: [2] Hear the terms of this covenant and proclaim them to the people of Judah and the citizens of Jerusalem. [3] Say to them, this is what YHWH, the God of Israel says: Cursed is anyone who does not obey the terms of this covenant.… [6] YHWH said to me, announce all these words in the cities of Judah and in the streets of Jerusalem. Tell them to obey the terms of this covenant and do them.… [8] But they would not listen or pay attention. Instead they went their own willful way. So I brought upon them all the punishments of this covenant. (11:1–3, 6, 8)[30]

---

its covenant and election arrangements, as well as long-established dynastic arrangements and land claims. The prose sermons, no less than the Jeremianic poetry, speak of a world under massive assault and of a people whose lives bristle with pain. See Stulman, *Order amid Chaos*, 11–98.

29. See Viktor Frankl's classic work, *Man's Search for Meaning* (New York: Washington Square Press, 1985), 11.

30. Biblical translations are mine.

[11] Now say to the people of Judah and the citizens of Jerusalem: This is what YHWH says: I am shaping evil against you. I am devising a plan against you. Each one of you turn from your evil ways and reform your ways and your actions. [12] But they said, "It's hopeless! We will follow our evil own plans and do what we want to do." (18:11–12)

[8] This is what you should say to this people: YHWH declares: I am setting before you the way of life and the way of death. [9] If you remain in the city, you will die by the sword, famine, and disease. If, however, you leave the city and surrender to the Babylonians, you will live. Yes, your lives will be spared. [10] I have set my face against this city for evil and not for good, declares YHWH. It will be delivered into the power of the king of Babylon, who will set it on fire. (21:8–10)

[8] Therefore, this is what YHWH of hosts says: Because you have not obeyed my words, [9] I am going to assemble all the tribes of the north and my servant King Nebuchadnezzar of Babylon, declares YHWH, and I will bring them against this country and its inhabitants as well as against all the surrounding nations. I will utterly destroy them and will make them an object of horror, shock, and ruin for all time. [10] I will put an end to the sounds of joy and laughter and the voices of the bride and the bridegroom. No more will you hear the sound of millstones or see the lamplight. [11] This whole land will be reduced to nothing. (25:8–11a)

In the most uncompromising of terms, Jeremiah the prose preacher speaks of a wayward and disobedient nation: Judah profanes the temple, breaks the covenant, rejects invitations to repent, refuses to heed God's warnings given through the prophets and the law, and is brazen in its defiance. In this morally exacting world, defiant Judah suffers the consequences of its many sins: a destruction as thorough as Shiloh's (7:12–15), unspeakable loss (11:11–13), God's adversarial judgment (18:11), and the inescapable horrors of war (21:3–10), which entails the abrogation of human joy and the end of culture (25:8–15).

Such accusations blame the victim rather than the perpetrator of violence, the Babylonian military machine. The Israel behind the text, as Douglas Knight and Amy-Jill Levine remind us, was actually "a tiny country buffeted by geopolitical forces it could scarcely repel."[31] The prose incli-

---

31. Douglas A. Knight and Amy-Jill Levine, *The Meaning of the Bible: What the Jewish Scriptures and Christian Old Testament Can Teach Us* (New York: HarperOne, 2011), 143.

nation to hold this "tiny country" responsible for virtually all its troubles, to explain its political misfortunes by way of moral causality, is a rigorous attempt to create symbolic coherence in times of social convulsion. For the sake of community survival, the text places war, military occupation, exile, and captivity—traumatic events in ancient as well as modern times—within a framework of meaning. More directly, this literature asserts that the nation's concentration of pain is not beyond the scope of God's concern or governance, nor is it the result of capricious geopolitical or mythic forces.

Scholars have long called attention to the surplus of guilt in the Jeremianic prose tradition and its depiction of Israel as a people disposed toward idolatry and moral failings.[32] Unfortunately, many believe it. That is, they assume a direct correspondence between literary depiction and historical reality, due in part to the text's extraordinary rhetorical force. Reading the prose tradition through the prism of trauma challenges this assumption and the resulting depiction of Judah as an immoral nation. This type of reading interprets Jeremiah's exacting speech as a mechanism for dealing with trauma, or, more specifically, as an attempt to create moral order and meaning out of a national disaster that defies symmetrical understandings. As disaster literature, the prose material tames the chaos of life through blame, a tendency that Smith-Christopher has recognized in contemporary communities traumatized by violence.[33] If this is indeed the case, Jeremiah's scathing prose sermons reflect a more primal concern than detailing Israel's social and religious conditions. The prose sermons reflect a sustained concern for survival: *the survival of the historical losers and the survival of their faith in God.*

In conclusion, the Deuteronomistic prose in the book of Jeremiah has been an easy target since Duhm and Mowinckel, largely because it bristles with blame, appears simplistic, and by and large rejects ambiguity. We should be slow, however, to dismiss this literature and slower to disparage it. In the first place, the Jeremiah tradition as a whole never privileges poetry over prose or prose over poetry. Rather, the book treats both as the word of God. Furthermore, both function as meaning-making expressions that support affiliated communities in the throes of war and captivity, although they represent two radically different social and symbolic worlds.

---

32. See Stulman, "Reading the Bible," in 183–86.
33. Smith-Christopher, *Biblical Theology of Exile*, esp. 75–123.

From the onset, the Jeremianic poetry pulsates with pain and vulnerability. The poetry's discordant voices express the unmanageable character of trauma itself. Its language of violence, sorrow, and rage gives voice to the palpable losses of war. The poetry portrays a wounded prophet, a world on the verge of collapse, a nation in denial and despair, and a suffering God; this portrayal names and reenacts pain too profound for ordinary categories of meaning. The Jeremianic poetry immerses readers in the unbearable world of traumatic violence—the violence of war, exile, and confinement.

The Deuteronomistic prose, no less than the poetry, attempts to help victims of violence survive the collapse of their worlds of meaning. The prose creates order amid social and symbolic chaos, translates the ravages of war into discursive language and provides solutions, teaches lessons and brings clarity and recognition to a world that is fractured seemingly beyond repair. The Deuteronomistic prose literature creates a metanarrative of a once seemingly unshakable world on the brink of destruction. The cumulative effect is to transform a victimized community into a community of active meaning-makers, albeit in terms starkly different from those employed in the poetry.

Together the prose and poetry of Jer 1–25 imagine an alternative world to that of realpolitik, a world in which God's purposes are realized through the contingencies of history, a world in which suffering people are not beyond the purview of divine power and concern, a world in which military might does not have the final say. The prose and poetry of Jer 1–25, despite their distinctive character, function as trauma literature for war-torn communities struggling to survive prolonged captivity in foreign lands.

Bibliography

Balentine, Samuel E. "The Prose and Poetry of Exile." Pages 345–63 in *Interpreting Exile: Displacement and Deportation in Biblical and Modern* Contexts. Edited by Brad E. Kelle, Frank Ritchel Ames, and Jacob L. Wright. AIL 10. Atlanta: Society of Biblical Literature, 2011.

Becker, Eve-Marie, Jan Dochhorn, and Else K. Holt, eds. *Trauma and Traumatization in Individual and Collective Dimensions: Insights from Biblical Studies and Beyond*. SANt 2. Vandenhoeck & Ruprecht, Göttingen, 2014.

Biddle, Mark. *Polyphony and Symphony in Prophetic Literature: Rereading Jeremiah 7–20*. Studies in Old Testament Interpretation 2. Macon, GA: Mercer University Press, 1996.

Bosworth, David A. "The Tears of God in the Book of Jeremiah." *Bib* 94 (2013): 24–46.

Bright, John. *Jeremiah: Introduction, Translation, and Notes.* AB 21. Garden City, NY: Doubleday, 1965.

Budde, Karl. "Das hebräische Klagelied." *ZAW* 2 (1882): 1–52.

Carr, David M. *Holy Resilience: The Bible's Traumatic Origins.* New Haven: Yale University Press, 2014.

Carroll, Robert P. *The Book of Jeremiah.* OTL. Philadelphia: Westminster, 1986.

Caruth, Cathy, ed. *Trauma: Explorations of Memory.* Baltimore: Johns Hopkins University Press, 1995.

———. *Unclaimed Experience: Trauma, Narrative, and History.* Baltimore: Johns Hopkins University Press, 1996.

Duhm, Bernhard. *Das Buch Jeremiah.* Tübingen: Mohr, 1901.

Frankl, Viktor. *Man's Search for Meaning.* New York: Washington Square Press, 1985.

Gerstenberger, Erhard S. "Elusive Lamentations: What Are They About?" *Int* 67 (2013): 121–32.

Gozdziak, Elzbieta M. "Refugee Women's Psychological Response to Forced Migration: Limitations of the Trauma Concept." http://tinyurl.com/SBL0689c.

Henderson, Joseph Michael. "Duhm and Skinner's Invention of Jeremiah." Pages 1–15 in *Jeremiah Invented: Constructions and Deconstructions of Jeremiah.* Edited by Carolyn J. Sharp and Else K. Holt. LHBOTS 595. New York: Bloomsbury T&T Clark, 2015.

———. "Jeremiah under the Shadow of Duhm: An Argument from the History of Criticism against the Use of Poetic Form as a Criterion of Authenticity." PhD diss., Fuller Theological Seminary, 2010.

Herman, Judith. *Trauma and Recovery: The Aftermath of Violence—from Domestic Abuse to Political Terror.* Rev. ed. New York: Basic Books, 1997.

Jones, Serene. *Trauma and Grace: Theology in a Ruptured World.* Louisville: Westminster John Knox, 2009.

Kelle, Brad E., Frank Ritchel Ames, and Jacob L. Wright, eds. *Interpreting Exile: Displacement and Deportation in Biblical and Modern Contexts.* AIL 10. Atlanta: Society of Biblical Literature, 2011.

Kira, Ibrahim Aref. "Taxonomy of Trauma and Trauma Assessment." *Traumatology* 7.2 (2001): 73–86.

Knight, Douglas A., and Amy-Jill Levine. *The Meaning of the Bible: What the Jewish Scriptures and Christian Old Testament Can Teach Us*. New York: HarperOne, 2011.

Kolk, Bessel van der. *The Body Keeps the Score: Brain, Mind, and Body in the Healing of Trauma*. New York: Penguin Books, 2015.

Lemaire, Jean-Marie. "Disconcerting Humanitarian Interventions, and the Resources for Collective Healing." Pages 71–77 in *Psychosocial and Trauma Response in War-Torn Societies: The Case of Kosovo*. Edited by Natale Losi. Psychosocial Notebook 1. Geneva: International Organization for Migration, 2000.

Leys, Ruth. *From Guilt to Shame: Auschwitz and After*. Princeton: Princeton University Press, 2007.

———. *Trauma: A Genealogy*. Chicago: University of Chicago Press, 2000.

Mowinckel, Sigmund. *Prophecy and Tradition: The Prophetic Books in the Light of the Study of the Growth and History of the Tradition*. Oslo: Dybwad, 1946.

———. *Zur Komposition des Buches Jeremia*. Kristiania: Dywad, 1914.

Nouwen, Henri. *The Living Reminder: Service and Prayer in Memory of Jesus Christ*. New York: HarperCollins, 1977.

O'Connor, Kathleen M. *Jeremiah: Pain and Promise*. Minneapolis: Fortress, 2011.

Reventlow, Henning Graf. *Liturgie und prophetisches Ich bei Jeremia*. Gütersloh: Gütersloher Verlagshaus, 1966.

Scarry, Elaine. *The Body in Pain*. Oxford: Oxford University Press, 1985.

Sebald, Winfried G. *On the Natural History of Destruction*. New York: Random House, 2003.

Smith-Christopher, Daniel L. *A Biblical Theology of Exile*. OBT. Minneapolis: Fortress, 2002.

Stulman, Louis. *Jeremiah*. AOTC. Nashville: Abingdon, 2005.

———. *Order amid Chaos: Jeremiah as Symbolic Tapestry*. BibSem 57. Sheffield: Sheffield Academic, 1998.

———. *The Prose Sermons of Jeremiah: A Redescription of the Correspondences with Deuteronomistic Literature in Light of Recent Text-Critical Research*. SBLDS 83. Atlanta: Scholars Press, 1986.

———. "Reading the Bible through the Lens of Trauma and Art." Pages 177–92 in *Trauma and Traumatization in Individual and Collective Dimensions: Insights from Biblical Studies and Beyond*. Edited by Eve-Marie Becker, Jan Dochhorn, and Else K. Holt. SANt 2. Vandenhoeck & Ruprecht, Göttingen, 2014.

Stulman, Louis, and Hyun Chul Paul Kim. *You Are My People: An Intro-duction to Prophetic Literature.* Nashville: Abingdon, 2010.

Wilder, Thornton. *The Bridge of San Luis Rey.* Perennial Classics. New York: HarperCollins, 2003.

Williams, Michael J. "An Investigation of the Legitimacy of Source Dis-tinctions for the Prose Material in Jeremiah." *JBL* 112 (1993): 193–210.

Wilson, Robert R. "Poetry and Prose in the Book of Jeremiah." Pages 413–27 in *Ki Baruch Hu: Ancient Near Eastern Studies in Honor of Baruch A. Levine.* Edited by Robert Chazan, William W. Hallo, and Lawrence H. Schiffman. Winona Lake, IN: Eisenbrauns, 1999.

3
Survival, Recovery, and Resilience in and through the Text: Ancient and Contemporary Contexts

Trauma, Psalmic Disclosure, and Authentic Happiness

Brent A. Strawn

The argument of the present essay contains four parts.[1] First, empirical studies have demonstrated that disclosure plays a key role in recovery from trauma (§1). Second, the Psalter is marked by extensive disclosure about traumatic events and the feelings of those who have been traumatized (§2). Third, insofar as the psalms are (re)read or (re)uttered texts, psalmic disclosure may function not only *descriptively*—as testimony to (or recovery from) past trauma—but also in a *prescriptive* fashion, that is, *therapeutically*, not just for the psalmists themselves but for all who (re)read or (re)utter these poems (§3). Fourth, the preceding points can be assessed in light of literature on post-traumatic growth (PTG) and Positive Psychology (§4), which suggests that, while far from hedonic, traumatic experiences may result in the later flourishing of individuals and greater resilience on their part. The traumatized, that is, may also live lives that can properly be described as happy, as long as that happiness is understood in its most authentic, eudaimonistic sense.[2] To come

---

1. This essay builds on previous work, including Brent A. Strawn, "The Triumph of Life: Towards a Biblical Theology of Happiness," in *The Bible and the Pursuit of Happiness: What the Old and New Testaments Teach Us about the Good Life*, ed. Brent A. Strawn (Oxford: Oxford University Press, 2012), 287–322; Strawn, "Poetic Attachment: Psychology, Psycholinguistics, and the Psalms," in *The Oxford Handbook to the Psalms*, ed. William P. Brown (Oxford: Oxford University Press, 2014), 404–23; and Strawn, "The Psalms and the Practice of Disclosure," in Walter Brueggemann, *From Whom No Secrets Are Hid: Introducing the Psalms*, ed. Brent A. Strawn (Louisville: Westminster John Knox, 2014), xiii–xxiv. I would like to thank Brad D. Strawn, David A. Bosworth, L. Juliana M. Claassens, Elizabeth Boase, and Christopher G. Frechette for assistance and encouragement along the way.

2. See, inter alia, Martin E. P. Seligman, *Authentic Happiness: Using the New Posi-*

full circle, the way traumatized persons find such happiness—or at least begin to move toward it—is often precisely through disclosure about their trauma. The psalms may be used to facilitate this process, and thus the psalms offer a way through trauma into happiness for those who read and/or pray them now.

1. The Role of Disclosure in Trauma Recovery

It is premature to discuss recovery from trauma without first discussing trauma proper. The English word *trauma* is a Greek loanword meaning "wound" or "hurt," though in recent discourse it is typically reserved for injuries of the most grievous physiological and psychological kind.[3] While many definitions can and have been offered for trauma, the following pastiche may suffice for now,[4] though it is far from complete: trauma is an overwhelming event or experience that (1) leaves people (whether individuals or groups) feeling helpless and dehumanized, without the capacities or categories to understand the trauma; (2) affects their emotions and memories in adverse and sometimes indirect ways; and (3) often profoundly and negatively impacts their behavior and interpersonal relationships. Recovery from trauma may then be defined as the various ways and means by which people (whether individuals or groups) somehow overcome the many ways trauma has wounded them, though recovery (healing) should never be confused with some totalizing cure.

Again, discussing recovery from trauma without further consideration of trauma proper seems abrupt. It is justifiable, however, for three reasons. The first of these is that post-traumatic recovery is an identifiable and discrete area of inquiry. Second, insofar as trauma involves grief

---

tive Psychology to Realize Your Potential for Lasting Fulfilment (New York: Simon & Schuster, 2002).

3. David M. Carr (*Holy Resilience: The Bible's Traumatic Origins* [New Haven: Yale University Press, 2014], 7–8) rightly avoids reducing "trauma" to "suffering," but there remains significant overlap between the two.

4. It is inspired from passages in Judith Herman, *Trauma and Recovery* (New York: Basic Books, 1992), 32–34, 51, 94; Cathy Caruth, "Recapturing the Past: Introduction," in *Trauma: Explorations in Memory*, ed. Cathy Caruth (Baltimore: Johns Hopkins University Press, 1995), 151–57; and Carole Beebe Tarantelli, "Life within Death: Toward a Metapsychology of Catastrophic Psychic Trauma," *International Journal of Psychoanalysis* 84 (2003): 915–28. I owe the latter two references to Carr, *Holy Resilience*, 7, insights from which are also incorporated above.

and the grieving process, the research discussed below under the general rubric of *recovery* is inextricably connected to trauma. Third, both trauma (or testimony about trauma) and recovery from trauma are at work in the text corpus under consideration here (the psalms), so for present purposes neither of these two entities is far removed from the other.

To return to and expand upon the second point, studies have shown that disclosure is not only a crucial part of recovery from trauma but also an important part of the grieving process. Disclosure plays a key role in the articulation of grief, and articulating grief, in turn, plays a key role in recovery. Judith Herman makes this point on the first page of her classic *Trauma and Recovery*: "Remembering and telling the truth about terrible events are prerequisites both for the restoration of the social order and for the healing of individual victims."[5] In fact, Herman identifies truth-telling as the second of three stages in recovery from trauma. In this second stage, "the survivor tells the story of the trauma … completely, in depth, and in detail."[6]

The benefits of full disclosure have been studied by James W. Pennebaker. In numerous publications, but especially in *Opening Up: The Healing Power of Expressing Emotions*, Pennebaker has demonstrated that honest disclosure—especially in written form and especially about traumatic events—bears concrete benefits for both physical and mental health. In terms of *physical health*, verbalizing traumatic experiences has direct and positive effects on the human immune system, whereas the opposite scenario obtains in the case of nonverbalization, or "inhibition."[7] As it turns out, keeping things back is hard work that eventually takes its toll on the human body and its defenses.[8] Keeping secrets prevents one from processing them, and this can result in physical ailments. In Pennebaker's words, "excessive holding back of thoughts, feelings, and behaviors can place people at risk for both major and minor diseases."[9] By way of contrast, "confronting our deepest thoughts and feelings can have remarkable short- and long-term health benefits…. Further, writing or talking about upsetting things can influence our basic values, our daily

---

5. Herman, *Trauma and Recovery*, 1.

6. Ibid., 175.

7. See James W. Pennebaker, *Opening Up: The Healing Power of Expressing Emotions*, rev. ed. (New York: Guilford, 1997), 37–38 and passim.

8. Ibid., 1–2 and passim.

9. Ibid., 2.

thinking patterns, and feelings about ourselves."[10] In brief, then, "not disclosing our thoughts and feelings can be unhealthy. Divulging them can be healthy."[11]

Herman has noted a similar dynamic. "The ordinary response to atrocities is to banish them from consciousness," she writes. "Certain violations of the social compact are too terrible to utter aloud: this is the meaning of the word *unspeakable*."[12] But, she goes on to point out, "atrocities ... refuse to be buried. Equally as powerful as the desire to deny atrocities is the conviction that denial does not work."[13] This conflict between denying horrific experiences and talking about them is what Herman calls "the central dialectic of psychological trauma."[14]

Pennebaker's empirical research is precisely at the interface of this dialectic as he delineates the psychosomatic effects of inhibition (holding back) versus confrontation (opening up):

- Inhibition *is physical work*: active inhibition of thoughts or feelings or behaviors requires physiological exertion.
- Inhibition *affects short-term biological changes and long-term health*: short-term effects include things such as increased perspiration during lie-detector tests, but over time inhibition takes a larger cumulative toll on the whole body.
- Inhibition *influences thinking abilities*: mostly by stymieing the chance to "think about the event in a broad and integrative way"; inhibition thus "prevents us from understanding and assimilating the event."[15]

But opening up about traumas can overcome the negative cognitive and psychological effects of inhibition:

---

10. Ibid.

11. Ibid.

12. Herman, *Trauma and Recovery*, 1, emphasis original.

13. Ibid.

14. Ibid. Cf. George A. Bonanno, *The Other Side of Sadness: What the New Science of Bereavement Tells Us about Life after Loss* (New York: Basic Books, 2009), 198.

15. Pennebaker, *Opening Up*, 9.

- Confrontation *reduces the effects of inhibition*: "The act of confronting a trauma immediately reduces the physiological work of inhibition."[16]
- Confrontation *forces a rethinking of events*: it "helps people to understand and ultimately, assimilate the event. By talking or writing about previously inhibited experiences, individuals translate the event into language. Once it is language-based, people can better understand the experience and ultimately put it behind them."[17]

One of Pennebaker's surprising findings is that, among survivors of childhood trauma, differences in the specific experience did not matter in terms of people's later health. "The only distinguishing feature" among those who were more sickly, who had been "diagnosed with virtually every major and minor health problem … cancer, high blood pressure, ulcers, flu, headaches, even earaches … was that the trauma had *not* been talked about to others. A sexual trauma that was not confided was no worse than a death in the family that was not discussed."[18] The conclusion, for Pennebaker, is that "early childhood traumas that are not disclosed may be bad for your health as an adult."[19] The same judgment holds true for those who experience trauma as adults, like the death of a spouse: "the more that people talked to others about the death of their spouse, the fewer health problems they reported having. Not talking with others about their spouses' death was clearly a health risk."[20]

In the case of adult trauma, Pennebaker notes two strategies that were frequently adopted by those who did not disclose and were, as a result, more ill: "the first was to move forward and try not to think about the spouse or the death"; the second was to pretend the traumatic experience had not happened.[21] Neither of these inhibition strategies was effective:

---

16. Ibid., 10.

17. Ibid.

18. Ibid., 19, emphasis added. This should not be understood as implying that there are no differences between something like sexual trauma and the death of a family member, only that the specific health outcomes measured by Pennebaker were the same in both cases.

19. Ibid., 20.

20. Ibid., 22.

21. Ibid., 23; cf. Bonanno, *The Other Side of Sadness*, 74, on "avoidance and distraction."

they did *not* lead to forgetting; quite the opposite, in fact. Those who did not talk about their trauma tended to become obsessed with it and ruminate on it. Rumination is correlated with poor physical health in the year following the death of a spouse.[22] In contrast, people who talked about their trauma actually thought about it less than those who did not. In the end, then, three factors were closely linked (see fig. 1).[23]

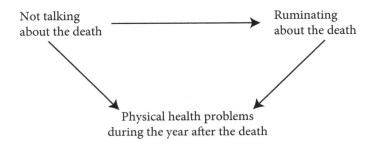

Figure 1. Factors of Nondisclosure in
Poor Health after the Death of a Spouse

More could be said about these matters, of course, and Pennebaker's research continues apace.[24] Even so, three main conclusions are clear: (1) trauma leaves marks on the human body and psyche;[25] (2) nondisclosure about trauma also takes a toll on body and mind; and (3) disclosure is crucial for both physical and mental health and an important step toward recovery.[26]

These conclusions hold true not only for physical and mental health but also for *spiritual* health. A final finding from Pennebaker's research is worth noting here and serves as a good segue to the psalms. Pennebaker has demonstrated that praying—to the extent that it involves opening up about pain—also helps trauma victims. "The more people prayed about their deceased spouses," for example, "the healthier they were. Prayer, in

---

22. Pennebaker, *Opening Up*, 23.

23. Ibid., 24.

24. For a listing, see Pennebaker's webpage at http://tinyurl.com/SBL0689d.

25. Cf. Herman, *Trauma and Recovery*, 238–40.

26. For important caveats on the research and the cause-effect problem, see Pennebaker, *Opening Up*, 25.

fact, worked the same way as talking to friends about the death. It is easy to see why this is true: *Prayer is a form of disclosure or confiding.*"[27]

2. PSALMIC DISCLOSURE

There are, of course, a host of texts from the psalms that could be considered as examples of disclosure as prayer and/or within the context of prayer. It would be a worthwhile and revealing project to assess the entire Psalter attending to this issue. There is not space for that here but, rather than stringing together a list of verse-length excerpts, I have chosen to focus on one psalm so as to probe it as an example of "psalmic disclosure." Psalm 35 is by no means the only example—it may not even be the most representative—but it suffices to highlight the dynamics of healing disclosure vis-à-vis trauma. The most pertinent verses follow:[28]

> Contend, O LORD, with those who contend with me;
> fight against those who fight me!
> Take hold of shield and buckler,
> and rise up to help me!
> Draw the spear and javelin against my pursuers
> say to my soul, "I am your salvation."
> Let them be put to shame and dishonor who seek after my life.
> Let them be turned back and confounded who devise evil against me.
> (35:1–4)

> For without cause they hid their net for me;
> without cause they dug a pit for my life. (35:7)

> All my bones shall say,
> "O LORD, who is like you?
> You deliver the weak from those too strong for them,
> the weak and needy from those who despoil them."

> Malicious witnesses rise up; they ask me about things I do not know.

---

27. Ibid., 24, emphasis added. See further L. VandeCreek et al., "Praying about Difficult Experiences as Self-Disclosure to God," *The International Journal for the Psychology of Religion* 12 (2002): 29–39; and Kimberly N. Snow et al., "Resolving Anger toward God: Lament as an Avenue toward Attachment," *Journal of Psychology and Theology* 39 (2011): 130–42. Not all prayer, of course, is primarily about disclosure.

28. All biblical translations are from the NRSV unless otherwise noted.

They repay me evil for good; my soul is forlorn.
But as for me, when they were sick, I wore sackcloth;
I afflicted myself with fasting.
I prayed with head bowed on my bosom,
as though I grieved for a friend or a brother;
I went about as one who laments for a mother,
bowed down and in mourning.

But at my stumbling they gathered in glee,
they gathered together against me;
ruffians whom I did not know
tore at me without ceasing;
they impiously mocked more and more,
gnashing at me with their teeth. (35:10–16)

Already the gist of the psalm is clear. Like so many other psalms, Ps 35 tantalizes with details that remain frustratingly ambiguous. The psalmist is clearly in distress and obviously has enemies, but the psalmist does not reveal the specific nature of the distress or the identity of the enemies.

However, the psalmist *does* reveal something, or rather several things, and in so doing reveals quite a lot. The basic thing the psalmist reveals is that she is in profound trouble.[29] Moreover, this threat is both a present (35:1–6) and past (35:7–8) reality. The terms used in the opening verses are contentious (*ryb*) and proceed to become militaristic and violent (*lḥm*, "shield and buckler," "spear and javelin," "pursuers," "net," and "pit"). They also concern shame and dishonor (35:4; see also 35:26).

The various threats posed to the psalmist account for why he begs for assistance, support, salvation (35:1–3), and payback (35:4–6), even of a talionic sort (35:7–8; cf. 35:3 with 35:6, both employing *rdp*). Such help will result in rejoicing and exultation (35:9), testimony (35:10), and thanksgiving (35:18). Moreover, the positive outcomes will extend beyond the enemies' downfall or the psalmist's own joy and will encompass the entire community that surrounds and supports her:

Let those who desire my vindication shout for joy and be glad,
and say evermore, "Great is the LORD,

---

29. Verses 25 and 27 speak of the psalmist with a third-person masculine singular suffix, but I vary the gender of the psalmist in my discussion below precisely because the psalm can be (re)uttered by others.

who delights in the welfare of his servant."
Then my tongue shall tell of your righteousness
and of your praise all day long. (35:27–28)[30]

Again (and alas), the specifics of the psalmist's pain remain elusive, but—whatever it was—it seems to qualify as trauma, at least of the interpersonal sort.[31] The varied metaphors used to evoke the psalmist's plight, many of which are quite violent, are proof of the point. The psalmist is *under attack*: people want him dead (35:4) and have set plans in motion to realize that goal (35:7); these enemies are "too strong" for the weak and are "those who despoil" the needy (35:10). The psalmist belongs to both categories, evidently, as all she can do is cry to God for help (35:1–3, 17, 19, 22–27).[32]

Amidst these fragmentary images (memories?) of malevolence, it becomes clear that the psalmist feels *betrayed*. This is recounted in the middle section of the psalm, which describes how the psalmist was accused by "malicious witnesses" of things about which he was innocent (35:11), with 35:12 serving as a summary of the situation and the psalmist's feelings about it:

> They repay me evil for good;
> my soul is forlorn [*šəkôl*]. (35:12)

The term *šəkôl* is perhaps better translated "bereaved"[33]—but of what: friends? interpersonal relations? human contact? all of the above? What-

---

30. Walter Brueggemann (*The Message of the Psalms: A Theological Commentary* [Minneapolis: Augsburg, 1984], 65) notes that the praise in Ps 35 is presented in terms of *withheld anticipations* of praise. This restrained praise might not be a bargaining or threatening device, however, so much as the result of the psalmist's broken trust caused by deep betrayal. If so, the psalmist's human relationships have wreaked havoc on her relationship with God.

31. See the definition of trauma offered above and the preceding note. The mention of maternal bereavement in 35:14 is also striking and unexpected—might it be a parapraxis? Verse 12 might also be compared at this point (see below). For a communal instance of trauma with disclosure, see Ps 137.

32. See David G. Garber Jr., "Trauma Theory," in *The Oxford Encyclopedia of Biblical Interpretation*, ed. Steven L. McKenzie, 2 vols. (Oxford: Oxford University Press, 2013), 2:422, who notes how oftentimes only religious language can suffice to speak about trauma.

33. Cf. the imagery in 35:14 (and n. 30 above) and the translations of 35:12 in NJPS and CEB.

ever the case, the betrayal is a deep cut because, when the tables were turned and the enemies were in trouble, the psalmist did everything in her power to intercede (35:13) and to sympathize (35:14). But when the psalmist "stumbled" (ṣl', 35:15),[34] all bets were off. At that point, these people suddenly become (or are joined by) "ruffians whom I did not know" (35:15), and the abuse the psalmist suffers at their hands—or at their words—can only be described with the harshest of terms: they "tore [qr'] at me without ceasing" (35:15), "gnashing [ḥrq] at me with their teeth" (35:16). No wonder these people are described as the most frightening of predators—lions!— and their work nothing less than "ravages" (35:17).[35]

The psalmist, then, is clearly traumatized and discloses that he feels that way. The psalmist's enemies are treacherous, hating him for no reason (35:19). They are untrustworthy or worse (35:20) and mock him (35:21). The psalmist fears being completely consumed by these people: "Do not let them say, 'We have swallowed you up [bl']'" (35:25b). That dread possibility can only be stopped by God; hence the psalmist's prayer.

Psalm 35, then, is an example—just one, but a good one—of psalmic disclosure. Much more could be said about this psalm, and books could be written to round out this example with others,[36] but the main points would remain the same:

- The psalmists have *experienced* events that are properly called traumatic—to greater and lesser degrees and in a wide variety of circumstances.
- The psalmists *describe* such things in their psalms, again to greater or lesser degrees and with various levels of transparency.

But is that the end of the matter? Do the psalms stop at description of traumatic experiences and feelings and go no further?

---

34. Elsewhere, ṣl' seems to have a stronger sense: "calamity" or "demise" (see Jer 20:10; Ps 38:17; Job 18:12).

35. The meaning of *miśśō'ēhem* is not certain; "ravages" (NRSV) depends on the Greek (κακουργια). See Hos 13:8 for another instance of lion imagery that also employs qr'.

36. See, e.g., Dennis Sylva, *Psalms and the Transformation of Stress: Poetic-Communal Interpretation and the Family*, LTPM 16 (Leuven: Peeters; Grand Rapids: Eerdmans, 1993); and Kristin M. Swenson, *Living through Pain: Psalms and the Search for Wholeness* (Waco, TX: Baylor University Press, 2005).

3. The Psalmic Process

Certainly not, the psalms do not stop at description of trauma. Psalm 35 alone is sufficient proof that the psalms go beyond simply describing (past) trauma. Since it is an individual lament, Ps 35 moves beyond description of trauma to description of postdeliverance praise (or the promise of such praise if the deliverance has not yet been [fully] experienced). Moreover, the (public) nature of the psalms as literary artifacts capable of (re)reading and (re)utterance indicates that the expression of trauma in the Psalter repeatedly presses beyond the experiences and description of the traumatized psalmist alone.[37] There are several reasons why this should be the case.

The first and most basic reason is that "trauma is contagious."[38] Among other things, this means that the expression of trauma often *mentions* others and typically *includes* others, even if only imaginatively.[39] Still further, confronting trauma, and recovering from it, usually implies the *presence of another*: a listener who can offer things such as "advice, attention, sympathy, financial assistance, and a way of excusing individuals from carrying out their normal responsibilities" as they grieve.[40] Even the more mundane of these offerings are significant because traumatized individuals do not recover in isolation but only in "renewed connections with other people," which permits the re-creation of "the psychological faculties that were damaged or deformed by the traumatic experience. These faculties include the basic capacities for trust, autonomy, initiative, competence, identity, and intimacy."[41] The presence of a listener or group of listeners is thus an integral part of the disclosure process. As George A. Bonanno puts it, "People confronted with the pain of loss need comfort.... They consistently fare better when they have other people to turn to."[42]

---

37. For (re)utterance, see, inter alia, Harold Fisch, *Poetry with a Purpose: Biblical Poetics and Interpretation* (Bloomington: Indiana University Press, 1990), 118, 127. See further below.

38. Herman, *Trauma and Recovery*, 140.

39. See Strawn, "Practice of Disclosure," xviii: disclosure "takes *courage* and, in turn ... *en*-courages—it can give others the courage to share their own stories."

40. Pennebaker, *Opening Up*, 27.

41. Herman, *Trauma and Recovery*, 133.

42. Bonanno, *The Other Side of Sadness*, 72.

It is no surprise, then, and of profound import, that Ps 35 opens up to address all others within earshot—or, better, within emotion-shot—of the psalmist:

> Let those who desire [ḥpṣ] my vindication shout for joy and be glad,
> and say evermore, "Great is the Lord,
> who delights [ḥpṣ] in the welfare [šālôm] of his servant." (35:27)

Nor is it insignificant that the psalmist promises her postdeliverance praise within "the great congregation" and in the midst of "the mighty throng" (35:18). The trauma the psalmist experienced was altogether isolating (note "me versus them" in 35:15–16, 19–21, 24–26), but recovery places the psalmist back within a community that cares for his well-being (35:27).

Two further points must be made about the presence of others who listen to traumatic disclosure in the psalms, one pertaining to the ancient context, one concerning the present. First, we might ponder the effects of psalmic disclosure on ancient audiences. What would the public articulation of trauma have done to listeners? One might imagine, building on Gerald T. Sheppard's work, that such disclosure functioned, among other things, to inculcate sympathy and protection.[43] Those overhearing trauma verbalized in a psalm might have been mobilized to provide the comfort, assistance, renewed connection, and psychological faculties that Bonanno, Pennebaker, and Herman assert traumatized persons need so badly. This seems a plausible if not probable result of listening to psalmic disclosure in antiquity.[44]

Second, what are the effects of overhearing psalmic disclosure now, in a contemporary context? Insofar as the psalms are (re)readable and (re)utterable, which is to say (re)performable,[45] they not only *describe* trau-

---

43. See Gerald T. Sheppard, "'Enemies' and the Politics of Prayer in the Book of Psalms," in *The Bible and the Politics of Exegesis: Essays in Honor of Norman K. Gottwald on His Sixty-Fifth Birthday*, ed. David Jobling, Peggy L. Day, and Gerald T. Sheppard (Cleveland: Pilgrim, 1991), 61–83.

44. Recall the communal aspects of Ps 35; cf. also Job 42:11. See further W. Derek Suderman, "Are Individual Complaint Psalms Really Prayers? Recognizing Social Address as Characteristic of Individual Complaints," in *The Bible as a Human Witness to Divine Revelation: Hearing the Word of God through Historically Dissimilar Traditions*, ed. Randall Heskett and Brian Irwin, LHBOTS 469 (New York: T&T Clark, 2010), 153–70.

45. For "(re)performance," see Brueggemann, *From Whom No Secrets Are Hid*, 1.

matic disclosure; they actually *prescribe* it or at least make it manifest. This is to say that every time someone (re)performs the psalms—says one out loud, for example, or prays one in some fashion—these ancient poems function to realize and manifest full traumatic disclosure in the speaker/ pray-er by means of this process.[46] Viewed this way, the psalms not only model the practice of full disclosure; they become the precise way contemporary readers or pray-ers disclose everything, including experiences of and feelings about trauma, whether that trauma be their own, the trauma of others, or the trauma of others-as-their-own.[47]

Elsewhere I have called this dynamic "the psalmic process" and defined it as the way the psalms can be seen, not simply as evidence of a therapeutic process but as that process itself.[48] If this is correct, the relevance and importance of the psalmic process to the matters of disclosure, trauma, and recovery should be obvious from the work of Herman, Pennebaker, and Bonanno. To say the least, the psalms can provide a script for those not yet comfortable with confronting upsetting truths regarding their own trauma. In this way, the psalms offer traumatized persons specific words to adopt as their own, even if the script is at some remove, a "trying out" of another person's (the psalmist's) disclosure. Even at such point in time when the words of the psalms are no longer needed or prove insufficient somehow, perhaps because a victim is finally ready to open up for himself or herself, the psalms remain useful working models for how to disclose traumatic experiences and feelings. The main point is that, whatever the specific case, whenever the psalms are (re)performed, they disclose; when that happens, we who (re)perform the psalms disclose with them. When that happens, we are on the path to recovery because disclosure is essential to recovery and a major facilitator of the same.

For the way canonicity and prayer formulation function to make reuse and rereading likely if not mandatory, see Strawn, "Poetic Attachment."

46. For the importance of repetition in lessening the intense feeling of trauma, see Herman, *Trauma and Recovery*, 195.

47. The latter is, of course, the primary effect of (re)performance.

48. See Strawn, "Poetic Attachment," 411–17, and the discussion of Ps 131 there as evidence that this process intends a therapeutic outcome.

4. Post-traumatic Growth, Authentic Happiness, and the Psalms

I conclude with three observations on how psalmic disclosure bears on studies of trauma, post-traumatic growth (PTG), and happiness as studied in Positive Psychology.

1. First, the psalms provide trauma researchers with additional and ancient data that should be taken into consideration in future studies. Much of the literature dealing with trauma and recovery focuses mainly, if not exclusively, on modern phenomena. Without minimizing the difficulties of working with ancient literary remains, especially on psychological matters, it remains clear that the psalms are important repositories of information about trauma and disclosure and demonstrate (if nothing else) the ubiquity of certain issues in trauma theory across wide cultural and chronological gaps.[49]

2. Second, the psalms may contribute to recent discussions of PTG and human resilience in the face of trauma and loss. PTG research has shown that even traumatic experiences may result in the later flourishing of individuals. On the basis of the preceding argument, evidently such later flourishing is dependent in no small way on disclosure. But the psalms also witness to other characteristics that have proven effective in coping with profound loss, things such as emotional flexibility, a secure attachment, and resilience.[50]

---

49. See, similarly, Garber, "Trauma Theory," 427; and Amy C. Cottrill, "The Traumatized 'I' in Psalm 102: A Feminist Biblical Theology of Suffering," in *After Exegesis: Feminist Biblical Theology; Essays in Honor of Carol A. Newsom*, ed. Patricia K. Tull and Jacqueline E. Lapsley (Waco, TX: Baylor University Press, 2015), 171–86. For cross-cultural studies of PTG, see Tzipi Weiss and Roni Berger, eds., *Posttraumatic Growth and Culturally Competent Practice* (Hoboken, NJ: Wiley & Sons, 2010); more generally, Lawrence G. Calhoun and Richard G. Tedeschi, eds., *Handbook of Posttraumatic Growth: Research and Practice* (Mahwah, NJ: Erlbaum, 2006); and the helpful appendix on "contemporary study of trauma and ancient trauma" in Carr, *Holy Resilience*, 253–70.

50. See, e.g., Bonanno, *The Other Side of Sadness*, 75–78; Sylva, *Psalms*, 38; and Strawn, "Poetic Attachment"; cf. Cottrill, "The Traumatized 'I' in Psalm 102," 173–75, on "a hermeneutic of creative resiliency." Some of these aspects may be best traced at the book level: how the different psalms, in the aggregate across the Psalter, evidence emotional flexibility and the like, as do those who read/pray all of them (or several of them). One should also not ignore the fact that some psalm(ist)s manifest far less resilience than others (see, e.g., Ps 88). It should occasion no surprise that the psalms manifest different responses to trauma.

3. Finally, one might consider Positive Psychology, which studies human flourishing, strengths, and virtues—happiness, that is, but not of a Pollyannaish type.[51] A pleasurable (hedonic) definition of the happy life is viable but is only one possible and rather shortsighted vision. Instead, positive psychologists favor a eudaimonistic definition of the good life as most comprehensive and helpful. In this light, if we are to talk about happiness in the psalms, it must be through a thick definition of the term, one dominated by eudaimonism, the good life, not one dominated by hedonism, the pleasurable life.[52]

An essay by Colleen Shantz on happiness in the Pauline epistles is illustrative at this point.[53] Shantz soberly considers the several and real impediments preventing Paul from experiencing happiness. Together, these problems prevent anyone from believing that Paul lived "a happy life" in any pleasurable or virtuous definition of that phrase.[54] "What is it," then, "that kept him from bitterness?"[55]

The answer to what kept Paul from bitterness lies in his construction of a *meaningful* life, one that looks "beyond oneself to a cause or purpose that transcends us," that "is devoted to something that is greater than one's own life."[56] The solution was Paul's creation of this kind of meaningful life that "created joy in the midst of otherwise unbearable hardships. Gratitude became the fuel for all of Paul's unconventional and difficult life—a life that can, despite its hardships, nevertheless be rightfully described as happy."[57]

What Shantz says about Paul can be applied, mutatis mutandis, to the psalmists. They, too, can be called "happy"—*despite* their traumas, whatever the specific and no doubt varied nature of that trauma. After all, as Brown has pointed out, the only people in the psalms who enjoy

---

51. See Seligman, *Authentic Happiness*. For PTG and Positive Psychology, see Stephen Joseph and P. Alex Linley, eds., *Trauma, Recovery, and Growth: Positive Psychological Perspectives on Posttraumatic Stress* (Hoboken, NJ: Wiley & Sons, 2008).

52. See Strawn, "Triumph of Life," 289, 295; further William P. Brown, "Happiness and Its Discontents in the Psalms," in Strawn, *The Bible and the Pursuit of Happiness*, 95–115.

53. Colleen Shantz, "'I Have Learned to Be Content': Happiness according to St. Paul," in Strawn, *The Bible and the Pursuit of Happiness*, 187–201.

54. Ibid., 197.

55. Ibid.

56. Ibid., 189; further, 197–200.

57. Ibid., 201; see also 200.

a life completely free of pain are the wicked (Ps 73:3–5, 12).[58] Or, as Tal Ben-Shahar has written, "the only people who don't experience … normal unpleasant feelings [like disappointment, sadness, or fear] are psychopaths. And the dead."[59]

The psalmists somehow knew these truths, although perhaps not in the way we know or articulate them today, and so disclosed their traumas; the Psalter as a whole now does the same. In so doing, both the psalmists and the book of Psalms offer us models for how we might begin the long and hard process of recovery from our own similar difficulties.

Bibliography

Bonanno, George A. *The Other Side of Sadness: What the New Science of Bereavement Tells Us about Life after Loss*. New York: Basic Books, 2009.

Ben-Shahar, Tal. *Being Happy: You Don't Have to Be Perfect to Lead a Richer, Happier Life*. New York: McGraw Hill, 2011.

Brown, William P. "Happiness and Its Discontents in the Psalms." Pages 95–115 in *The Bible and the Pursuit of Happiness: What the Old and New Testaments Teach Us about the Good Life*. Edited by Brent A. Strawn. Oxford: Oxford University Press, 2012.

Brueggemann, Walter. *From Whom No Secrets Are Hid: Introducing the Psalms*. Edited by Brent A. Strawn. Louisville: Westminster John Knox, 2014.

———. *The Message of the Psalms: A Theological Commentary*. Minneapolis: Augsburg, 1984.

Calhoun, Lawrence G., and Richard G. Tedeschi, eds. *Handbook of Posttraumatic Growth: Research and Practice*. Mahwah, NJ: Erlbaum, 2006.

Caruth, Cathy. "Recapturing the Past: Introduction." Pages 151–57 in *Trauma: Explorations in Memory*. Edited by Cathy Caruth. Baltimore: Johns Hopkins University Press, 1995.

Carr, David M. *Holy Resilience: The Bible's Traumatic Origins*. New Haven: Yale University Press, 2014.

Cottrill, Amy C. "The Traumatized 'I' in Psalm 102: A Feminist Biblical Theology of Suffering." Pages 171–86 in *After Exegesis: Feminist Bibli-*

---

58. Brown, "Happiness and Its Discontents in the Psalms," 96–97.

59. Tal Ben-Shahar, *Being Happy: You Don't Have to Be Perfect to Lead a Richer, Happier Life* (New York: McGraw Hill, 2011), 15.

cal Theology; Essays in Honor of Carol A. Newsom. Edited by Patricia K. Tull and Jacqueline E. Lapsley. Waco, TX: Baylor University Press, 2015.

Fisch, Harold. *Poetry with a Purpose: Biblical Poetics and Interpretation*. Bloomington: Indiana University Press, 1990.

Garber, David G., Jr. "Trauma Theory." Pages 421–28 in vol. 2 of *The Oxford Encyclopedia of Biblical Interpretation*. Edited by Steven L. McKenzie. 2 vols. Oxford: Oxford University Press, 2013.

Herman, Judith. *Trauma and Recovery*. New York: Basic Books, 1992.

Joseph, Stephen, and P. Alex Linley, eds. *Trauma, Recovery, and Growth: Positive Psychological Perspectives on Posttraumatic Stress*. Hoboken, NJ: Wiley & Sons, 2008.

Pennebaker, James W. *Opening Up: The Healing Power of Expressing Emotions*. Rev. ed. New York: Guilford, 1997.

Seligman, Martin E. P. *Authentic Happiness: Using the New Positive Psychology to Realize Your Potential for Lasting Fulfilment*. New York: Simon & Schuster, 2002.

Shantz, Colleen. "'I Have Learned to Be Content': Happiness according to St. Paul." Pages 187–201 in *The Bible and the Pursuit of Happiness: What the Old and New Testaments Teach Us about the Good Life*. Edited by Brent A. Strawn. Oxford: Oxford University Press, 2012.

Sheppard, Gerald T. "'Enemies' and the Politics of Prayer in the Book of Psalms." Pages 61–83 in *The Bible and the Politics of Exegesis: Essays in Honor of Norman K. Gottwald on His Sixty-Fifth Birthday*. Edited by David Jobling, Peggy L. Day, and Gerald T. Sheppard. Cleveland: Pilgrim, 1991.

Snow, Kimberly N., et al. "Resolving Anger toward God: Lament as an Avenue toward Attachment." *Journal of Psychology and Theology* 39 (2011): 130–42.

Strawn, Brent A. "Poetic Attachment: Psychology, Psycholinguistics, and the Psalms." Pages 404–23 in *The Oxford Handbook to the Psalms*. Edited by William P. Brown. Oxford: Oxford University Press, 2014.

———. "The Psalms and the Practice of Disclosure." Pages xiii–xxiv in Walter Brueggemann, *From Whom No Secrets Are Hid: Introducing the Psalms*. Edited by Brent A. Strawn. Louisville: Westminster John Knox, 2014.

———. "The Triumph of Life: Towards a Biblical Theology of Happiness." Pages 287–322 in *The Bible and the Pursuit of Happiness: What the Old and New Testaments Teach Us about the Good Life*. Edited by Brent A. Strawn. Oxford: Oxford University Press, 2012.

Suderman, W. Derek. "Are Individual Complaint Psalms Really Prayers? Recognizing Social Address as Characteristic of Individual Complaints." Pages 153–70 in *The Bible as a Human Witness to Divine Revelation: Hearing the Word of God through Historically Dissimilar Traditions*. Edited by Randall Heskett and Brian Irwin. LHBOTS 469. New York: T&T Clark, 2010.

Swenson, Kristin M. *Living through Pain: Psalms and the Search for Wholeness*. Waco, TX: Baylor University Press, 2005.

Sylva, Dennis. *Psalms and the Transformation of Stress: Poetic-Communal Interpretation and the Family*. LTPM 16. Leuven: Peeters; Grand Rapids: Eerdmans, 1993.

Tarantelli, Carole Beebe. "Life within Death: Toward a Metapsychology of Catastrophic Psychic Trauma." *International Journal of Psychoanalysis* 84 (2003): 915–28.

VandeCreek, L. et al. "Praying about Difficult Experiences as Self-Disclosure to God." *The International Journal for the Psychology of Religion* 12 (2002): 29–39.

Weiss, Tzipi, and Roni Berger, eds. *Posttraumatic Growth and Culturally Competent Practice*. Hoboken, NJ: Wiley & Sons, 2010.

Legislating Divine Trauma[*]

Samuel E. Balentine

In her landmark book on trauma, psychiatrist Judith Herman records verbatim the "crisis of faith" experienced by a combat veteran of the Vietnam War:

> I could not rationalize in my mind how God could let good men die. I had gone to several ... priests. I was sitting there with this one priest and said, "Father, I don't understand this: How does God allow small children to be killed? What is this thing, this war, this bullshit? I got all these friends who are dead." That priest, he looked me in the eye and said, "I don't know, son, I've never been to war." I said, "I didn't ask you about war, I asked you about God."[1]

The veteran's words are revealing. It is the one outside the religious establishment who asks about God's role in his traumatizing experience. It is the priest who speaks from inside the religious establishment who fails to understand that his counsel will be inadequate if he cannot say something about God. As Herman says, traumatic experiences breach all relationships—with family, friends, and God. They create a sense of alienation and disconnection so profound that the meaning of life, indeed the meaning of the entire created order, seems irrevocably shattered.

---

* I am grateful to Cathy Caruth for reading an early draft of this paper. I hope it will be evident how much I have benefitted from her wisdom even when not indicated.

1. Judith Herman, *Trauma and Recovery: The Aftermath of Violence—From Domestic Abuse to Political Terror*, rev. ed. (New York: Basic Books, 1997), 55. See also Shoshanna Felman, who speaks of the "larger, more profound, less definable '*crisis of truth*'" that trauma generates within history itself ("Education and Crisis, or the Vicissitudes of Teaching," in *Trauma: Explorations in Memory*, ed. Cathy Caruth [Baltimore: Johns Hopkins University Press, 1995], 17, emphasis added).

Neither Herman, nor most others working in trauma studies, including those in the field of religion and theology, gives substantive attention to the originating cause or source of the traumatic experience.[2] With this in mind, I have two objectives in this essay. The first is to pose a question: How do we exegete trauma when/if God is the perpetrator of the abusing experience?[3] The second is to seed a proposition that I hope will bear fruit. I suggest that what biblical studies should and can contribute to trauma studies is to provide a hermeneutic for studying, understanding, and responding to the roles played by God, religion, and religious institutions in creating traumatic (literally, "wounding") experiences.[4] It may be that for persons experiencing trauma the external source "has gone inside,"[5] but this does not mean that the outside/external source of the wound has been removed, until and unless the ethical imperative to do so becomes painfully clear.[6]

---

2. Trauma study gives primary attention to the victim, not the victimizer, in two ways: by focusing on the wounding experience itself and its traumatic shattering of a person previously whole; and by focusing on how the victim of trauma may survive and live meaningfully beyond the experience. For an overview of these two approaches and brief bibliography, see Cathy Caruth, *Unclaimed Experience: Trauma, Narrative, and History* (Baltimore: Johns Hopkins University Press, 1996), 131 n. 2.

3. A second and no less important aspect of this issue is how to exegete biblical texts in which the narrativized God becomes the *victim* of traumatic experience. This study, however, must be deferred for another occasion.

4. Numerous studies deal with (divine) violence in scripture, almost always with the objective of constructing a defense (theodicy) for God's behavior (e.g., Eric Seibert, *The Violence of Scripture: Overcoming the Old Testament's Troubling Legacy* [Minneapolis: Fortress, 2012]; Seibert, *Disturbing Divine Behavior: Troubling Old Testament Images of God* [Minneapolis: Fortress, 2009]; Jerome Creach, *Violence in Scripture* [Louisville: Westminster Kohn Knox, 2013]). For a cross-disciplinary discussion, see Michael Bergman, Michael J. Murray, and Michael C. Rea, eds., *Divine Evil? The Moral Character of the God of Abraham* (Oxford: Oxford University Press, 2013). This paper deals with similar issues but from a different perspective.

5. Caruth, *Unclaimed Experience*, 59.

6. The question of moral agency is an important issue in sociological approaches to cultural trauma; see, e.g., Angela Kühner, *Kollektive Traumata—Annahmen, Argumente, Konzepte: Eine Bestandsaufnahme nach dem 11. September* (Berlin: Berghof Forschungszentrum für Konstruktive Konfliktbearbeitung, 2002). Who injured the victim? Who or what caused the trauma? Directly related to this is identification of the institutional arena and the hierarchy of power within which the trauma has occurred (e.g., Jeffrey C. Alexander, *Trauma: A Social Theory* [Cambridge: Polity, 2012]; Kai Erikson, *A New Species of Trouble: Explorations in Disaster, Trauma, and Community* [New York: Norton, 1994]).

1. The Jurisprudence of Catastrophe

Hebraic legal materials, principally the Decalogue and the Book of the Covenant, provide an important index of ancient Israel's history and values.[7] This is especially instructive when Israel's laws are examined in relation to what was likely its most traumatic experience: the mass deportation of the population to Babylon in 586 BCE. The presenting question in what follows is this: Does the formative logic of the covenant, by which God promises reward and threatens punishment, effectively use law to legitimate divine violence?

The narrative that reports the events surrounding 586 BCE is curiously brief. The siege of Jerusalem and the consequent famine, mass slaughter, and forced deportation to Babylon require a mere eleven verses, 2 Kgs 25:1–11. About originating causes or traumatic effects, the historical record contains not a word. Whether this rises to the level of a "conspiracy of silence" should remain an open question, but the noiselessness of the narrative signals at the very least what trauma theorists call a "collapse of witnessing."[8] The burden of explaining a traumatic experience that is marginalized by the historical record falls to the Deuteronomistic Historians, who use covenantal law (torah) to bridge the gap between the silence of history and the collapse of understanding.

The question from Herman's war veteran may be reframed as the repeating question the Deuteronomistic History seeks to answer: "Why has the Lord done such a thing to this land and to this house?" (1 Kgs 9:8; cf. Deut 29:24; Jer 9:12; 16:10; 22:8).[9] The Deuteronomistic History's answer is straightforward and consistent: "Because they have forsaken the Lord their God, who brought their ancestors out of the land of Egypt and

---

7. Theodore Ziolkowski notes that medieval law collections were described as "mirrors" because they provided the "truest reflection of their respective societies and societal values" (*The Mirror of Justice: Literary Reflections of Legal Cases* [Princeton: Princeton University Press, 1997], 4).

8. I borrow the phrase "conspiracy of silence" from Stanley B. Frost, who uses it to describe the lack of information in the Hebrew Bible concerning the death of Josiah in 609 BCE ("The Death of Josiah: A Conspiracy of Silence," *JBL* 84 [1968]: 369–82). For the notion of a "collapse of witnessing," see Dori Laub's discussion of the Holocaust as a historical enigma that defies understanding ("Truth and Testimony: The Process and the Struggle," in Caruth, *Trauma*, 61–75).

9. All biblical translations are from the NRSV unless otherwise noted.

embraced other gods ... therefore the Lord has brought this disaster upon them (1 Kgs 9:9; see also Deut 29:25–28; Jer 9:13–16; 16:11–13; 22:9).[10]

This answer in the Deuteronomistic History is lodged within the logic of Israel's covenantal laws, which according to the narrative were first given to Moses at Mount Sinai (Exod 19–24), then reiterated in Deut 5–30.[11] The basic construction of the Sinai legal corpus is well known and needs little comment. The Decalogue comprises unconditional imperatives from God ("Do not do X" or "Do X") that can only be satisfied by Israel's strict compliance. The Book of the Covenant, with its "if ... then" approach to case law, spells out clearly the rewards for obedience and the punishments for disobedience. This legal framework rests on the unquestioned affirmation that God's ways are "perfect," "just," and "without deceit" (Deut 32:4).

The accompanying blessings and curses are integral aspects of a system of justice that sanctions God's authority to mete out deserved rewards and penalties. I cite here a sampling of the curses that God is empowered to execute, if the people do not observe the law:[12]

> The LORD will send upon you disaster, panic, and frustration in everything you attempt to do....
> The LORD will afflict you with consumption, fever, inflammation, with fiery heat and drought, and with blight and mildew....
> Your corpses shall be food for every bird of the air and animal of the earth....
> You shall be continually abused and robbed, without anyone to help....
> Your sons and daughters will be given to another people while you look on....
> You shall become an object of horror, a proverb, and a byword among all people. (Deut 28:20, 22, 26, 29, 32, 37)[13]

---

10. The eleven verses devoted to the description of the destruction of Jerusalem stand in marked contrast with the 181 chapters of the Deuteronomistic History that "ethicizes" its impact (David Janzen, *The Violent Gift: Trauma's Subversion of the Deuteronomistic History's Narrative*, LHBOTS 561 [New York: T&T Clark, 2012], 237).

11. On Deuteronomy's "repetition" of the Exodus law, see Bernard M. Levenson, *Deuteronomy and the Hermeneutics of Legal Innovation* (New York: Oxford University Press, 1997).

12. On the taxonomy and social function of curses uttered by deities in ancient Near Eastern and Hebrew texts, see Anne Marie Kitz, *Cursed Are You! The Phenomenology of Cursing in Cuneiform and Hebrew Texts* (Winona Lake, IN: Eisenbrauns, 2014), 134–52.

13. Correspondence between the curses in Deut 28 and the cursing sections in the

Legal processes typically require a trial before verdicts are rendered. Israel's covenantal law follows this model. Deuteronomy reports that, after Moses proclaimed the covenant requirements and their respective sanctions, God instructed him to write the "words of the law [tôrâ]" (Deut 31:24) as a "witness ['ēd] for me [God] against the Israelites" (31:19; cf. 31:21, 26, 28). In the "Song of Moses" (Deut 32) this "witness" takes the shape of a covenant lawsuit in which Moses summons heaven and earth to hear God's indictment of Israel.[14] The indictment begins by establishing God's legal standing as the plaintiff in the case. God is a "rock"; his work is "perfect" and "just;" his judgments are true, never false (32:4). Israel, the defendant in the case, has forsaken this "rock" and abandoned the God who gave them life for other gods they had never known (32:15, 18). The consequence for the violation of covenant partnership is God's justified anger, imaged as a fire that devours the earth and erases Israel from human history (32:22–26). The punishment is consistent with God's role as the superintendent of covenantal sanctions. The God who has authority to

---

Neo-Assyrian Vassal Treaties of Esarhaddon (VTE), which are connected to Assyrian siege warfare and its horrors, including exile and damage to subsistence systems, has long been noted (e.g., Hans Ulrich Steymans, "Eine assyrische Vorlage für Deuteronomium 28:20–44," in *Bundesdokument und Gesetz: Studien zum Deuteronomium*, ed. Georg Braulik, HBS 4 [Freiburg: Herder, 1995], 119–41; Steymans, *Deuteronomium 28 und die Adê zur Thronfolgeregelung Asarhaddons: Segen und Fluch im Alten Orient und in Israel*, OBO 145 [Göttingen: Vandenhoeck & Ruprecht, 1995]). These "correspondences" have not gone unquestioned (e.g., Carly L. Crouch, *Israel and the Assyrians: Deuteronomy, the Succession Treaty of Esarhaddon, and the Nature of Subversion*, ANEM 8 [Atlanta: Society of Biblical Literature, 2014]).

What is most significant about these correspondences for the purpose of this essay is that the attributes of God are derived from, or at least consonant with, indigenous Mesopotamian attributes of kings. Indeed, conceptualization of YHWH as a sovereign king to whom absolute loyalty is due is a dominant relational metaphor for God in the Old Testament (Marc Zvi Brettler, *God Is King: Understanding an Israelite Metaphor*, JSOTSup 76 [Sheffield: Sheffield Academic, 1989]; Shawn W. Flynn, *YHWH Is King: The Development of Divine Kingship in Ancient Israel*, VTSup 159 [Leiden: Brill, 2013]). The royal metaphor thus assumes a rough imitative correspondence between divine ethics and human ethics.

14. On covenantal lawsuits in the Hebrew Bible, legal language, and ancient Near Eastern antecedents, see Kenneth A. Kitchen and Paul J. N. Lawrence, *Treaty, Law and Covenant in the Ancient Near East*, 3 vols. (Wiesbaden: Harrassowitz, 2012). Deuteronomy 32 does not rigidly follow the lawsuit pattern but instead plays with it, ironically transforming it into a lyrical *ex post facto* affirmation of divine justice. See below.

bless and curse those standing before the divine bench is the God who has unrestricted power to deal life and death, to wound and to heal (32:39; see also Exod 4:11; Isa 45:7; Lam 3:37–38; Sir 33:14–15).[15]

Two matters merit attention here. First, the literary context of Deut 32 presents the future of Israel's covenantal relationship as open-ended; the determination about blessings and curses remains to be decided in accord with Israel's future behavior; a trial in which disputes about obedience or disobedience can be fairly adjudicated is a promise yet to be tested. The compositional history of Deut 32 makes it clear, however, that it is a late addition to the core narrative, almost certainly from the exilic period.[16] Thus in terms of real-time history, this is a report of a trial that has already occurred and a verdict that has already been rendered. The trial is there-fore not so much a search for the truth about why Jerusalem was destroyed in 586 BCE as a finalizing of the answer. Second, it is important to note that in this trial God is both plaintiff and judge. The legal process has no autonomy. There is no distinction between law and moral obligations: to sin against God is to break the law. God both presents the evidence of guilt and decides that this evidence is sufficient for the verdict God seeks. As the defendant, Israel has no voice, no say in the trial.[17]

Legal scholars refer to this use of the law as the "jurisprudence of catastrophe."[18] When catastrophes overturn normative order, the law serves two principal functions: either it explains the catastrophe as a tool

---

15. There is also, however, a certain moral inconsistency in God's decision. The rationale for punishing Israel—they have sinned against God—transposes into a ratio-nale for saving them, because God worries that Israel's enemies will misinterpret their demise as a sign of God's failure to protect them (Deut 32:27, 36, 41, 43). By this logic, it is better for God's reputation, and coincidentally for Israel's welfare, to demonstrate overpowering compassion instead of overpowering anger, in which case the question becomes, Whose justice is being served, God's or Israel's?

16. Distinguishing the so-called *Urdeuteronomium*, presumably the first edition of the book, from its multiple redactions continues to be a complex matter. It is suf-ficient for my purposes to note the near consensus that Deuteronomy in its present form is the product of nearly two hundred years of scribal activity. For a survey of the discussion, see Braulik, *Bundesdokument und Gesetz*.

17. Covenant lawsuits typically present God as plaintiff and Israel or other nations as the defendant (e.g., Hos 4:1–2; Mic 6:1–8). There are limited but astonishing exam-ples where the roles are reversed, in which case one wrongly accused summons God to court (e.g., Jer 12:1–6). In Job, perhaps the boldest such text, the futility of this move is made abundantly clear (e.g., Job 9–10).

18. Lawrence Douglas, Austin Sarat, Martha M. Umphrey, "A Jurisprudence of

of justice, in which case the law affirms the rules that govern life by enacting meaningful and just penalties for their violation, or the law responds to a catastrophe by (re)asserting its sovereignty over life and death, in which case it seeks to control and counter trauma through strategies of anticipation, prevention, and amelioration. What nature overturns, the law can put right. Considering both these functions, Old Testament law can also be described as a "jurisprudence of catastrophe."

2. Law as a Vehicle of Trauma

Robert Cover, a distinguished legal scholar at Yale Law School, argues that all law codes are located within a master narrative that gives them meaning.

> For every constitution there is an epic, for every decalogue a scripture. Once understood in the context of the narratives that give it meaning, law becomes not merely a system of rules to be observed, but a world in which we live.[19]

The "scripture" that gives ancient Israel's Decalogue and Covenant Code meaning is the master narrative about the reciprocal relationship between YHWH and Israel. When the people agree to the categorical imperatives of the covenant, they do so with the conviction that their behavior must mirror God's: "*I am* your God. ... *You shall be* my people" (Jer 11:4; 24:7; 30:22; 31:33; 32:28; Ezek 11:20; 14:11; 36:28; 37:23, 27; cf. Exod 6:7; 19:4–6; 20:1–2). Divine ethic determines human ethic.

This covenantal logic, however, raises several questions. If God works in history by imposing a *quid pro quo* system of rewards and punishments, then should not humans seek to shape history, in conformity with God's will, by enacting a similar retributive law in their relationships with others?[20] If an orderly society depends on a legal system that sanctions harsh penalties for disobedience to unconditional commandments, then

---

Catastrophe: An Introduction," in *Law as Catastrophe*, ed., Austin Sarat, Lawrence Douglas, and Martha M. Umphrey (Stanford: Stanford University Press, 2007), 1–18.

19. Robert Cover, "Nomos and Narrative," in *Narrative, Violence, and the Law: The Essays of Robert Cover*, ed. Martha Minnow, Michael Ryan, and Austin Sarat (Ann Arbor: University of Michigan Press, 1995), 95–96.

20. For one example of how human retribution may imitate divine retribution, at least conceptually, see the petitions in the imprecatory psalms, in which suppliants implore God to crush their enemies (Pss 17:13–14; 35:4–6; 58:6–9; 137:7–9).

is there not a legal, if not a divine, imperative to use, when necessary, violent behavior to correct violent misbehavior? If it is a legal, ethical, and moral necessity for God to use "disaster, panic, and frustration," to "abuse," "crush," and "rob" in order to keep order, then why should humans not do the same?[21] In commenting on the requisites of law and government in Greek society, Plato sharply frames the ethical question: "If because I do evil You [gods] punish me with evil, what is the difference between You and me?"[22]

Shoshana Felman uses psychoanalysis and literary criticism to examine the hidden links between trauma and law.[23] Her focus is the 1961 trial in Jerusalem of Nazi war criminal Adolf Eichmann. Horrific acts of violence such as those identified with the Holocaust rupture history; they open up a gap between experience and understanding, between suffering and the capacity to moralize. The courtroom becomes a place where the experience can be identified, remembered, and articulated. Alleged perpetrators and victims have fair and equal opportunities to make their case before an impartial judge and jury. The verdict rendered is meant to balance the scales of justice, to colonize extreme misfortune as an injustice that can be legally remedied. The irony of this justice-by-law process is that the courtroom may become the site of a reenactment that requires both perpetrators and victims to relive the experience; traumatic events, buried in wounded memory, are resuscitated; their effects must be endured once again. In short, the trial that is meant to contain the trauma becomes a vehicle for sustaining it.

Felman illustrates with a dramatic moment in the Eichmann trial. A man known by the pseudonym K-Zetnick (a slang term for a concentration camp inmate) was called to testify because he met Eichmann in Auschwitz. In response to the prosecutor's questions, K-Zetnick quickly

---

21. On the perverse moralism of (human) violence, see Cathy Caruth, "An Interview with Robert Jay Lifton," in Caruth, *Trauma*, 128–47.

22. Plato, *Complete Works*, ed. John M. Cooper (Indianapolis: Hackett, 1977). Plato counsels caution when using the gods as moral and ethical exemplars because the master narrative of Greece, especially as constructed by poets such as Homer and Hesiod, is full of stories about the frivolous cruelty and violence of the gods. Because repetition of such stories encourages imitation by unformed minds, it is better to pass over them in silence. Some theologies, in other words, must be censored for the greater good of society (see Plato, *Republic* 2.380B; *Laws* 10.901A).

23. Shoshanna Felman, *The Juridical Unconscious: Trials and Traumas in the Twentieth Century* (Cambridge: Harvard University Press, 2002).

slipped into a trance-like narrative of what he experienced in two years of living on the "planet of Auschwitz," where people neither lived nor died in accordance with the law. When the presiding judge tried to steer him back to the protocols of the court, K-Zetnick stood up, then suddenly fainted and collapsed on the floor beside the witness stand. Police rushed to his side, a cry went out from the audience, the judge called for order, an ambulance was called, and K-Zetnick was rushed to the hospital. The court went into recess.[24]

Felman invites us to interpret law through the lens of trauma, what she calls the "ghost in the house of justice."[25] The ghost in the courtroom is K-Zetnick's speechlessness. Like the history that muted the cries from Auschwitz, the court has (inadvertently) silenced the witness. The silence itself now becomes the witness that not only interrupts the legal process but also brings it to a halt. It is not only history that has been placed on trial; now the law itself must stand trial.[26] The protocols of the court have retraumatized the witness, thus exposing the limits of the law. In Felman's words, "The trial has attempted to articulate the trauma so as to *control* its damage. But it is the structure of trauma … that in the end controls the trial."[27]

When we view covenantal law through the lens of trauma, an unsettling picture begins to take shape. In God's courtroom, the only witnesses called are heaven and earth, and they are summoned on God's behalf. The one cursed/punished by law has no voice, not even a fainting presence. The relationship between suffering and meaning remains unarticulated. Indeed, the one aggrieved is not the defendant, Israel, but instead God, the prosecutor, who has been abused by a perverse people (Deut 32:5, 15–17). If the Eichmann trial reenacts the trauma of Auschwitz, the trial envisioned in Deut 32 effectively reenacts the erasure of the trauma of exile from the court's records. Whereas 2 Kgs 25 gives eleven verses to the exile report, Deut 32, whether proleptic or retrospective, gives no report at all. If in the Eichmann trial the witness to trauma collapses, in the covenant trial the law itself seems to lose consciousness. It proceeds from divine indictment to divine justification to divine verdict without so much as a conscious pause for any word from or on behalf of the accused. The

---

24. Ibid., 136–37.
25. Ibid., 131–66.
26. Ibid., 16.
27. Ibid., 60, emphasis original.

only interruption is an introspective moment when God ponders whether the verdict could be misunderstood (32:27), in which case the worry is about God's judicial reputation, not the defendant's welfare. The lingering ghost in the covenant house of justice is the silenced voice of the *I* who is condemned by divine law to suffer "disaster ... wasting hunger ... burning consumption ... bitter pestilence ... for young man and woman alike, nursing child and old gray beard" (32:23–25). If the law is a gift from God meant to delight the heart, as the psalmist declares (Pss 1, 119), then it is a "violent gift" wrapped in Israel's traumatic experience of exile.[28]

3. A Traumatizing God?

It is easy to be sympathetic with the Deuteronomistic master narrative. It chronicles a radical and consequential transformation in history when a group of slaves revolted against a despotic Egyptian Pharaoh, cast their lot with a God whose like had never been known in quite the same way before, and thus embarked on the journey of monotheism. Perhaps such a journey requires both an encounter with imperial power and an unquenchable desire to escape from it. How does one escape from the highest power regnant in the land if not with the help of a still higher power, a God above all gods, a God beyond all imaginable comparison, an exclusive, sovereign God? The political mechanism for the alliance between this God and the people delivered from Egyptian oppression was the covenant, which makes receiving the continuing benefits of God's power contingent upon unconditional obedience to divine imperatives. By this logic, punishment is an expression of God's covenantal fidelity. For God to survive exile as God, with power untarnished, Israel would have to be punished and eventually restored, if the redemptive *telos* of the master narrative was to be validated. Even the worst punishments, those exacted through the destruction of Jerusalem and Babylonian captivity, serve primarily to reinforce God's overwhelming sovereignty. The more horrific the punishment, the more this YHWH God demonstrates unrivaled power that commands grateful submission.[29] In the final analysis, according to the Deuteronomistic

---

28. Janzen, *The Violent Gift*, 3.

29. On the covenant as a political mechanism that sacralizes trial by adversity, see Marcel Gauchet, *The Disenchantment of the World: A Political History of Religion*, trans. Oscar Burge (Princeton: Princeton University Press, 1997), 107–15. See further David Carr, who posits that Israel's "traumatic chosenness," which implicitly requires

master narrative, the violent enactment of the exile is more about the vindication of God's justice than Judah's suffering.

Nonetheless, trauma theorists remind us that all master narratives that attempt a totalizing explanation for horrific suffering will inevitably be challenged by on-the-ground realities. Perpetrators of violence may take cover in a variety of defenses—denial, silence, rationalization, and prerogative[30]—but ultimately "the unbelievable cannot be made believable."[31] When the traumatizing power is a force of nature (e.g., an earthquake, tornado, flood), we think of it as a natural disaster; in the jargon of the insurance industry it is called, ironically, an "act of God." When the traumatizing agent is another human being, we speak of cruelty, brutality, or barbarism. The perpetrator can be convicted as a criminal; the law can exact punishment and provide compensation; an acceptable equilibrium between justice and injustice can be restored. But what happens when the force behind the trauma is the court of justice itself? What if the court metes out excessive penalties? What if its protocols deny the accused a fair hearing? What if the accused is never given a chance to plead "not guilty"? In the modern world, such issues can be referred to a court of appeal. In ancient Israel, they had to be resolved by covenant justice.

How do we exegete texts that describe God's use of traumatizing penalties to enforce obedience to the law? Our colleagues in the social sciences may claim exemption from this question. They have no need for a hermeneutic of divine agency. They operate effectively by privileging a scientific investigation of causality. In one way or another, human beings are both the perpetrators and the victims of horrific violence. The discipline of biblical studies does not have this option. Even biblical scholars who insist on defined boundaries between historical-critical research and theological reflection have to deal with texts in which God has, at the very least, a narrativized role in history.

Trauma study has migrated from the medical field to literary studies and now to biblical studies. I believe it is now time for those of us in biblical studies to be more intentional about what we bring to this ongoing conversation. Indeed, it is debatable whether trauma studies was ever

---

"devotion to a devastating God," helps to shape a resilient Judaism (*Holy Resilience: The Bible's Traumatic Origins* [New Haven: Yale University Press, 2014], 124–27, 248.

30. Herman identifies these and other "predictable apologies" perpetrators offer (*Trauma and Recovery*, 8).

31. Janzen, *The Violent Gift*, 60.

really a secular endeavor from its beginning. What is enigmatic in trauma can never be reduced to, or explained in terms of, a secular psychology. There is necessarily the intrusion of some catalyzing "Other," whether divine or human, when traumatic experiences fracture life.[32] As we continue to learn from trauma theorists, we should aspire to contribute something of our own expertise that could be helpful to them and generative for us. Where to begin? I offer the following suggestions with the hope that they will invite further reflection.

(1) We should resist the notion that there is one, unified trauma *theory* and recognize, even exploit, the multiple *theories*, each one bleeding into the other, that are at work. Whether the operating hermeneutic is psychological, sociological, or *theological*, its reach will likely exceed its grasp. No single approach can persuasively render the meaningless meaningful.

(2) Even so, of these multiple approaches, a theological approach may be particularly positioned to make a significant contribution. Because theology intentionally situates itself at the intersection of God (gods), world, and humankind, it necessarily deals with the collision of the mundane and the transcendent, the explicable and the inexplicable, in short, precisely with the arenas of thought and behavior in which traumatic experiences occur.

(3) Biblical scholars work with a deposit of texts that convey a variety of *master narratives of suffering* not only within the Deuteronomistic History but also in prophetic literature, psalms, and wisdom literature.[33] Embedded within each are counternarratives, sometimes faint, sometimes robust, that dispute and defy proffered interpretations of suffering. Our task is to examine critically the underlying assumptions about God (gods), world, and humankind that provide context for both the master and counternarratives. Whose interests do they serve? What belief and behavior do they advocate and why? When and if they are persuasive, for either ancient or contemporary "carrier groups,"[34] what are the cultural, political, and religious consequences?

---

32. I owe this insight to Cathy Caruth.

33. See, for example, the collection of essays in Eve-Marie Becker, Jan Dochhorn, and Else K. Holt, eds., *Trauma and Traumatization in Individual and Collective Dimensions: Insights from Biblical Studies and Beyond*, SANt 2 (Göttingen: Vandenhoeck & Ruprecht, 2014).

34. Alexander, *Trauma*, 20.

(4) A biblical or theological hermeneutic for trauma cannot avoid dealing with both the *victims* of violence and the *perpetrators* of violence.[35] It is the latter that present a special challenge and a fraught opportunity, precisely because Hebrew scriptures so often describe God as the agent of trauma. If psychological approaches to trauma focus on the *survival of victims*, then biblical approaches must examine the *survival of theism* in the face of extraordinary suffering.[36]

The challenge before us is to develop a clear and rigorous methodology for exegeting traumatic violence in religious texts and in religious institutions that use these texts to define their ethical imperatives. For such a task we need not claim all wisdom when we seek to transcend our mortal-minded limitations.[37] Rather, like Odysseus, who resisted Calypso's temptation to become godlike because his human journey was too important, we should exploit our possibilities.[38]

---

35. For a cogent warning about yielding to the "intuitive tyranny of the victim's view," see Roy F. Baumeister, *Evil: Inside Human Violence and Cruelty* (New York: Henry Holt, 1997), 32–59.

36. See Louis Stulman on how reading the prophets through the lens of trauma reveals primal concerns about the "*survival of God, the survival of faith, the survival of the community*" ("Reading the Bible through the Lens of Trauma and Art," in Becker, Dochhorn, and Holt, 189, emphasis original).

37. The carriers of (religious) master narratives of suffering typically defend their propositions by stressing the limitations of human understanding, for example: "What is proper to oneself is an offense to one's God…. Who knows the will of the gods in heaven? Who understands the plans of the underworld gods? Where have mortals learnt the way of God?" (Ludlul Bel Nemeqi [I Will Praise the Lord of Wisdom], II, 34–38, trans. from *BWL*, 41; Mesopotamian text, ca. seventh century BCE, likely a copy of a text from the second millennium BCE); "Can you find out the deep things of God? Can you find out the limit of the Almighty? It is higher than heaven—what can you do? Deeper than Sheol—what can you know? … A stupid person will get understanding when a wild ass is born human" (Zophar to Job, Job 11:7–9, 12); "No man as he toils knows whether in the end his enterprise will turn out well or ill…. We mortals have no knowledge, only vain belief; the gods fix everything to suit themselves" (Hesiod, *Theogony* 135–136, 141–142 [Most, LCL]; seventh century BCE).

38. Homer, *Odyssey* 5.180–185, 188–197. On this point, see Martha C. Nussbaum, "Transcending Humanity," in her *Love's Knowledge: Essays on Philosophy and Literature* (New York: Oxford University Press, 1990), 365–91.

Bibliography

Alexander, Jeffrey C. *Trauma: A Social Theory.* Cambridge: Polity, 2012.

Baumeister, Roy F. *Evil: Inside Human Violence and Cruelty.* New York: Henry Holt, 1997.

Becker, Eve-Marie, Jan Dochhorn, and Else K. Holt, eds. *Trauma and Traumatization in Individual and Collective Dimensions: Insights from Biblical Studies and Beyond.* SANt 2. Göttingen: Vandenhoeck & Ruprecht, 2014.

Bergman, Michael, Michael J. Murray, and Michael C. Rea, eds. *Divine Evil? The Moral Character of the God of Abraham.* Oxford: Oxford University Press, 2013.

Brettler, Marc Zvi. *God Is King: Understanding an Israelite Metaphor.* JSOTSup 76. Sheffield: Sheffield Academic, 1989.

Carr, David. *Holy Resilience: The Bible's Traumatic Origins.* New Haven: Yale University Press, 2014.

Caruth, Cathy. "An Interview with Robert Jay Lifton." Pages 128–47 in *Trauma: Explorations in Memory.* Edited by Cathy Caruth. Baltimore: Johns Hopkins University Press, 1995.

———. *Unclaimed Experience: Trauma, Narrative, and History.* Baltimore: Johns Hopkins University Press, 1996.

Cover, Robert. "Nomos and Narrative." Pages 95–172 in *Narrative, Violence, and the Law: The Essays of Robert Cover.* Edited by Martha Minnow, Michael Ryan, and Austin Sarat. Ann Arbor: University of Michigan Press, 1995.

Creach, Jerome. *Violence in Scripture.* Louisville: Westminster Kohn Knox, 2013.

Crouch, Carly L. *Israel and the Assyrians: Deuteronomy, the Succession Treaty of Esarhaddon, and the Nature of Subversion.* ANEM 8. Atlanta: Society of Biblical Literature, 2014.

Erikson, Kai. *A New Species of Trouble: Explorations in Disaster, Trauma, and Community.* New York: Norton, 1994.

Felman, Shoshanna. "Education and Crisis, or the Vicissitudes of Teaching." Pages 13–73 in *Trauma: Explorations in Memory.* Edited by Cathy Caruth. Baltimore: Johns Hopkins University Press, 1995.

———. *The Juridical Unconscious: Trials and Traumas in the Twentieth Century.* Cambridge: Harvard University Press, 2002.

Flynn, Shawn W. *YHWH is King: The Development of Divine Kingship in Ancient Israel.* VTSup 159. Leiden: Brill, 2013.

Frost, Stanley B. "The Death of Josiah: A Conspiracy of Silence." *JBL* 84 (1968): 369–82.

Gauchet, Marcel. *The Disenchantment of the World: A Political History of Religion*. Translated by Oscar Burge. Princeton: Princeton University Press, 1997.

Herman, Judith. *Trauma and Recovery: The Aftermath of Violence—From Domestic Abuse to Political Terror*. Rev. ed. New York: Basic Books, 1997.

Hesiod. *Hesiod 1: Theogony, Works and Days, Testimonia*. Edited and translated by Glenn W. Most. LCL 57. Cambridge: Harvard University Press, 2006.

Janzen, David. *The Violent Gift: Trauma's Subversion of the Deuteronomistic History's Narrative*. LHBOTS 561. New York: T&T Clark, 2012.

Kitchen, Kenneth A., and Paul J. N. Lawrence. *Treaty, Law and Covenant in the Ancient Near East*. 3 vols. Wiesbaden: Harrassowitz, 2012.

Kitz, Anne Marie. *Cursed Are You! The Phenomenology of Cursing in Cuneiform and Hebrew Texts*. Winona Lake, IN: Eisenbrauns, 2014.

Kühner, Angela. *Kollektive Traumata—Annahmen, Argumente, Konzepte: Eine Bestandsaufnahme nach dem 11. September*. Berlin: Berghof Forschungszentrum für Konstruktive Konfliktbearbeitung, 2002.

Laub, Dori. "Truth and Testimony: The Process and the Struggle." Pages 61–75 in *Trauma: Explorations in Memory*. Edited by Cathy Caruth. Baltimore: Johns Hopkins University Press, 1995.

Levenson, Bernard M. *Deuteronomy and the Hermeneutics of Legal Innovation*. New York: Oxford University Press, 1997.

Nussbaum, Martha C. *Love's Knowledge: Essays on Philosophy and Literature*. New York: Oxford University Press, 1990.

Plato. *Complete Works*. Edited by John M. Cooper. Indianapolis: Hackett, 1977.

Seibert, Eric. *Disturbing Divine Behavior: Troubling Old Testament Images of God*. Minneapolis: Fortress, 2009.

———. *The Violence of Scripture: Overcoming the Old Testament's Troubling Legacy*. Minneapolis: Fortress, 2012.

Steymans, Hans Ulrich. "Eine assyrische Vorlage für Deuteronomium 28:20–44." Pages 119–41 in *Bundesdokument und Gesetz: Studien zum Deuteronomium*. Edited by Georg Braulik. Herders biblische Studien 4. Freiburg: Herder, 1995

————. *Deuteronomium 28 und die Adê zur Thronfolgeregelung Asarhaddons: Segen und Fluch im Alten Orient und in Israel.* OBO 145. Göttingen: Vandenhoeck & Ruprecht, 1995.

Stulman, Louis. "Reading the Bible through the Lens of Trauma and Art." Pages 177–92 in *Trauma and Traumatization in Individual and Collective Dimensions: Insights from Biblical Studies and Beyond.* Edited by Eve-Marie Becker, Jan Dochhorn, and Else K. Holt. SANt 2. Vandenhoeck & Ruprecht, Göttingen, 2014.

Ziolkowski, Theodore. *The Mirror of Justice: Literary Reflections of Legal Cases.* Princeton: Princeton University Press, 1997.

Trauma and Recovery:
A New Hermeneutical Framework
for the Rape of Tamar (2 Samuel 13)

L. Juliana M. Claassens

There probably are few stories that portray the reality of rape and sexual assault in the Bible as vividly as the story of Tamar and her half-brother Amnon as narrated in 2 Sam 13. Many feminist interpreters justifiably have portrayed Tamar as victim of the traumatic experience of being raped by her half-brother, silenced by the male community, and living out her days in her brother Absalom's house a ruined woman.[1] For instance, on the aftermath of Tamar's rape, Pamela Cooper-White writes as follows in her imaginative retelling of Tamar's story from the perspective of Absalom's daughter Tamar, who is said to have been born several years after her namesake aunt died:[2]

> They tell me that after that Tamar went quietly around their house like a ghost, pale and ill and weeping. She was like an empty shell. Even her

---

* Portions of this essay appear in the chapter "Resisting the Violence of Rape," in L. Juliana M. Claassens, *Claiming Her Dignity: Female Resistance in the Old Testament* (Collegeville, MN: Liturgical Press, 2016).

1. Phyllis Trible, "Tamar: The Royal Rape of Wisdom," in *Texts of Terror: Literary-Feminist Readings of Biblical Narratives*, OBT 13 (Philadelphia: Fortress, 1984), 37–57; Alice A. Keefe, "Rapes of Women/Wars of Men," *Semeia* 61 (1993): 79–97; Athalya Brenner, "A Double Date: We Are Tamar and Tamar," in *I Am: Biblical Women Tell Their Own Stories* (Minneapolis: Fortress: 2004), 133–46.

2. Pamela Cooper-White (*The Cry of Tamar: Violence against Women and the Church's Response* [Minneapolis: Fortress, 1995], 9) interprets the reference that Absalom named his only daughter after Tamar (2 Sam 14:27) as an indication that Tamar possibly died early, seeing that in some Jewish traditions such naming is only done in memory of a deceased relation.

outrage had been beaten out of her.… My mother says that when Absalom came and told how he'd had Amnon killed, Tamar turned even paler and fell down screaming and crying. That night they all formed a caravan and fled. Tamar was so weak she couldn't ride and became so ill that when they arrived at Geshur, she no longer even knew who any of them were. She died a few days later.[3]

An interpretation such as this one is filling in the narrative gaps by focusing on Tamar as a victim who never was able to recover from her ordeal. Indeed, we are told quite little in the biblical text about what happened to Tamar after the rape or how she experienced both the violation and the aftermath in the days, months, and years following the traumatic occurrence. I propose that one could fill in the narrative gaps differently by focusing not only on the trauma associated with Tamar's rape but also on the recovery that one hopes would follow upon an event of such magnitude.

In this regard, Judith Herman's seminal *Trauma and Recovery* offers us a framework to imagine Tamar's story differently, in order not to deny the horrifying event of being raped by one's half-brother but to highlight those instances in the narrative that point to the victim as resisting violence in whichever way possible.[4] By focusing on both the traumatic aspect of the rape as well as the potential for survival or recovery, this essay sets out to do justice to the victim's perspective but at the same time not to focus so much on the victim aspect of the person that the survival or recovery part of the traumatic occurrence is negated.

As part of a larger project on female resistance in the Old Testament, this essay reads the narrative of Tamar's rape by her half-brother Amnon in 2 Sam 13 through the lens of trauma theory with special attention to Herman's exploration of trauma and post-traumatic stress syndrome, on the one hand, and her discussion of the fundamental stages of recovery, on the other.[5]

---

3. Ibid., 4.

4. Judith Herman, *Trauma and Recovery: The Aftermath of Violence—From Domestic Abuse to Political Terror*, rev. ed. (New York: Basic Books, 1997).

5. There is a growing body of literature on trauma theory that has advanced our understanding of traumatic events. See, e.g., Cathy Caruth, *Unclaimed Experience: Trauma, Narrative and History* (Baltimore: Johns Hopkins University Press, 1996); Shoshana Felman, "Education and Crisis: Or, the Vicissitudes of Teaching," in *Trauma: Explorations in Memory*, ed. Cathy Caruth (Baltimore: Johns Hopkins University Press, 1995), 13–60; Kai Erikson, "Notes on Trauma and Community," in Caruth, *Trauma,*

1. Defining Trauma

Herman describes the psychological effects of the trauma associated with rape. In the aftermath of rape, victims complain of symptoms resembling those of combat veterans: insomnia, nausea, startled responses, nightmares, and dissociative and numbing responses.[6] Herman calls the posttraumatic stress condition associated with rape "rape trauma syndrome," and she identifies in it the following characteristics, among others. First, the psychological trauma associated with rape is marked by a profound sense of helplessness. Herman argues that at the moment of trauma the victim is rendered helpless by the overpowering force associated with the violence of rape, which dramatically affects the person's ability to function.[7] For instance, when an individual is completely powerless, she may go into a state of surrender, escaping the trauma by altering her state of consciousness. In the words of a rape survivor cited by Herman: "I couldn't scream. I couldn't move. I was paralyzed … like a rag doll."[8]

Second, Herman describes the dehumanizing nature of traumatic occurrences. She writes that, whereas many trauma survivors would say "'I am now a different person,' the most severely harmed stated simply: 'I am not a person.'"[9] The reason for this is that trauma, in essence, negates the individual's point of view. With regard to rape, Herman argues that "the purpose of the attack is precisely to demonstrate contempt for the victim's autonomy and dignity."[10]

Third, Herman explains how trauma affects the victim's emotions and memories: "The traumatized person may experience intense emotion but without clear memory of the event, or may remember everything in detail

---

183–99; Jeffrey Alexander, *Trauma: A Social Theory* (Cambridge: Polity, 2012); Jeffrey Kauffman, ed., *Loss of the Assumptive World: A Theory of Traumatic Loss* (New York: Brunner-Routledge, 2002). See also the following works in biblical studies that fruitfully utilize trauma theory: Daniel L. Smith-Christopher, *A Biblical Theology of Exile*, OBT (Minneapolis: Fortress, 2002); Kathleen O'Connor, *Jeremiah: Pain and Promise* (Minneapolis: Fortress, 2011); Eve-Marie Becker, Jan Dochhorn, and Else Holt, eds., *Trauma and Traumatization in Individual and Collective Dimensions: Insights from Biblical Studies and Beyond*, SANt 2 (Göttingen: Vandenhoeck & Ruprecht, 2014).

6. Herman, *Trauma and Recovery*, 31.

7. Ibid., 33. See also Erikson, "Notes on Trauma and Community," 83.

8. Herman, *Trauma and Recovery*, 42.

9. Ibid., 94.

10. Ibid., 53.

but without emotion."[11] Moreover, long after the danger has passed, a traumatized person may relive the event through flashbacks or nightmares "as
though it were continually recurring in the present." Herman argues: "They
cannot resume the normal course of their lives, for the trauma repeatedly
interrupts. It is as if time stops at the moment of trauma."[12]

Finally, Herman also shows how traumatic events have a devastating
effect upon the victim's basic human relationships, markedly changing the
way the individual relates to family and friends.[13] Herman elaborates:

> Traumatized people feel utterly abandoned, utterly alone, cast out of the
> human and divine systems of care and protection that sustain life. There-
> after a sense of alienation, of disconnection, pervades every relationship,
> from the most intimate familial bonds to the most abstract affiliations of
> community and religion. When trust is lost, traumatized people feel that
> they belong more to the dead than to the living.[14]

2. TAMAR AS TRAUMA VICTIM

The above-mentioned portrayal of the traumatic nature of rape is a helpful
interpretative tool for reading the narrative of Tamar's violation. In 2 Sam
13 there are several textual details that are reminiscent of the description
of trauma outlined above. For instance, Tamar is portrayed as helpless in
the face of the overpowering violence enacted by Amnon. The actual rape
is preceded by a long buildup in which Amnon and his crafty friend Jona-
dab work together to conceive a plot that would leave Tamar little room
for escape. Tamar is, in the friends' carefully constructed plan, the object
of repeated commands ("take," "bring," and "give"), which she obeys without a word. After she had prepared food in Amnon's sight and brought it
to him in his bedchamber, he proceeds violently to grab hold of her, as
indicated by the use of the verbal root *ḥzq* in verses 11 and 14. The rape
in 13:14 is narrated with a mere two verbs that follow upon one another
in quick succession: "he raped her" (*way'annehā*) and "he laid (with) her"

---

11. Ibid., 34.

12. Ibid., 37. See also Cathy Caruth, who defines trauma as a series of thoughts,
dreams, and hallucinations that "possesses the receiver and resists psychoanalytic
interpretation and cure" ("Trauma and Experience: Introduction," in Caruth, *Trauma*,
5–6).

13. Herman, *Trauma and Recovery*, 51.

14. Ibid., 52.

(*wayyiškab 'ōtāh*). Both of these verbs indicate the extent to which Tamar is objectified.[15] Frank Yamada further points out how the use of the impersonal demonstrative *zō't* in Amnon's exclamation, "Take *this* away from me" (13:17), contributes to Tamar's dehumanization. As Yamada argues, "After the rape Amnon adds more humiliation to Tamar's shame by failing to recognize her humanity."[16]

We also see how Tamar's other (male) family members fail to offer a supportive network of care, inadvertently contributing to her anguish. David is portrayed as the absent father who would rather mourn for the death of his rapist son than his daughter's violation, and Absalom, using familial language in 13:20, silences Tamar in order to protect the family secret: "Her brother Absalom said to her, 'Has Amnon your brother been with you? Be quiet for now, my sister; he is your brother; do not take this to heart.'"[17]

Finally, the concluding words of the narrative offer a most dramatic depiction of the effects of the trauma experienced by Tamar: "Tamar remained, a desolate woman, in her brother Absalom's house" (2 Sam 13:20). Much has been written about the term *šōmēmâ* and its significance. Ulrike Bail draws a connection between this reference and its use in Isa 54:1, where *šōmēm* is used to describe a state of barrenness; two verses later, in Isa 54:3, *šōmēm* is used with reference to the devastated and ruined city or land that has become uninhabitable.[18] With this in mind, Bail argues that Tamar, after the violation by her brother Amnon, lived out her days in Absalom's house utterly "destroyed," or, one could say "a ruined woman," which in German is rendered well with the phrase "eine lebendige Begrabene" (a person buried alive).[19] On the one hand, one could

---

15. Trible notes how "the Hebrew omits the preposition to stress his brutality" ("Tamar," 46).

16. Frank M. Yamada, *Configurations of Rape in the Hebrew Bible: A Literary Analysis of Three Rape Narratives*, StBibLit 109 (New York: Lang, 2009), 120. Trible argues that Tamar has become "a disposable object" for Amnon, "a thing, a 'this' he wants to throw out. She is trash" ("Tamar," 48).

17. Biblical translations are from the NRSV.

18. Ulrike Bail, *Gegen das Schweigen Klagen: Eine Intertextuelle Studie zu den Klagepsalmen Ps 6 und Ps 55 und der Erzählung von der Verwaltigung Tamars* (Gütersloh: Gütersloher Verlagshaus, 1998), 196; Ilse Müllner, *Gewalt im Hause Davids: Die Erzählung von Tamar und Amnon (2 Sam 13, 1–22)* (Freiburg: Herder, 1997), 324.

19. Bail, *Gegen das Schweigen Klagen*, 155, 198; Cooper-White, *The Cry of Tamar*, 8.

thus argue that the trauma had a devastating effect on Tamar, who lived out the rest of her years in Absalom's house. This reading is warranted, particularly if one heeds Herman's warning that, if a rape victim avoids the recovery process, this may result in "a narrowing of consciousness, a withdrawal from engagement with others, and an impoverished life."[20] On the other hand, would it not make a difference if one were to give Tamar a life beyond the walls of her brother Absalom's compound, as some interpreters have sought to do? Aided by Judith Herman's description of the different elements of the recovery process, would it not be possible to imagine Tamar's recovery from rape trauma syndrome? Particularly if one takes into consideration Ilse Müllner's point that, insofar as sexual violence is aimed at the extinction of the person, the mere act of survival on the part of the victim may be understood as an act of resisting (sexual) violence.[21]

3. Recovery from Trauma

Herman outlines three stages in the process of recovery that ought to follow upon a traumatic event: (1) establishing safety; (2) remembering and mourning the traumatic event; (3) reconnecting with ordinary life.[22] This process of recovery does not occur in a straightforward linear fashion but rather can be likened to a marathon: a test of endurance with the survivor little by little gaining a sense of safety that may allow her to move on to the next steps of the recovery process.[23] Moreover, Herman writes that one never completely recovers from trauma: "The impact of a traumatic event continues to reverberate throughout the survivor's lifecycle."[24]

In the following section these stages of recovery are used as an interpretative framework for the story of Tamar. Of course, one could argue that psychological treatment that is associated with this recovery process as proposed by Herman is a modern-day invention and anachronistic in terms of the biblical portrayal of Tamar. Still, as Herman rightly points out, psychologists have learned much regarding the recovery process from the great number of trauma survivors worldwide who have never received any kind of formal treatment. Those survivors who manage to recover

---

20. Herman, *Trauma and Recovery*, 42.
21. Bail, *Gegen das Schweigen Klagen*, 204; Müllner, *Gewalt im Hause Davids*, 348.
22. Herman, *Trauma and Recovery*, 3, 155.
23. Ibid., 174.
24. Ibid., 211.

invent their own coping mechanisms, which include drawing upon the networks of relationships in their own communities that may serve as a source of support.[25]

3.1. Safety

The first task of the recovery process is for the victim to reach a place of safety. Herman notes that, for survivors of a single traumatic event, a basic sense of safety can be obtained reasonably soon, if the victim possesses adequate social support.[26] Establishing safety is particularly important in the case of rape, in which it quite often occurs that the victim knows her attacker—as also in the case of Tamar. Interpreters have mostly interpreted the reference to Tamar finding refuge in Absalom's house in a negative fashion. However, they have overlooked the fact that, as Herman points out, in the case that the rapist enjoys a higher status than the victim, it may be necessary for the victim to withdraw from some part of her social world in order to escape the perpetrator.[27] Phyllis Trible also argues that, even though a surface reading of Absalom's response to Tamar after the rape would have Absalom minimizing the crime and excusing Amnon, Absalom really serves as an advocate of Tamar, taking the place of their father to ensure her safety.[28]

Moreover, as indicated earlier, the biblical text also focuses narrowly on the response of the *male* relatives to Tamar's ordeal. Conceivably there also were supportive *female* family members and friends who could offer the necessary care and protection that, according to Herman, might have a strong healing effect on the traumatized person.[29] We know at least that Absalom named his daughter after his sister, which is indicative of a significant familial relationship. Together Absalom and his wife might have provided a supportive network for Tamar so that she could gradually progress toward the second and third stages of recovery: remembering and mourning the traumatic event and engaging once more with the broader community.[30]

---

25. Ibid., 241.
26. Ibid., 165.
27. Ibid., 62.
28. Trible, "Tamar," 52.
29. Herman, *Trauma and Recovery*, 63.
30. Ibid., 162.

3.2. Mourning

The second important stage of the recovery process is for the victim to reconstruct the traumatic event and mourn its losses. Herman argues that it is vital for the victim to give herself over to grief, as a failure to mourn may result in the victim's becoming trapped in the traumatic process.[31]

Herman notes that the ultimate goal of the second stage is to put the traumatic event into words. She argues that, in the telling of the traumatic event, "the trauma story becomes testimony," which constitutes an essential part of the recovery process.[32] At first, it may be difficult for the trauma survivor to use words, or the first attempts to narrativize the traumatic event may be convoluted. However, Herman proposes that in the process of reconstructing the trauma event "an ordinary person becomes a theologian, a philosopher, a jurist."[33] Part of the sense-making process of the traumatic event is that the survivor interprets what has happened to her in terms of the values and beliefs that she held before the trauma broke into her life.

The act of mourning, moreover, serves as a means by which the trauma survivor may resist the violence that has befallen her. Herman describes this link between mourning and resistance as follows:

> Reclaiming the ability to feel the full range of emotions, including grief, must be understood as an act of resistance rather than submission to the perpetrator's intent. Only through mourning everything that she has lost can the patient discover her indestructible inner life.[34]

By mourning, the trauma survivor is able to reclaim her voice and to become a subject once more, resisting the dehumanization experienced on account of the traumatic event. In this regard, Herman notes that it is important for those close to the victim "to affirm the dignity and value of the survivor."[35]

---

31. Ibid., 69.
32. Ibid., 25.
33. Ibid., 179.
34. Ibid., 188.
35. Ibid., 179. Felman argues that "to testify is to engage, precisely, in the process of re-finding one's own proper name, one's signature" ("Education and Crisis," 53).

Even though the biblical text focuses less on Tamar's experience after the rape than on her male relatives' responses to this tragic event, there are several instances in the text that point to Tamar's resistance during and after the terrifying ordeal. I argue that these hints of resistance are important for the ensuing process of recovery that, one hopes, followed Tamar's rape.[36]

3.2.1. Tamar's Resistance during the Rape

A clear link between resistance and the recovery process has been shown to exist. In this regard, Herman argues that "the women who remained calm, used many active strategies, and fought to the best of their abilities were not only more likely to be successful in thwarting the rape attempt but also less likely to suffer severe distress symptoms even if their efforts ultimately failed."[37]

When her brother seeks to force himself upon her, Tamar responds by saying no four times:

> She answered him, "No, my brother, do not force me; for such a thing is not done in Israel; do not do anything so vile! As for me, where could I carry my shame? And as for you, you would be as one of the scoundrels in Israel. Now therefore, I beg you, speak to the king; for he will not withhold me from you." (2 Sam 13:12–13)

Within Tamar's response we see how she in the first instance uses the language "my brother" so as to try and reason with Amnon, reminding him that his intended sexual deed would be considered incest. She then proceeds to name the trauma when she uses the technical term for rape ('al ta'annēnî) in order to describe her impending violation. Next, she continues the act of narrativizing the traumatic occurrence when she makes a moral judgment on Amnon's intended action, calling it "foolish" or "senseless" (nəbālâ), moreover saying that such a thing is considered shameful in Israel. Tamar further begs Amnon to consider the effects that this violent deed will have on her (13:13: "Where would I carry my shame?") and also

---

36. Trible, "Tamar," 45; Cooper-White, *The Cry of Tamar*, 13.

37. Herman, *Trauma and Recovery*, 59. Herman notes that "women who were immobilized by terror and submitted without a struggle were more likely not only to be raped but also to be highly self-critical and depressed in the aftermath."

upon him as the perpetrator. Echoing the term "folly" she used earlier to describe the act of rape, Tamar warns Amnon that he will become one of the fools (hannəbālîm) in Israel. According to Yamada, Tamar is seeking to resist Amnon's abusive act by means of a shaming speech, by naming the shameful act for what it is: "folly" (nəbālâ).[38] When all of this fails, Tamar proposes a pragmatic solution, seeking the blessing of their father that would enable both parties to save face. One could make sense of Tamar's action by considering Herman's point that many rape victims attempt "to appeal to the humanity of the rapist or to establish some form of empathetic connection with him." However, as Herman notes: "These efforts were almost universally futile."[39]

Even though Tamar's resistance indeed proves to be futile—Amnon proceeds in the next verses to rape her violently, then send her away in shame—we do see in her resistance aspects of what has been described as a vital part of the recovery process. In contrast to the other rape narratives in the Hebrew Bible (e.g., the story of the Levite's concubine in Judg 19 and Dinah in Gen 34), Tamar has a voice, and she uses it. According to Fokkelien van Dijk-Hemmes, Tamar in her resistance comes across as exceedingly strong. Van Dijk-Hemmes argues: "Determined to save her honour, she unmasks the true meaning of Amnon's action and reveals his true form: as one of the 'shameful' fools in Israel."[40] In this regard, Müllner proposes that the narrator actually places Israel's ethics, a sense of what is right and what is wrong, in Tamar's mouth.[41]

Immediately after the rape, Tamar's resistance continues when she begs Amnon not to send her away, once again finding the words to name his atrocious treatment of her.[42] In 13:16 she calls Amnon's intention of sending her away a "wrong" (rā'â), which one could translate in stronger terms as "evil"—even greater than Amnon's act of sexual violence against her.[43]

---

38. Yamada, Configurations of Rape, 115–17.

39. Herman, Trauma and Recovery, 59.

40. Fokkelien van Dijk-Hemmes, "Tamar and the Limits of Patriarchy: Between Rape and Seduction (2 Samuel 13 and Genesis 38)," in Anti-covenant: Counter-reading of Women's Lives in the Hebrew Bible, ed. Mieke Bal, JSOTSup 81 (Sheffield: Almond, 1989), 145.

41. Müllner, Gewalt im Hause Davids, 343.

42. Trible, "Tamar," 47.

43. Yamada, Configurations of Rape, 120. In her appeal to Amnon, Tamar is using legal language in an attempt to prohibit Amnon from sending her away. According to

We thus see how Tamar, in the midst of the traumatic experience of being raped, resists the violence to which she has been subjected. I propose that we see in Tamar's resistance, the first signs of recovery: an attempt to find words to narrate the traumatic occurrence and to engage in an act of interpretation that offers a moral judgment of the deed of sexual violation. One would hope that Tamar continued this process of naming and interpreting the traumatic events as she left Amnon's living quarters and found a refuge in the house of Absalom.

3.2.2. Lament and Resistance after the Rape

In the aftermath of the rape, Tamar's vivid display of mourning regarding the trauma just experienced can be understood in terms of Herman's second stage of the recovery process: "But Tamar put ashes on her head, and tore the long robe that she was wearing; she put her hand on her head, and went away, crying aloud as she went" (2 Sam 13:19).

All these actions performed by Tamar may be considered classic mourning rituals, and the elaborate description of her mourning highlights the intensity and duration of her anguish.[44] The loud weeping and crying at the top of her voice, as suggested by the root *zʿq*, belongs to the vocabulary of lament.[45] Even though we do not hear the content of Tamar's lament, the act of tearing her robe makes visible the violence to which she has been subjected. By means of this symbolic action, Amnon's violation of Tamar is brought into the open. Moreover, according to Bail, *zʿq* is typically used in the context of the judiciary, constituting the basic cry of those who find themselves without justice. In German this link between lament and judgment is expressed well with the words "Klage" and "Anklage."[46]

---

the law in Deut 22:28–29, an Israelite male who had sex with an unmarried woman was now married to her, responsible for her well-being, and could not divorce her.

44. Brenner, "A Double-Date," 141. See also Yamada, *Configurations of Rape*, 121–22. Flora Keshgegian writes about the importance of lament to give "people a framework for naming their experience as trauma" (*Time for Hope: Practices for Living in Today's World* [New York: Continuum, 2006], 104).

45. Bail, *Gegen das Schweigen Klagen*, 147. See also my work on the mourning or wailing women in Jer 9 (L. Juliana M. Claassens, "Calling the Keeners: The Image of the Wailing Woman as Symbol of Survival in a Traumatized World," *JFSR* 26 [2010]: 63–78; and Claassens, *Mourner, Mother, Midwife: Reimagining God's Liberating Presence* [Louisville: Westminster John Knox, 2012], 18–30).

46. Bail, *Gegen das Schweigen Klagen*, 147.

Tamar's lament thus serves as a public indictment against the injustice of Amnon's behavior.

We are told in 13:20 that Tamar's lament is heard by Absalom. Absalom thus serves as a witness to Tamar's trauma. However, his act of silencing her stands in sharp contrast to what Herman would say are the core tasks of the second stage of the recovery process: remembering the traumatic event and mourning its losses.[47] In an attempt to discover how the text breaks through Absalom's silencing of Tamar in order to give Tamar a voice, Bail imagines the lament psalms as an interpretative context for Tamar's lament.[48] Bail argues that, for instance, Ps 6 on a literary level can represent Tamar's lament. In an imaginative act of reading, she suggests that one could include the trauma of sexual violence in the situation of disease and injustice evoking the lament in this psalm.[49] In this regard, Bail offers that lament is an act of resistance that gives to the one who suffers the dignity of speech.[50] Moreover, one could argue that underlying the lament in Ps 6 is the presumption that God hears the lament of the one who calls upon God, an act that further serves to counter the perpetrator's attempts of silencing the victim.

According to Bail, in the context of the lament psalms, and specifically in the words of Ps 6, one finds that Tamar receives a voice, continuing the process of mourning already started in the biblical text itself.[51] So one indeed sees in Ps 6 a vivid description of the victim mourning a traumatic occurrence, which, as has been shown above, forms a necessary aspect of the recovery process: "I am weary with my moaning; every night I flood

---

47. Bail (ibid., 157) writes that the final act of violence is by Absalom, who banishes Tamar into the "sprachliche Nichts" (linguistic nothingness).

48. According to Bail (ibid., 24), lament has the function of bringing violence into speech. In the Old Testament, the lament psalms attest to the social, physical, and psychological well-being of the individual being disturbed.

49. Bail (ibid., 159) imagines a heading for Ps 6 that can be translated as: "a lament of Tamar, who was violated in body and speech, to speak against the silence."

50. Bail writes that the cry of those in need is the most elementary form of resistance which stands at the heart of what it means to be human (*Gegen das Schweigen Klagen*, 49, 59–61). See also Claus Westermann, "The Role of the Lament in the Theology of the Old Testament," *Int* 28 (1974): 31.

51. See also Brenner ("A Double-Date," 141), who imagines Tamar sitting in Absalom's compound mourning her virginity, her life, and the loss of her sense of family and protection.

my bed with tears; I drench my couch with my weeping. My eyes waste away because of grief; they grow weak because of all my foes" (Ps 6:6–7).

Bail's imaginative reading makes it possible to contemplate life beyond trauma, a process of mourning and resistance that may lead to the vital third stage of the recovery process: once again reconnecting with every-day life.

3.3. Reconnection

The third and final task of the recovery process is for the victim to reestab-lish connections with the wider community. Judith Herman describes this part of the recovery process as follow:

> Having come to terms with the traumatic past, the survivor faces the task of creating a future. She has mourned the old self that the trauma had destroyed; now she must develop a new self. Her relationships have been tested and forever changed by the trauma; now she must develop new relationships. The old beliefs that gave meaning to her life have been challenged; now she must find a new sustaining faith.[52]

In terms of Tamar's story, there is no way of knowing whether she ever did reach this stage of the recovery process. Adrien Bledstein's creative inter-pretation of the text, which imagines Tamar as writing stories, poetry, and prayers for healing, expresses such hope for recovery when she writes that she would "like to imagine that Tamar ... came to understand her trauma and to use her gifts to benefit all Israel."[53]

Bledstein's imaginative reading sounds a lot like what Herman would say regarding the recovery process: "While there is no way to compensate for an atrocity, there is a way to transcend it, by making it a gift to others."[54] Thus Herman argues that the rape survivors who "recover most success-fully are those who discover some meaning in their experience that tran-scends the limits of personal tragedy."[55]

---

52. Herman, *Trauma and Recovery*, 196.

53. Adrien Janis Bledstein, "Tamar and the 'Coat of Many Colors,'" in *Samuel and Kings*, ed. Athalya Brenner, FCB 2/7 (Sheffield: Sheffield Academic, 2000), 82.

54. Herman, *Trauma and Recovery*, 207.

55. Herman writes regarding the women who were active in the antirape move-ment as a means of transcending the suffering: "In refusing to hide or to be silenced, in

Moreover, Herman notes that "in the third stage of recovery, as the survivor comes to terms with the trauma in her own life, she may also become more open to new forms of engagement with children.... If she does not have children, she may begin to take a new and broader interest in young people. She may even wish for the first time to bring children in the world."[56]

Most interpreters assume that Tamar would not have had children, even though this is something that lies beyond the scope in the narrative.[57] However, the reference to Absalom naming his daughter Tamar, who like her aunt is said to be beautiful, is a significant connection to the wider community and attests to the reestablishment of life-giving connections that is so important for recovery.[58] Herman's citation of the testimony of a Vietnam veteran describing the feeling of seeing his combat buddy holding his newborn son at his baptism voices the significance of such newfound connections: "In the middle of the ritual, I was overcome with a sense of ... winning!"[59]

4. TAMAR AS SURVIVOR

This essay read Tamar's story from the dual perspective captured in the title of Judith Herman's work, *Trauma and Recovery*. On the one hand, it is important to focus on the trauma aspect of Tamar's tragic narrative. As Herman writes about the significance of remembering the trauma experienced by victims of the Vietnam War: "These veterans refused to be forgotten. Moreover, they refused to be stigmatized. They insisted upon the rightness, the dignity of their distress."[60] To narrativize the trauma of rape as does Tamar's story could conceivably play an important role in raising awareness regarding the reality of rape that persists to this day, making it possible, as Herman notes, "for women to overcome the barriers of denial, secrecy, and shame that has prevented them from naming their injuries."[61]

---

insisting that rape is a public matter, and in demanding social change, survivors create their own living monument" (*Trauma and Recovery*, 73).

56. Ibid., 206–7.

57. Cooper-White, *The Cry of Tamar*, 8–9.

58. See also Trible's suggestion that in his daughter "Absalom has created a living memorial for his sister" ("Tamar," 55).

59. Herman, *Trauma and Recovery*, 207.

60. Ibid., 27.

61. Ibid., 28–29.

At the same time, this essay has argued that it is important also to consider Tamar's recovery from the traumatic experience of being raped by her half-brother. To retell Tamar's story from the victim's perspective with a focus on survival and recovery is an act of resistance in itself. To imagine Tamar's recovery is to give her agency, to contemplate her mourning the tragic events, and to interrupt the process of victimization and erasure of the subject started in the biblical account.

No reading can undo the violence perpetrated against Tamar nor the hundreds of thousands of men, women, and children who have experienced the pain and humiliation of sexual violence on a regular basis. However, the act of reading Tamar's story in terms of its honest portrayal of her trauma as well as her potential recovery affirms her narrative as a living monument, raising awareness and challenging readers then and now to resist (sexual) violence.

BIBLIOGRAPHY

Alexander, Jeffrey C. *Trauma: A Social Theory*. Cambridge: Polity, 2012.

Bail, Ulrike. *Gegen das Schweigen Klagen: Eine Intertextuelle Studie zu den Klagepsalmen Ps 6 und Ps 55 und der Erzählung von der Verwaltigung Tamars*. Gütersloh: Gütersloher Verlagshaus, 1998.

Becker, Eve-Marie, Jan Dochhorn, and Else K. Holt, eds. *Trauma and Traumatization in Individual and Collective Dimensions: Insights from Biblical Studies and Beyond*. SANt 2. Vandenhoeck & Ruprecht, Göttingen, 2014.

Bledstein, Adrien Janis. "Tamar and the 'Coat of Many Colors.'" Pages 65–83 in *Samuel and Kings*. Edited by Athalya Brenner. FCB 2/7. Sheffield: Sheffield Academic, 2000.

Brenner, Athalya. *I Am: Biblical Women Tell Their Own Stories*. Minneapolis: Fortress: 2004.

Caruth, Cathy. "Trauma and Experience: Introduction." Pages 3–12 in *Trauma: Explorations in Memory*. Edited by Cathy Caruth. Baltimore: Johns Hopkins University Press, 1995.

———. *Unclaimed Experience: Trauma, Narrative, and History*. Baltimore: Johns Hopkins University Press, 1996.

Claassens, L. Juliana M. "Calling the Keeners: The Image of the Wailing Woman as Symbol of Survival in a Traumatized World." *JFSR* 26 (2010): 63–78.

————. *Claiming Her Dignity: Female Resistance in the Old Testament*. Collegeville, MN: Liturgical Press, 2016.

————. *Mourner, Mother, Midwife: Reimagining God's Liberating Presence*. Louisville: Westminster John Knox, 2012.

Cooper-White, Pamela. *The Cry of Tamar: Violence against Women and the Church's Response*. Minneapolis: Fortress, 1995.

Dijk-Hemmes, Fokkelien van. "Tamar and the Limits of Patriarchy: Between Rape and Seduction (2 Samuel 13 and Genesis 38)." Pages 135–56 in *Anti-covenant: Counter-reading of Women's Lives in the Hebrew Bible*. Edited by Mieke Bal. JSOTSup 81. Sheffield: Almond, 1989.

Erikson, Kai. "Notes on Trauma and Community." Pages 183–99 in *Trauma: Explorations in Memory*. Edited by Cathy Caruth. Baltimore: Johns Hopkins University Press, 1995.

Felman, Shoshana. "Education and Crisis: Or, the Vicissitudes of Teaching." Pages 13–60 in *Trauma: Explorations in Memory*. Edited by Cathy Caruth. Baltimore: Johns Hopkins University Press, 1995.

Herman, Judith. *Trauma and Recovery: The Aftermath of Violence—From Domestic Abuse to Political Terror*. Rev. ed. New York: Basic Books, 1997.

Kauffman, Jeffrey, ed. *Loss of the Assumptive World: A Theory of Traumatic Loss*. New York: Brunner-Routledge, 2002.

Keefe, Alice A. "Rapes of Women/Wars of Men." *Semeia* 61 (1993): 79–97.

Keshgegian, Flora. *Time for Hope: Practices for Living in Today's World*. New York: Continuum, 2006.

Müllner, Ilse. *Gewalt im Hause Davids: Die Erzählung von Tamar und Amnon (2 Sam 13, 1–22)*. Freiburg: Herder, 1997.

O'Connor, Kathleen M. *Jeremiah: Pain and Promise*. Minneapolis: Fortress, 2011.

Smith-Christopher, Daniel L. *A Biblical Theology of Exile*. OBT. Minneapolis: Fortress, 2002.

Trible, Phyllis. *Texts of Terror: Literary-Feminist Readings of Biblical Narratives*. OBT 13. Philadelphia: Fortress, 1984.

Westermann, Claus. "The Role of the Lament in the Theology of the Old Testament." *Int* 28 (1974): 20–38.

Yamada, Frank M. *Configurations of Rape in the Hebrew Bible: A Literary Analysis of Three Rape Narratives*. StBibLit 109. New York: Lang, 2009.

Reading Biblical Texts through the Lens of Resilience

Robert J. Schreiter

Reading scriptural texts through the lens of trauma studies is proving to be an exciting development in biblical studies and the study of other ancient Mediterranean and Near Eastern texts. The first forays into *theological* texts through the lens of trauma are promising as well, although this lens would seem, at least at this point, not to provide the far-reaching consequences that it may well have in biblical studies.[1] I come to this literature in biblical studies not as an expert in that field but as a systematic theologian who has become interested in trauma studies, especially as it plays itself out in post-conflict situations in international peace-building. In the development of my work in this area, I have become especially interested in *resilience*, or the capacity to live under and respond to oppressive or violent situations over longer periods of time. Resilience is related to, but stands somewhat over against, *resistance*, or the capacity to withstand onslaughts of violence or oppression. Resistance in its different forms has been explored in socio-logical and anthropological studies such as James C. Scott's well-known *Weapons of the Weak* and is a prominent category in postcolonial writing.[2] In the course of its use over the last decades, resistance sometimes has become romanticized, for example, in the popular European imagination in countries such as France or the Netherlands, where at one point the majority of the population had been viewed as part of the resistance

---

1. I am thinking here of studies of postbiblical texts as found in collections such as Eve-Marie Becker, Jan Dochhorn, and Else Holt, eds., *Trauma and Traumatization in Individual and Collective Dimensions: Insights from Biblical Studies and Beyond*, SANt 2 (Göttingen: Vandenhoeck & Ruprecht, 2014).

2. James C. Scott, *Weapons of the Weak: Everyday Forms of Peasant Resistance* (New Haven: Yale University Press, 1985).

against Fascism in World War II. More careful recent research has now shown that only a small part of those populations was actually involved in the struggle against the Nazis.

Resilience is only now coming to the fore as an important category in other fields beyond psychology, health studies, the humanities, and the social sciences. It is appearing in biology and in environmental studies, as researchers anxiously explore issues around maintaining biodiversity in the midst of climate change.

The term *resilience* does occur in the study of trauma in the biblical texts, although generally in passing. Such is the case in a work on trauma and Jeremiah by Kathleen O'Connor. There she speaks of the book of Jeremiah as "a work of resilience, a book of massive theological imagination, and a kind of survival manual for a destroyed society."[3] David Carr entitles his study of the formation of the Hebrew and (to some extent) Christian Bible as *Holy Resilience*. He does not go extensively into the dimensions of resilience but does focus on important aspects of resilience, such as integrating catastrophe into one's foundational narrative and the "resilient power" bestowed by certain concepts such as chosenness.[4] That it has not been examined more closely in biblical studies to this point is not surprising. Even in the psychological and psychiatric literature on trauma, the meaning of resilience is taken for granted as the capacity to "bounce back" after disaster. Such is the case in a recent book on post-traumatic stress disorder (PTSD) by one of the foremost researchers into traumatic stress, the psychiatrist Bessel van der Kolk.[5]

My interest in resilience revolves around how people come to identify their sources of strength that allow them to maintain their humanity in the midst of harrowing disaster or long-term oppression, what practices get them in touch with their resilient power, and how resilience might be strengthened or enhanced. It has arisen out of my work in helping societies rebuild after armed conflict.

Recently a book by the Austrian social ethicist and theologian Clemens Sedmak addressed these questions from the points of view of philoso-

---

3. Kathleen O'Connor, *Jeremiah: Pain and Promise* (Minneapolis: Fortress, 2011), x.

4. David Carr, *Holy Resilience: The Bible's Traumatic Origins* (New Haven: Yale University Press, 2014), 122.

5. Bessel van der Kolk, *The Body Keeps the Score: Brain, Mind and Body in the Healing of Trauma* (New York: Penguin Books, 2015).

phy, the humanities, and theology. Entitled *Innerlichkeit und Kraft: Studie über epistemische Resilienz* (*Interiority and Strength: A Study of Epistemic Resilience*) the book addresses principally the development of individual, rather than collective or social, resilience.[6] Moreover, Sedmak focuses especially, but not exclusively, on the cognitive (or, as he likes to call them, *epistemic*) dimensions. Nonetheless, this study represents an important resource for studying resilience as a significant dimension of how people are able to recover from traumatic experiences and build the capacity to engage such experiences when they recur in the future.

As a way of making a small contribution to the use of the literature on trauma to study biblical texts and to expand the use of it for theology in a wider sense, I would like to examine resilience more closely, by exploring here three of its aspects: what resilience is, how it is achieved, and how to live from it. In doing this, I draw upon what I have learned from biblical scholars in their use of trauma literature in the study of biblical texts and the work of Sedmak and others. I conclude with some suggestions of the impact trauma studies can have on some questions in Christian theology.

What Is Resilience?

For providing a theoretical description of resilience, I turn here to Sedmak's work. Sedmak is writing in German and discovered, as I did some years ago, that there is no exact German equivalent for the English word *resilience*. He uses the loanword *Resilienz* and another formulation of his own making (as far as I can tell): *Widerstandskraft*, which may be translated roughly as "capacity to resist." The latter formulation points out that resilience is related to resistance but is yet something different: resilience tries to formulate the *capacities* that make resistance possible and help to sustain it. Sedmak's understanding of resilience highlights the power of interiority that builds the capacity to withstand adversities (*Widrigkeiten*) and to engage them.[7] He goes on to review the psychological literature and notes three convergences there in the developing study of resilience: (1) resilience is more a process that brings diverse systems in the context into interaction with one another than a discrete characteristic or attribute; (2) resilience is something that can be learned and taught; key to

---

6. Clemens Sedmak, *Innerlichkeit und Kraft: Studie über epistemische Resilienz* (Freiburg: Herder, 2013).

7. Ibid., 7.

this is strengthening a sense of agency; and (3) resilience is built through a combination of psychological, social, cultural, spiritual, and contextual factors. In other words, resilience is a complex process rather than a static condition.[8]

For Sedmak, resilience is anchored in an interiority that is marked by a strong sense of identity and a confidence in one's agency. The building blocks for both identity and agency include an affirmation of meaning, a sense of being in control, and a strong sense of the direction in which one is moving. When these are in place, the result is a sense of (meaningful) community or connectedness, personal and social agency, and goal-directedness.[9] Put into the language of the psychological literature of trauma, resilience can disengage victims from the sense of isolation that comes with trauma, overcome the paralysis of action that usually accompanies trauma, and restore a sense of a meaningful future in the face of feeling completely under the power of past trauma.

David Janzen ably summarizes the "trauma literature" that examines what trauma does to human experience in *The Violent Gift*. There he shows how language becomes unmoored from experience and loses its capacity to give form and meaning to experience, how past and present become disconnected, how temporality itself is suppressed, and how the loss of capacity to place traumatic experience in a framework of causality and ethics destroys the capacity for making meaning.[10] This summary indicates what has to be done in the healing of trauma: language has to be recovered as a vehicle for processing experience, the tyranny of past events that freezes us in an unending past and that blocks out the present and the future must be overcome, and a sense of meaning and a framework for right behavior must be restored.

Biblical texts in which the undoing of trauma and evidence of resilience can be found are, among other places, in Lamentations and in the psalms of lament. Especially in the latter, the texts begin with a cry of abandonment, followed by a recitation of the isolation, the desolation,

---

8. Ibid., 21–22.

9. Ibid., 31–32.

10. David Janzen, *The Violent Gift: Trauma's Subversion of the Deuteronomic History's Narrative*, LHBOTS 561 (New York: T&T Clark, 2012), 44. The English-language biblical studies using trauma literature draw especially upon Anglophone literature on the topic. For a biblical study that draws also upon the German-language literature, see Ruth Poser, *Das Ezechielbuch als Trauma-Literatur*, VTSup 154 (Leiden: Brill, 2012).

and the abandonment that goes beyond the psalmist's capacity to give them expression:

> My God, my God, why have you forsaken me,
> Why are you so far from helping me, from the words of my groaning?
> O my God, I cry by day, but you do not answer, and by night, but find
> no rest. ...
> I am poured out like water, and all my bones are out of joint;
> my heart is like wax; it is melted within my breast;
> my mouth is dried up like a potsherd, and my tongue sticks to my jaws;
> you lay me in the dust of death.
> For dogs are all around me; a company of evildoers encircles me.
> My hands and feet have shriveled; I can count all my bones.
> They stare and gloat over me. (Ps 22:1–2, 14–17)[11]

This well-known text conveys the sense of isolation, and it struggles with words to express the consequences of feeling abandoned.

Other texts show resilience, such as Jeremiah's letter to those in exile in Babylon:

> Thus says the LORD of hosts, the God of Israel, to all the exiles whom I have sent into exile from Jerusalem to Babylon: Build houses and live in them; plant gardens and eat what they produce. Take wives and have sons and daughters; take wives for your sons and give your daughters in marriage, that they may bear sons and daughters; multiply there and do not decrease. (Jer 29:4–6)

The injunctions given here show the opposite of a feeling of abandonment, a loss for words to express the isolation, and a lack of any orientation to the future. Building houses suggests permanency, as does cultivating a garden. Marrying, having children, and seeing that the children marry indicate a future orientation rather than remaining frozen in an exilic present.[12]

---

11. Translations of biblical texts are taken from the NRSV.

12. Sedmak actually uses this passage as a sign of resilience (*Innerlichkeit und Kraft*, 32).

Resilience: How to Get There

When trauma strikes, the first order of business is to overcome the paralyzing effects of trauma. The studies that I have read that explore the Bible as trauma literature explore how the texts are a witness to struggling with trauma *in medias res*. I have found this most illuminating as a way of reading those texts. Even though the use of contemporary literature on trauma is a cultural and historical transposition of late twentieth- and early twenty-first-century research onto a different time and place, what students of the Bible have done with the recent trauma literature is, I believe, warranted. Cross-cultural studies of trauma in our contemporary setting suggest that the symptoms of trauma (the experience of fragmentation and isolation, the loss of agency, the inadequacy of language to express the pain, the burden of a past that negates the present and blots out hope for the future, the sense of meaninglessness) vary little across cultural boundaries. Likewise, the condition of having been healed from trauma (a renewed sense of agency, meaning, purpose, and community) seems to be fairly invariant. What is more culture-specific are the *means* that help move populations from a traumatized state to a post-traumatic one.[13]

So what I am looking at here in terms of reading the Bible through the lens of trauma is not a negation of what has been developed in the literature on trauma and the Bible thus far. This brief study is, rather, intended to explore one aspect of the whole phenomenon of trauma and the treatment of trauma: the place and role of resilience in approaching the Bible and questions in Christian theology. From the point of view of method, what is presented here is intended to extend or complement the work on trauma and the Bible done thus far. In terms of method, this work differs somewhat from what has been done to date, which, as far as I am able to tell from my reading in the area of study of the Bible and trauma, has been built on individual authors' summaries of their own research into the trauma literature. What I present here relies upon Sedmak's effort to synthesize the literature on trauma into a coherent framework that empha-

---

13. The Turkish Cypriot psychoanalyst Vamik Volkan has done some of the most extensive work in this area across a wide variety of cultures. See, for example, Vamik Volkan, *Enemies on the Couch: A Psychopolitical Journey through War and Peace* (Durham, NC: Pitchstone Books, 2013). This assertion also comes out of my own experience working among traumatized people in places as different as Croatia, South Sudan, Sri Lanka, the Philippines, and Colombia.

sizes the cognitive or epistemic dimensions that make for a resilient capacity as they are developed within individuals. I now outline that task. In the next section, when I explore the way resilience is enacted, the features arising from resilience will come to the fore.

Sedmak sees resilience as an enhanced sense of identity and agency, built up by a cultivation of interiority, that is, those inner capacities that give us direction or orientation, enhance our capacity to act, and provide frameworks of causality and ethical action. In trauma we are cut off from these inner capacities. He speaks here of vulnerability (*Verwundbarkeit*). As he understands it, vulnerability is an openness that makes us susceptible to grace and to assistance. He sees this as different from resistance, which projects a certain invulnerability.[14] A word of caution needs to be given here. Obviously, trauma is a form of woundedness, and the vulnerability of which Sedmak speaks is not intended to be understood as a naïve standing in the way of trouble. The vulnerability of which he speaks is a preparedness to deal with wounds as they come to us. It might be understood as a predisposition to have some of the means necessary to address the wounds of trauma when they occur. Such vulnerability is not some automatic antidote to the toxins that trauma releases in the body, whether for individuals, groups, or the body politic. Rather, it is a kind of preparedness to engage trauma so as not to be a sheer victim of it, in order to become (in the language of Judith Herman and others) a *survivor* and not remain a victim.[15]

Sedmak frames this cultivation of interiority epistemically with three activities: thinking, remembering, and believing. Thinking is understood here as work of the imagination that allows us to develop alternative possibilities, to take cognitive distance from what has occurred, to put things in context, to consider what is essential and what is peripheral, to give order to things, and to reframe the current situation. It is at once a cognitive and a therapeutic kind of action.[16]

Biblical examples of such imaginative thinking can be found in the visions of a different kind of future in the prophetic literature. Two of the best-known examples would be Isa 11:6–9, the vision of the peaceable kingdom, and Ezek 37:1–14, the vision of the dry bones. In each of

---

14. Sedmak, *Innerlichkeit und Kraft*, 156.

15. Judith Herman, *Trauma and Recovery: The Aftermath of Violence—From Domestic Abuse to Political Terror*, rev. ed. (New York: Basic Books, 1997).

16. Sedmak, *Innerlichkeit und Kraft*, 240.

visions the prophet goes beyond what looks to be the case now and imagines something different in the future. This move from the present into the future is most explicit in the Ezekiel passage, where the prophet is bidden by YHWH to so prophesy (Ezek 37:4).

Second, Sedmak notes the importance of remembering. Memory is not an archive of the past; it is rather our relationship with the past from the vantage point of the present. Memory is the basis for identity. Indeed, as Sedmak puts it, memory forms the bridge between the interior of a person and the social reality in which the person is situated, the construction of an intangible infrastructure that holds together the commonweal.[17] Memory provides a "sacramental" view of the world; that is, it endows the present, visible world with a deeper meaning, as the signs in the present point to a "deep grammar" at the basis of reality.

Biblical scholars interested in trauma have explored in detail the role of memory in trauma, using especially the work on cultural memory of Jan Assmann and the theory of cultural trauma of Jeffrey Alexander.[18] In the theories of both of these scholars, one an Egyptologist and the other a sociologist, the tasks of creating coherence and developing narrativity are central. Coherence is important because traumatic memory is often fragmented and therefore undigested. It then becomes an obstacle to identity until it can be absorbed into a coherent network of memory. That network is most commonly framed in narrative. Sedmak speaks of this as "anamnestic resilience," where a trauma that has been assimilated into a narrative results in the subject becoming able to domesticate that traumatic memory by putting it into a chain of causality and meaning.[19] The Bible is replete with narratives that recount what God has done for Israel's ancestors. Here one thinks of Deut 26:5–9, the formula for remembering what God has done for Israel, from the call of Abraham through deliverance from Egypt and entry into the promised land. Similarly, Ps 126, a history performed as a litany in gratitude for God's everlasting mercy, is intended to be recited together by the people to strengthen collective remembrance.

---

17. Ibid., 271.

18. Jan Assmann, *Religion and Cultural Memory*, trans. Rodney Livingstone (Stanford, CA: Stanford University Press, 2006); Jeffrey Alexander, *Trauma: A Social Theory* (Cambridge: Polity, 2012).

19. Sedmak, *Innerlichkeit und Kraft*, 266.

The third element going into the interiority that leads to resilience is believing. To believe is to take the risk of affirming and depending upon an "other." It bespeaks the trust that is at the basis of human interdependence and community. Trust also represents the flowering of the vulnerability of which Sedmak speaks. Trust is an openness that acknowledges our finitude and expresses itself in gratitude for the dependability that only God provides. In the psalms of lament mentioned earlier, the complaint and lament of the psalmist are interlaced or at times "turned" by an affirmation of trust in God and praise of God for God's faithfulness to those who are in distress:

> Yet you are holy, enthroned on the praises of Israel.
> In you our ancestors trusted, and you delivered them.
> To you they cried, and were saved;
> in you they trusted, and they were not put to shame. (Ps 22:3–5)

Indeed, such "turning," which resolves or concludes some of the psalms of lament, makes these psalms an exercise in building resilience, since they take those who recite the psalm through the full trajectory from the isolation and fragmentation caused by trauma, through the struggle to find words to express the feeling of woundedness, to a renewed trust in God and hope for a better future:

> Posterity will serve him,
> future generations will be told about the Lord,
> and proclaim his deliverance to a people yet unborn,
> saying that he has done it. (Ps 22:30–31)

Living from Resilience

I turn to my third point: how to live from resilience, or how resilience manifests itself. Resilience shows itself in a "performative" act of identity affirmation; in other words, by the act of affirming, identity is not only recognized but enhanced further. It is evident in three ways, which are often related to one another.

It manifests itself first of all by focusing upon narratives of the group from the group's distant past that witness to its founding and having overcome adversity in those ancient times, as well as in subsequent encounters with trauma-inducing events. David Carr notes how focusing on these stories allows current trauma to be integrated into a group's narrative. He cites Isa 51 as an example:

> Listen to me, you that pursue righteousness,
> you that seek the LORD.
> Look to the rock from which you were hewn,
> and to the quarry from which you were dug.
> Look to Abraham your father,
> and to Sarah who bore you;
> for he was but one when I called him,
> but I blessed him and made him many. (Isa 51:1–2)[20]

Second, out of these narratives, concepts are elicited that express distinctive characteristics of the resilient identity of the group. Carr notes chosenness as one such resilient characteristic; O'Connor notes recurrent themes in Jeremiah's characterization of Israel's identity: the temple, the covenants, and the Sabbath.[21] One might include also the role of promise in the trauma literature of the Bible. These themes constitute nodes in the network of meaning that connect the strings of narration of a people's past and present and how they continue to interconnect with one another.

Third, the founding narratives are recounted in a ritual context. Ritual is important in dealing with trauma in two distinctive ways. First of all, engaging in ritual is a setting off from routine or day-to-day time and space, denoting that what is being dealt with cannot be treated effectively with normal, mundane activity. Thus, throughout the Hebrew Scriptures any attempt to address God is done in a ritual rather than a casual manner. Second, within the special spatiotemporal setting, ritual allows us to move through time in a different way; most notably, ritual makes possible moving backward in time to an earlier moment.[22] Certainly a most striking ritual enactment is Ezra's reading of the "rediscovered" Torah scroll to the people in Neh 8.[23]

---

20. Carr, *Holy Resilience*, 92.

21. O'Connor, *Jeremiah*, 93.

22. Robert J. Schreiter, "The Catholic Social Imaginary and Peacebuilding: Ritual, Sacrament, and Spirituality," in *Peacebuilding: Catholic Theology, Ethics, and Praxis*, ed. Robert Schreiter, R. Scott Appleby, and Gerard F. Powers (Maryknoll, NY: Orbis, 2010), 221–39.

23. See Carr, *Holy Resilience*, 98.

Such practices are evident still in our contemporary situation. A student of mine some years ago explored the resilience of the Parkari Kholi people, a small tribe of Hindus who live as indentured servants to their Muslim feudal overlords in Pakistan. There the ritual enactment is the wedding ceremony, which takes a week to perform. During the week, the entire history of the Parkari Kholi is recounted, with episodes of their overcoming adversity in the past receiving special emphasis.[24] In 2012, the Sikh community in the suburb of Oak Creek in Milwaukee County, Wisconsin, suffered the murder of six of their members in their temple by a deranged (non-Sikh) assailant. To recover from this, they read their entire Scripture, the Guru Granth Sahib, aloud, a process that takes forty-eight hours to complete. Their story is replete with persecution and overcoming adversity in the past.

The ritual of the readings that form part of the Roman Catholic (and other) celebrations of the Easter vigil falls into this performative tradition of resilience. The first reading in the cycle, taken from the first account of creation in the book of Genesis, is a Priestly account written after the exile, in which creation happens in a measured, stately procession of deeds, built over the "formless void" that holds the remains of slain figures from mythology of the ancient Near East. Such an orderly unfolding of "the beginning" bespeaks a new sense of meaning and purposefulness in postexilic Israel that is guaranteed by the utter sovereignty of God. The third reading is the hymn of Moses and the Israelites about how YHWH has rescued the Israelites from the hand of Pharaoh (Exod 15), certainly the defining act of rescue of Israel by God. The cycle of readings culminates in the proclamation of the resurrection. The readings can be construed as a response to the trauma of Christ's crucifixion. It begins with the orderliness of the Priestly account of creation and moves forward through history to the resurrection of Christ.

Conclusion: Some Consequences for Theology

The reading of the Scriptures through the lens of trauma has been instructive for me as a theologian and suggestive of how a number of theological issues might be revisited. Let me list briefly four of them.

---

24. Tomás King, "Resilience and Resistance as the Foundations of a Practical Theology for an Oppressed People" (DMin thesis project, Catholic Theological Union, 2008).

First of all, trauma theory can help us rethink the central soteriological claim of Christian faith, namely, that we are saved through the suffering, death, and resurrection of Jesus Christ. Why is our rescue through the death of Jesus so important to Christian faith? Salvation in the next life is important in the other two Abrahamic faiths, in Judaism and Islam, but in those traditions salvation comes about through righteous living, not the horrific death of some person. How central soteriology is to Christian faith comes out particularly when Christians engage in interreligious dialogue: Christians routinely think that such dialogues must begin with the soteriological question, something that would not be a starting point for other religious traditions. Does trauma theory help us understand how the early disciples of Jesus struggled to understand the meaning of Jesus's cruel death and integrate it into their memory of Jesus, as well as the rationale for their continuing together as a community?

Trauma theory can be utilized to refocus how that soteriological tradition took shape in the first decades of the Jesus movement. Scholars have detected in the New Testament writings three strands that developed to explain the death of Jesus on the cross.[25] One was that Jesus suffered the rejection (and death) that was the lot of so many of Israel's prophets. This helped the followers of Jesus situate the trauma of his humiliating death in the longer history of Israel, something alluded to in some of the speeches in the Acts of the Apostles (Acts 2:22–24; 5:30–31; 10:40). The second strand indicates that Jesus "had" to die (*dei*), as though it were in God's plan (see Mark 8:31; 9:12). The third strand, which comes to fruition in the Pauline corpus and the book of Hebrews, is that Jesus's death was a sacrifice that effected a cosmic reconciliation of all creation back to God (e.g., Col 1:19–20). The fact that these accounts of why Jesus died on the cross emerged more or less simultaneously suggests that they were varied attempts to deal with the traumatic memory of Jesus's death. They did this by linking it back to other traumas (persecution of the prophets, especially by religious authorities) and by finding a hidden meaning in God's action rather than simply the willful action of evil authorities. Finally, these accounts assigned the violent death of Jesus ultimate meaning by putting the story in a whole different key as a cosmic ritual by making it a sacrifice that brings all things back together in God. Trauma theory helps account

---

25. Edward Schillebeeckx, *Jesus: An Experiment in Christology*, trans. Hubert Hoskins (New York: Crossroad, 1979).

for these developments and suggests perhaps why the third strand—of cosmic ritual and reconciliation—came to be the predominant one. The theory's predominance arises from the fact that it embeds the crucifixion into the widest possible network of meaning—the mystery of the entire cosmos itself. What appears to be a cruel and violent act meant to terminate a flow of meaning becomes instead the key to ultimate meaning.

A second theme that the reading of Scriptures through the lens of trauma prompts is a rethinking of atonement theory and sacrifice. Contemporary Western attitudes toward the concept of sacrifice are deeply ambivalent, if not altogether negative. For some, sacrifice legitimates religious violence. For others, it legitimates the image of an angry God who demands the death of Jesus, thereby legitimating parental (more specifically, paternal) violence against children.

Sacrifice is an admittedly complex phenomenon. The Bible itself shows ambivalence about the efficacy of sacrifice (e.g., Hos 6:6). Yet sacrifice is, to my mind, essentially about attempts at communication between two unequal worlds: the human world and the divine world. Two sets of biblical texts that deal with aspects of trauma may provide some way forward here. The first are the Servant Songs of Second Isaiah. They explore one aspect of sacrifice that is troublesome to Westerners' sense of autonomy: how one person can take on the suffering of others. The second is the book of Hebrews, which was possibly written to a beleaguered community suffering persecution. Christ's sacrifice allows him to break through all the obstacles to direct communication with God.[26] The sacrifice is intended to offer consolation to a community that finds itself hedged in on all sides.

A third theme suggested by trauma theory might help us reconsider eschatological language, which has been dominated by a theology of hope since the 1960s. While there is much that is legitimate in such theologies, these theologies have not dealt well with the apocalyptic dimensions of Christian eschatological language, especially its violent character.[27]

---

26. Robert J. Schreiter, *In Water and in Blood: A Spirituality of Solidarity and Hope* (Maryknoll, NY: Orbis, 2006), 103–15.

27. Klaus Koch, *Ratlos vor der Apokalyptik* (Gütersloh: Mohn, 1970). A useful point of entry into considering the healing potential of violent language can be found in Christopher G. Frechette, "Destroying the Internalized Perpetrator: A Healing Function of the Violent Language against Enemies in the Psalms," in Becker, Dochhorn, and Holt, *Trauma and Traumatization*, 71–84.

Fourth and finally, trauma theory raises some cautions about a too-easy embrace of postmodernism as a suitable framework for theology. Graham Ward has asked whether we have come to the limits of postmodern thinking for theology.[28] At the conclusion of his work on resilience, Sedmak, as a social ethicist, asks whether nihilism might be lethal for the building and sustaining of resilience in a world beset with so much suffering.[29] Thinking backward from trauma theory to how to help communities recover from trauma and build their resilience within, in the face of future trauma, suggests that we perhaps should not have made so uncritical an embrace of the end of metanarratives.

In whatever manner theology may revisit these issues, I as a theologian am grateful for how biblical studies has been opening up for us the prospects that trauma studies may offer. This opening may help us rethink some important and at times vexing topics.

BIBLIOGRAPHY

Alexander, Jeffrey C. *Trauma: A Social Theory*. Cambridge: Polity, 2012.
Assmann, Jan. *Religion and Cultural Memory*. Translated by Rodney Livingstone. Stanford, CA: Stanford University Press, 2006.
Becker, Eve-Marie, Jan Dochhorn, and Else K. Holt, eds. *Trauma and Traumatization in Individual and Collective Dimensions: Insights from Biblical Studies and Beyond*. SANt 2. Göttingen: Vandenhoeck & Ruprecht, 2014.
Carr, David M. *Holy Resilience: The Bible's Traumatic Origins*. New Haven: Yale University Press, 2014.
Frechette, Christopher G. "Destroying the Internalized Perpetrator: A Healing Function of the Violent Language against Enemies in the Psalms." Pages 71–84 in *Trauma and Traumatization in Individual and Collective Dimensions: Insights from Biblical Studies and Beyond*. Edited by Eve-Marie Becker, Jan Dochhorn, and Else K. Holt. SANt 2. Göttingen: Vandenhoeck & Ruprecht, 2014.
Herman, Judith. *Trauma and Recovery: The Aftermath of Violence—From Domestic Abuse to Political Terror*. Rev. ed. New York: Basic Books, 1997.

---

28. Graham Ward, "Theology and Postmodernism: Is It Over?" *JAAR* 80 (2012): 466–84.
29. Sedmak, *Innerlichkeit und Kraft*, 361–72.

Janzen, David. *The Violent Gift: Trauma's Subversion of the Deuteronomistic History's Narrative.* LHBOTS 561. New York: T&T Clark, 2012.

King, Tomás. "Resilience and Resistance as the Foundations of a Practical Theology for an Oppressed People." DMin thesis project, Catholic Theological Union, 2008.

Koch, Klaus. *Ratlos vor der Apokalyptik.* Gütersloh: Mohn, 1970.

Kolk, Bessel van der. *The Body Keeps the Score: Brain, Mind, and Body in the Healing of Trauma.* New York: Penguin Books, 2015.

O'Connor, Kathleen M. *Jeremiah: Pain and Promise.* Minneapolis: Fortress, 2011.

Poser, Ruth. *Das Ezechielbuch als Trauma-Literatur.* VTSup 154. Leiden: Brill, 2012.

Schillebeeckx, Edward. *Jesus: An Experiment in Christology.* Translated by Hubert Hoskins. New York: Crossroad, 1979.

Schreiter, Robert J. "The Catholic Social Imaginary and Peacebuilding: Ritual, Sacrament, and Spirituality." Pages 221–39 in *Peacebuilding: Catholic Theology, Ethics, and Praxis.* Edited by Robert Schreiter, R. Scott Appleby, and Gerard F. Powers. Maryknoll, NY: Orbis, 2010.

———. *In Water and in Blood: A Spirituality of Solidarity and Hope.* Maryknoll, NY: Orbis, 2006.

Scott, James C. *Weapons of the Weak: Everyday Forms of Peasant Resistance.* New Haven: Yale University Press, 1985.

Sedmak, Clemens. *Innerlichkeit und Kraft: Studie über epistemische Resilienz.* Freiburg: Herder, 2013.

Volkan, Vamik. *Enemies on the Couch: A Psychopolitical Journey through War and Peace.* Durham, NC: Pitchstone Books, 2013.

Ward, Graham. "Theology and Postmodernism: Is It Over?" *JAAR* 80 (2012): 466–84.

BETWEEN TEXT AND TRAUMA:
READING JOB WITH PEOPLE LIVING WITH HIV

Gerald O. West

" 'Every South African has been damaged by apartheid,' Michael Lapsley and his colleagues of the Institute for Healing of Memories used to say when they facilitated the first Healing of Memories workshops in the late 1990s."[1] As we enter the third decade of liberation and democracy "we realise," argues Philippe Denis, another pioneer of memory work in the South African context, "that, as part of the legacy of apartheid, a host of challenges face South African society. We are also damaged by HIV and AIDS, domestic violence, sexual abuse, violent crime, xenophobia, corruption and various forms of discrimination." In sum, "People suffer from multiple wounds."[2]

This essay situates itself within our multiple woundedness and the associated trauma. Drawing on eclectic strands of trauma theory, all of which have been used within the South African context, this essay analyzes how a Bible-reading methodology linked to liberation theology locates itself alongside more mainstream approaches to the treatment of trauma. Within the South African context, Debra Kaminer and Gillian Eagle reflect on three broad categories of response to trauma. First, there are the mainstream approaches of cognitive behavior therapy, narrative therapy, psychodynamic therapy, and integrative therapeutic approaches.[3] Second, there are indigenous responses, including traditional African

---

1. David Tuesday Adamo, "The Use of Psalms in African Indigenous Churches in Nigeria," in *The Bible in Africa: Transactions, Trajectories and Trends*, ed. Gerald O. West and Muse Dube (Leiden: Brill, 2000), 336–49.

2. Ibid.

3. Debra Kaminer and Gillian Eagle, *Traumatic Stress in South Africa* (Johannesburg: Wits University Press, 2010), 88.

healers such as the *inyanga* and *isangoma* (to use the isiZulu terms), who play significant roles as traumatic stress practitioners.[4] Third, there are a range of "community interventions, rituals and memorials," practices that involve various groups of people forming communities of various kinds that are designed "to collectively mark and mourn what has been lost and to recreate some sense of social cohesion."[5]

It is within the third category, local community forms of intervention, that what has come to be called Contextual Bible Study makes a contribution to healing in the context of trauma. This essay reflects on the ways in which Contextual Bible Study may be considered a therapeutic practice, or, more precisely, a therapeutic praxis. In many of the areas in which the Ujamaa Centre for Community Development and Research works with Contextual Bible Study processes, individual therapy is not an option for people affected by trauma. Most cannot afford private counseling, and state services often do not have sufficient personnel or the capacity to work in all the local languages.[6] Contextual Bible Study is resolutely local, drawing on local resources and local participants, and the processes are facilitated in local languages.

As has already become apparent, my essay weaves its understanding and use of trauma theory (as appropriated in the South African context) around Contextual Bible Study processes. The essay uses a particular set of Contextual Bible Study, on the book Job, as a case study.

THE ANATOMY OF A CONTEXTUAL BIBLE STUDY

There are various ways of describing the Contextual Bible Study praxis,[7] but here I focus briefly on a series of interconnected methodological "movements" that shape the collaborative reading process. While a little

---

4. Ibid., 114.

5. Denis, "Storytelling and Healing," 10, referring to Kaminer and Eagle, *Traumatic Stress in South Africa*, 119–20.

6. Denis, "Storytelling and Healing," 10.

7. Gerald O. West, "The Contribution of Tamar's Story to the Construction of Alternative African Masculinities," in *Bodies, Embodiment, and Theology of the Hebrew Bible*, ed. Tamar Kamionkowski and Kim Wonil (London: T&T Clark, 2010), 184–200; West, "Do Two Walk Together? Walking with the Other through Contextual Bible Study," *Anglican Theological Review* 93 (2011): 431–49; West, "Deploying the Literary Detail of a Biblical Text (2 Samuel 13:1–22) in Search of Redemptive Masculinities," in *Interested Readers: Essays on the Hebrew Bible in Honor of David J.A. Clines*, ed. James

abstract at this point in the essay, these movements take on a fuller form when we consider a particular case of Contextual Bible Study.

The overarching movement is that of See-Judge-Act, a process formed in the worker-priest movement in Europe in the 1930–1940s.[8] This movement begins within the organized formations of the poor and marginalized as they analyze (See) their context *from below*. This analysis of *reality* is then brought into dialogue with the *prophetic* voices of the Bible, enabling "the God of life" to address (Judge) the social reality. Through this dialogue with the Bible "the shape of the gospel" is used to plan a series of actions (Act) that will bring about transformation of the social reality, so that all may have life, and have it abundantly.

Within this overarching movement there is another movement, from community-consciousness to critical-consciousness to community-consciousness. The See moment of social analysis generates a particular contextual concern that becomes the local community-based *theme* that provides the initial engagement with the biblical text, allowing every participant to share his or her particular understanding of the text. This moment not only makes it clear to the participants that the Bible study belongs to them; it also offers a reception history of that text's presence in a particular community. The Bible study then moves into a series of rereadings of the text, slowing down the process of interpretation, using the resources of socially engaged biblical scholarship (critical-consciousness). After a series of critical-consciousness questions, the Bible study moves back into community-consciousness, as the participants appropriate the biblical text for the particular social project identified in the See moment.

With respect to the particular biblical *criticisms*, there is a third layer of movement. Within the moment of critical-consciousness, but overlapping with the initial moment of community-consciousness, is a first moment in which the generative contextual theme of the community workshop is brought into dialogue with the semiotic-thematic features

---

K. Aitken, Jeremy M. S. Clines, and Christl M. Maier (Atlanta: Society of Biblical Literature, 2013), 297–312.

8. James R. Cochrane, "Questioning Contextual Theology," in *Towards an Agenda for Contextual Theology: Essays in Honour of Albert Nolan*, ed. McGlory T. Speckman and Larry T. Kaufmann (Pietermaritzburg: Cluster, 2001), 67–86 (76–77); Gerald O. West, *Biblical Hermeneutics of Liberation: Modes of Reading the Bible in the South African Context* (Maryknoll, NY: Orbis; Pietermaritzburg: Cluster, 1995), 188–93.

of (or in front of) a particular biblical text. The interpretive process then slows down,[9] as literary "on-the-text" questions are introduced that offer access to (in a second moment) the (literary) detail of the text. In most cases, literary engagement leads (in a third moment) "behind the text" to a sociohistorical engagement with the text, as participants probe the world that produced the text, seeking for lines of connection between both the literary dimensions and the sociohistorical dimensions of the text and their contextual realities. These critical reading resources "re-member" the biblical text, drawing attention to detail that may not have been engaged with. This critical rereading of the text then moves into a fourth moment of critical appropriation, as the participants appropriate particular features of the reread text, leading to new forms of community-consciousness and then community-based action.

Together, as the case study that follows in the next section of the essay illustrates, these concentric and intersecting movements constitute the Contextual Bible Study process.

So Contextual Bible Study begins and ends under the control of a particular local community, who uses the resources of the Contextual Bible Study, along with a range of other local resources, to plan for and implement community-based action. The socially engaged biblical scholar is already involved in the struggles of particular communities for survival, liberation, and life, so that the invitation to do Contextual Bible Study together comes from within this larger praxis. The presence of the Bible, too, as an artifact of considerable sacral power in African contexts, has the potential to contribute toward the formation of a safe and sacred space.

Journeying with Job

In our work with people living with HIV who are overt about their HIV-positive status, the Ujamaa Centre for Community Development and Research has turned to the book of Job. Our collaborative Contextual Bible Studies with the Siyaphila ("We are well/alive") community-based organization of people living with HIV and AIDS focused initially on biblical texts from the gospels that affirmed the solidarity of God and Jesus with those who are HIV-positive, over against the condemnatory stigmatization

---

9. John Riches, *What Is Contextual Bible Study? A Practical Guide with Group Studies for Advent and Lent* (London: SPCK, 2010), 41.

they experienced from their families, the church, and society in general.[10] But too many funerals and too much of Job 1:21 ("The LORD gave and the LORD has taken away; blessed be the name of the LORD" [NRSV]) as part of most South African funeral liturgies prompted the Ujamaa Centre to facilitate Contextual Bible Studies in which local communities would read on into the poetry.[11] Working with my colleague, Bongi Zengele, who coordinated the Ujamaa Centre's HIV and AIDS work, we met with a local Siyaphila support group and set about constructing our first Contextual Bible Study on Job, working on Job 3.

As we explored Job 3 together in that formative Contextual Bible Study, a young man, one of the few men at that time to participate in a Siyaphila group, voiced his despair, declaring that he knew exactly how Job felt fantasizing about his death. Trembling with emotion, he told us how he had had to fight the desire to take his own life after he was diagnosed as HIV-positive. He had managed, he continued, to live "positively," drawing deeply on the support of the Siyaphila network. But, he declared, turning directly to me as one of the facilitators, our reading of Job 3 on this day had reignited his smoldering desire for death. Why should he not, he asked, take his own life?

So I followed the process, moving into the Judge moment by re-turning to the text, saying that, although Job, like him, had fantasized about his own death, using an array of images (which the group had already identified), Job had not contemplated taking his own life. He had directed, instead, his desire for death toward God, imagining the many ways in which God might have brought about his death at birth (3:3–19) or before he had experienced his current troubles (3:20–26). Although Job continued to lament about his life in chapter 3 and in his other speeches, I said, he seemed to accept that his life was in God's hands.

Remarkably, my turn to the text (a Judge moment) seemed to satisfy the young man, and he nodded and sat among us again. The whole group now seemed more engaged; he had clearly articulated what many others felt in their bodies. As one of the facilitators, I then sought to affirm his irruption, fearing that he might feel he had done "the wrong thing" by so

---

10. Gerald O. West, "Reading the Bible in the Light of HIV/AIDS in South Africa," *The Ecumenical Review* 55 (2003): 335–44.

11. Gerald O. West, "Newsprint Theology: Bible in the Context of HIV and AIDs," in *Out of Place: Doing Theology on the Crosscultural Brink*, ed. Jione Havea and Clive Pearson (London: Equinox, 2011), 161–86.

openly lamenting. Our churches regularly refuse opportunities to engage the lamenting portions of the biblical tradition, insisting rather on superficial forms of celebration. So I carried on, following the poetic narrative through to the end, summarizing briefly how Job refused to restrain his lament in the face of his friends' arguments (throughout his many poetic speeches), how Job even refused to retract his lament when finally face to face with God (38:1–42:6), and how in the prose epilogue God commended Job for "having spoken of/to God what is right" (42:7). It seemed to me, I concluded, that both what and how Job had spoken to/of God was right/appropriate/just, given Job's reality.

Others now rejoined the discussion, sharing their own doubt, fear, and despair. Some time later, after nearly three hours, Bongi Zengele brought our time together to a conclusion, inviting us to breathe deeply in unison and to pray for one another. Flowing from this liturgical moment, she then invited the Siyaphila participants to write, in their own language, their own version of Job 3. Quietly, each participant found a space in the room and wrote. When the participants had had enough time to express themselves, we asked them if they would be willing to share what they had written with others outside of the group. They were unanimous, making it clear that what they had written must be shared with others. Just as Job 3 expressed a traumatized Job's struggle with his reality, so, too, what they had written expressed their reality and their trauma, and they wanted this reality to be heard and understood by their families, churches, and communities. They also made it clear that they wanted their names to be associated with what they had expressed, but without a particular name being associated with a particular personal lament. We have honored their wishes, making known what is not known, hoping that others living with HIV will find in these laments the resources with which to express their own laments and hoping that the families, churches, and communities of those living with HIV will hear and understand and change.[12]

By the end of our workshop, we were exhausted but strangely at peace. Significantly, as we contemplated the Act aspect of the Contextual Bible Study process, we were asked whether we would be willing to do this same Contextual Bible Study with their families. The group yearned for their

---

12. Gerald O. West, "The Poetry of Job as a Resource for the Articulation of Embodied Lament in the Context of HIV and AIDS in South Africa," in *Lamentations in Ancient and Contemporary Cultural Contexts*, ed. Nancy Lee and Carleen Mandolfo, SBLSymS 43 (Atlanta: Society of Biblical Literature, 2008), 195–214.

families to share their experience with lament. Since then we have done the Contextual Bible Study on Job 3 often, and together with the Siyaphila support network Bongi Zengele has established programs to draw the families of those living with HIV alongside them as they continue the struggle to live positively.[13]

What follows is the shape of our Contextual Bible Study on Job 3. It has been through numerous revisions, changing shape as the reality of those living with HIV changes. As indicated above, these shaping questions follow the flow of the Contextual Bible Study methodologies and are embedded within forms of liturgical scaffolding.

1. Job 1:21, "The LORD gave, and the LORD has taken away; blessed be the name of the LORD," is a biblical text often read at funerals. Have you heard this text being read at funerals? Why do pastors and priests read this biblical verse at funerals? What does it say about people who have died of AIDS-related illnesses? What does it say to people living with HIV and AIDS?

2. Listen to Job 3. What is Job trying to say in this text? What images or metaphors does Job use in his lament?

3. How does this text resonate with people living with HIV? Which of Job's images or metaphors are particularly relevant?

4. What is God's view of how Job has spoken in chapter 3 (and elsewhere)? Read Job 42:7.

5. What would be your own version of Job 3? Share it with those in the group.

6. How can you share your version of Job 3 with your local church or community or family?

THE CONTOURS OF TALKING ABOUT TRAUMA

Within the Ujamaa Centre we have long claimed that the Contextual Bible Study processes contribute to constructing a safe and sacred space in which the embodied experiences and theologies of marginalized sectors might find expression and articulation. In our work on gender violence,

---

13. Gerald O. West and Bongi Zengele, "The Medicine of God's Word: What People Living with HIV and AIDS Want (and Get) from the Bible," *JSTA* 12 (2006): 51–63.

for example, we have been quite careful about doing our Contextual Bible Study on the story in 2 Sam 13 of the rape of David's daughter Tamar.[14] Experience has taught us that this text, read through the processes of Contextual Bible Study, is a text with the capacity to reinvoke the trauma of sexual abuse.

So I should not have been surprised by the response of the young man to our Contextual Bible Study on Job 3. Bongi Zengele, a trained social worker and the staff person responsible for working with the Siyaphila network on a regular basis, was not surprised that the traumas associated with living with HIV were reinvoked by this text. Indeed, she had anticipated that this text might be an appropriate resource for an enabling engagement with trauma. She understood that, once a safe and sacred space has been forged, storytelling has the capacity to contribute to the healing of trauma.[15]

Two South African sister projects with which we were both familiar and with which Bongi Zengele had worked had pioneered storytelling as a resource for the healing of traumatic memories. The Institute for the Healing of Memories (established in 1998), which grew out of the Chaplaincy Project of the Trauma Centre for Victims of Violence and Torture, was a response to the partial work done by the Truth and Reconciliation Commission (1996–1997).[16] The Sinomlando Centre for Oral History and Memory Work in Africa was established in 1994 to add indigenous oral history to the public record, focusing in particular on the silenced memories of the Christian communities who suffered under apartheid. In 2000, in the wake of the HIV and AIDS pandemic wracking South Africa, the Sinomlando Centre, inspired by work in Uganda and Tanzania, set up a "memory box" program to provide psychosocial support to those living with HIV, their families, and especially the orphans affected by HIV and AIDS. Just as oral-history work enabled the telling of the oral stories of marginalized communities, so memory-box work enabled the passing on of stories from a generation dying of AIDS-related illnesses to their

---

14. West, "Contribution of Tamar's Story," 186.

15. Gerald O. West, "Contextual Bible Study: Creating Sacred (and Safe) Spaces for Social Transformation," *Grace and Truth* 16 (1999): 51–62; Undine Kayser, "Creating a Space for Encounter and Remembrance: The Healing of Memories Process" (Centre for the Study of Violence and Reconciliation and the Institute for the Healing of Memories, 2000), 6; Denis, "Storytelling and Healing," 11.

16. See http://tinyurl.com/SBL0689e.

families, particularly their children.[17] Using a range of methodologies, including oral history, life-story work, narrative therapy, and child counseling, the memory-box project included children affected by HIV in the stories of their families. As the shape of the epidemic shifted, with more HIV-positive people having access to antiretroviral treatment, memory work became less a preparation for and a response to death and more of a resource "to assist people living with HIV/AIDS to live positively and to hold on to life."[18]

Like Bongi Zengele, Philippe Denis recognizes the "therapeutic value of memory work in situations affected by sickness, trauma and death." And, Denis continues, "the main requirement is the setting up of a safe space for the telling of the story."[19] "Once a safe space has been created," Denis argues, "two other key processes are at work: the elaboration of the painful experience and its validation through empathetic listening."[20] "By developing a better understanding of their own history [through these processes], the wounded people gain control over their lives."[21] Together with this recovery of agency, wounded people also develop resilience, and resilience is a particularly important capacity for children affected by trauma.[22]

In this essay, I build on this work, including the biblical text as a resource within the process of the healing of traumatic memories.

A Safe and Sacred Space

In African contexts the Bible already has power before it is opened. The Bible as artifact or icon is an object of "strange power"[23] and is used in a range of ways to wield healing power.[24] The presence of the Bible contributes to the potential for a site to be recognized by the group as sacred. But a

---

17. Philippe Denis, ed., *Never Too Small to Remember: Memory Work and Resilience in Times of AIDS* (Pietermaritzburg: Cluster, 2005).

18. Philippe Denis, "Memory Work and Resilience," in Denis, *Never Too Small*, 7.

19. Ibid.

20. Denis, "Storytelling and Healing," 11.

21. Ibid., 12.

22. Denis, "Memory Work and Resilience," 8–18.

23. Jean Comaroff and John Comaroff, *Christianity, Colonialism and Consciousness in South Africa*, vol. 1 of *Of Revelation and Revolution* (Chicago: University of Chicago Press, 1991), 182.

24. Adamo, "The Use of Psalms."

sacred space is not always a safe space, as those struggling to live positively with HIV know only too well.

For a site to be a safe space, other conditions are required. Among the primary conditions is that the site is sequestered by the group themselves. Here I lean heavily on sociopolitical theory, more so than on psychosocial theory. In most cases Contextual Bible Study takes place within an already-secured site. We, in line with early forms of Latin American liberation theology,[25] have always emphasized the importance of working with organized groups of the marginalized, in this case those traumatized by the struggle to live positively with HIV. Part of the reason for this is that the organized marginalized have "a shared interest in jointly creating a discourse of dignity, of negation, and of justice." "They have, in addition," James Scott continues, "a shared interest in concealing a social site apart from domination where such a hidden transcript can be elaborated in comparative safety."[26] The Siyaphila network's weekly meetings are such sites.

As Scott indicates, a safe social site enables an articulation. Put differently, the question of whether or not the subaltern *can* speak should be recast as a question that takes space seriously.[27] A more appropriate question would be: *Where* can the subaltern speak? For, as James Scott so eloquently argues, subordinate classes are less constrained at the level of thought and ideology than they are at the level of political action and struggle, "since they can in secluded settings speak with comparative safety."[28] Human dignity, I have argued, even in the most damaged and denigrated subaltern, demands some form of "speaking."[29] *How* the subaltern speaks depends almost entirely on local "sectoral" control of space.

25. Jose Miguez Bonino, *Doing Theology in a Revolutionary Situation* (Philadelphia: Fortress, 1975).

26. James Scott, *Domination and the Arts of Resistance: Hidden Transcripts* (New Haven: Yale University Press, 1990), 114.

27. Gayatri C. Spivak, "Can the Subaltern Speak?" in *Marxism and the Interpretation of Culture*, ed. Cary Nelson and Lawrence Grossberg (London: Macmillan, 1988), 271–313.

28. Scott, *Domination and the Arts of Resistance*, 91.

29. West, "Newsprint Theology," 162.

HETEROTOPIC SPACE

At this point in the essay, Foucault's notion of the heterotopia is useful, for he identifies a heterotopia as a "counter-site," but in an unusual sense. Foucault is not, like Scott, contrasting marginal sites with dominant sites. For Foucault, a heterotopic site is "counter" to a utopian site. "Utopias," argues Foucault, reflecting perhaps on notions of utopia prevalent in liberation theologies in the 1970s,[30] "are sites with no real place."[31] But, continues Foucault, there are also "real places—places that do exist ... which are something like counter-sites, a kind of effectively enacted utopia in which the real sites, all the other real sites that can be found within the culture, are simultaneously represented, contested, and inverted."[32]

Characterized in this way, Contextual Bible Study processes are part of the infrastructure of the heterotopic space forged by Siyaphila support groups.[33] Such sites provide the scaffolding within which a common vocabulary can be constructed from the weekly shared stories and other embodied discourses of the Siyaphila members. This corporately constituted vocabulary can then be incorporated and used by each person to tell her or his own story. My use of notions such as *embodied* and *incorporation* draws on a range of theory,[34] as I will briefly illustrate, including the political theory of James Scott, the sociological theory of John Holloway, the anthropological theory of Jean and John Comaroff, the liberation theology theory of James Cochrane, and the trauma theory of Philippe Denis.

Scott offers a thick description of how marginalized sectors such as the HIV-positive construct their own discourse among themselves, describing how the first articulation by a member of the group has the potential to set in motion a "crystallization" whereby the other members of the group recognize "close relatives" of their own trauma, connecting them to a

---

30. See, for example, Bonino, *Doing Theology in a Revolutionary Situation*, 132–53.

31. Michel Foucault, "Of Other Spaces: Heterotopias" (1984); available from http://tinyurl.com/SBL0689f.

32. Ibid.

33. Gerald O. West, "The Not So Silent Citizen: Hearing Embodied Theology in the Context of HIV and AIDS in South Africa," in *Heterotopic Citizen: New Research on Religious Work for the Disadvantaged*, ed. Trygve Wyller (Göttingen: Vandenhoeck & Ruprecht, 2009), 23–42.

34. West, "Newsprint Theology," 162–76.

"single power grid."[35] Adopting a theoretical stance similar to that of Scott, John Holloway describes how the revolt of the dignity of the marginalized "derives its strength from the uniting of dignities." "Dignity resonates. As it vibrates, it sets off vibrations in other dignities, an unstructured, possibly discordant resonance."[36] Drawing on the work of the Comaroffs, Cochrane describes the "incipient theology" of marginalized and traumatized sectors as residing in the continuum between the conscious and the unconscious: "the realm of partial recognition, of inchoate awareness, of ambiguous perception, and, sometimes of creative tension: that liminal space of human experience in which people discern acts and facts but cannot or do not order them into narrative descriptions or even into articulate conceptions of the world."[37] "Through a long process of self-constitution that depends upon a history of growing consciousness through communicative action," Cochrane goes on to argue, organized groups such as the Siyaphila support groups develop "a foregrounded subjectivity" with the capacity both to speak to one another and to speak to others outside the community.[38]

From within trauma theory, Denis argues that safe space that facilitates both "the elaboration of the painful experience and its validation through empathetic listening" enables a narrative of the traumatic experience to take shape.[39] "Perhaps," continues Denis, "with difficulty and not without tears, they find the words to tell their story."[40] When someone tells a story within the carefully facilitated processes of a Healing of Memories workshop,[41] "the incoherent succession of events, perceptions and feelings that characterised the original event is reorganised into a coherent narrative."[42] Validation is a vital component of this process and so has become a key concept in trauma theory. As Charles Whitfield puts it, "validation is healing." He goes on to affirm that validation "usually happens in

---

35. Scott, *Domination and the Arts of Resistance*, 223–24.

36. John Holloway, "Dignity's Revolt," http://tinyurl.com/SBL0689g. See also Holloway, "Dignity's Revolt," in *Zapatista! Reinventing Revolution in Mexico*, ed. John Holloway and Eliona Peláez (London: Pluto, 1998), 159–98.

37. James R. Cochrane, *Circles of Dignity: Community Wisdom and Theological Reflection* (Minneapolis: Fortress, 1999), 88.

38. Ibid., 111.

39. Denis, "Storytelling and Healing," 11.

40. Ibid., 12.

41. Ibid., 11; see also Sean Field, "Beyond 'Healing': Trauma, Oral History and Regeneration," *Oral History* 34 (2006): 31–42.

42. Denis, "Storytelling and Healing," 12.

a safe environment" and that when it does the "validation of our experience by others allows us to open ourselves to a painful memory, explore it and work through it."[43]

I address in the next section of the essay whether we can consider biblical narrative as an "other" that has the capacity to offer an extended vocabulary with which to articulate a traumatic experience and potential narrative shape to voice and validate a traumatic experience.

HETEROTOPIC HERMENEUTICS

For many African readers of the Bible, and I suspect for (faithful) readers of the Bible in general, there is an immediacy of encounter with the Bible. African theology has reflected on this dimension of African Bible reading quite specifically and has developed a particular trajectory within African theology based on the "recognition" between contemporary "primal" African culture and ancient "primal" biblical cultures.[44]

As already indicated, when it comes to working (critically) with the biblical text, Contextual Bible Study incorporates four moments within a coherent movement. The first moment is in-front-of-the-text, a direct and unmediated semiotic-thematic encounter between text and reader. The second and third moments introduce or offer (more) critical modes of reading into the process, beginning with literary analysis and then sociohistorical analysis. The fourth moment returns to appropriation, but appropriation of a different, historically distanced, text. The fact that appropriation takes place demonstrates an important aspect of Foucault's notion of heterotopia. Through distantiation[45] the text becomes (more)

---

43. Charles Whitfield, *Memory and Abuse: Remembering and Healing the Effects of Trauma* (Deerfield Beach: Health Communications, 1995), 12.

44. John Mbiti, "Christianity and Culture in Africa," in *Facing the New Challenges: The Message of Pacla (Pan African Christian Leadership Assembly); December 9–19, 1976, Nairobi*, ed. Michael Cassidy and Luc Verlinden (Kisumu, Kenya: Evangel, 1978), 272–84; Lamin Sanneh, *Translating the Message: The Missionary Impact on Culture* (Maryknoll, NY: Orbis, 1989); Kwame Bediako, "John Mbiti's Contribution to African Theology," in *Religious Plurality in Africa: Essays in Honour of John S. Mbiti*, ed. Jacob K. Olupona and Sulayman S. Nyang (Berlin: de Gruyter, 1993), 367–90; Bediako, *Christianity in Africa: The Renewal of a Non-Western Religion* (Edinburgh: Edinburgh University Press; Maryknoll, NY: Orbis, 1995).

45. Using Paul Ricoeur's term from "The Hermeneutical Function of Distanciation," *Philosophy Today* 17 (1973): 129–41.

other and therefore another potential heterotopic site. In other words, the Contextual Bible Study processes open up space for a heterotopia through the contribution of critical biblical studies resources. As Foucault observes, one of the features of heterotopias is that they "are most often linked to slices of time" that "open onto what might be termed ... heterochronies."[46] However, because Foucault believes, incorrectly, that time, unlike space, "was detached from the sacred in the nineteenth century"[47]—betraying his European social location—he is unable to recognize fully[48] that sacred heterotopias are sites that connect across sanctified time. This means that, for example, a Contextual Bible Study can connect contemporary South Africans living with HIV with the biblical Job.

It was clear from our Contextual Bible Study on Job 3 that the biblical text offered participants images and metaphors that contributed toward a vocabulary through which to talk about their trauma. Job's trauma, so vividly articulated, also validated their incipient stories. They were not alone. Not only were they validated by each other, they were validated by a sacred ancestor in the faith who refused to be silent, who asserted his agency, and who struggled to make sense of his traumatic loss. As Denis notes, drawing on narrative therapy work,[49] survivors of trauma often see themselves "as victims, overpowered by pain, confusion and guilt." But through Healing of Memories workshops, "they begin to construct another story of their lives. After all, they survived. They resisted. They are heroes."[50]

Job 3 also provides other *literary* resources. The first is a narrative resource. By reading Job 3, an unfamiliar biblical text is recovered that tells the story of how the Job of 1:21, who quietly accepted his suffering, is not the whole story about responding to trauma. Most of the Siyaphila group participants were completely unaware of Job 3 and so had not realized that Job's story continued. Job 1:21 is part of a larger and longer narrative, they discovered, even through the "narrative" shifts into poetry.

---

46. Foucault, "Of Other Spaces."

47. Ibid.

48. But see ibid.

49. Michael White and David Epston, *Narrative Means to Therapeutic Ends* (New York: Norton, 1990); Michael White, *Re-authoring Lives: Interviews and Essays* (Adelaide: Dulwich Centre Publications, 1995); Jill Freedman and Gene Combs, *Narrative Therapy: The Social Construction of Preferred Realities* (New York: Norton, 1996).

50. Denis, "Storytelling and Healing," 13.

The second is a genre resource. Storytelling is not always easy for those who are severely traumatized. Their lives cannot yet be characterized or plotted in a coherent manner. That Job chooses poetry rather than narrative is itself a potential resource. The rhythm and cadence of Job 3 offered Siyaphila participants another way of working with this text, hearing the resonances between the poetry of Job and the poetry of African protest music.[51]

The third literary resource is the syntactic shape of the poem. The alternation of assertions and questions provided a potential shape to their own emerging articulations, for most of the participants included both in their own laments. For example, one of the participants writes:

> My God my God why did you allow me to have AIDS? Why did you give me this one child, when you know that my life-span is short? I will soon die and leave him with no parent! I wish I were not even born into this world! I am an orphan and unemployed. It would be better if I did not even exist in this world![52]

A fourth resource was the shape of the book of Job as a whole. Most "ordinary readers" do not have a clear sense of the overall shape of the book. The book is proclaimed in fragments. Providing an overall sense of shape to the book as a whole seemed a potentially useful resource. While Job 3 (as the start of the complication, in narrative terms)[53] offered resources to break their silence about their trauma, as Job had broken his silence, so Job 42:7 (as the start of the narrative resolution) offered resources to recognize that God did not disapprove of the resisting agency of Job. Indeed, God had publicly affirmed that Job had spoken of/to God "what is right."

But narrative resolution is not the same as the resolution of trauma. Our work together on Job 3 did not provide a definitive resolution of their trauma. "Valuable as they are," says Denis, "interventions based on storytelling should have no claim to having an immediate healing power."[54] In

---

51. West, "The Poetry of Job," 210–12.

52. Ibid., 204–5.

53. Aristotle, *Poetics*, trans. Gerald F. Else (Ann Arbor: University of Michigan Press, 1967), 30.

54. Denis, "Storytelling and Healing," 14.

her work on trauma and recovery, Judith Lewis Herman cautions: "resolution of the trauma is never final; recovery is never complete."[55]

RESILIENCE AS RESOLUTION

In enumerating the limitations of story-based therapeutic processes, Philippe Denis recognizes that often the most that can be hoped for is some form of resilience, a key concept in trauma theory.[56] Resilience is a substantial capacity for those struggling to live with trauma, especially for children affected by HIV and AIDS.[57] Resilience is in itself a form of healing.

The Siyaphila support groups are a site in which resilience is nurtured. Their weekly meetings, and the buddy system they use each day to remind each other about their antiretroviral treatment times, provide a rhythm of/for resilience. Having worked with Siyaphila support groups since the mid-1990s, we in the Ujamaa Centre can make a case for Contextual Bible Study as a resource in the construction of resilience. Our encounter with the young man who wanted to know why he should not take his life is an example of how Siyaphila members draw on the Bible in their struggle to live positively with HIV.[58]

The regular fortnightly Contextual Bible Studies facilitated by Bongi Zengele during the most difficult days of the epidemic provided participants with the time to articulate and rearticulate their trauma. Denis notes how important duration/time is in the building of resilience, but he recognizes that there are time constraints. The Healing of Memories workshops tend to be only of a weekend's duration, with perhaps one follow-up meeting a few months later.[59] However, the regularity of Siyaphila support group meetings and their own *local* control of the agenda of each meeting provide regular opportunities for members to retell their trauma. Denis argues that "it is only when the narrators 're-story' their lives and find a

---

55. Judith Herman, *Trauma and Recovery: The Aftermath of Violence—From Domestic Abuse to Political Terror* (New York: Basic Books, 1997), 211.

56. Denis, "Storytelling and Healing," 14–15.

57. Denis, "Memory Work and Resilience," 8–12.

58. See also West and Zengele, "The Medicine of God's Word," 56–63.

59. Denis, "Storytelling and Healing," 15. See also Philippe Denis, "The Healing of Memories and Reconciliation Consortium," in *A Journey towards Healing: Stories of People with Multiple Woundedness in Kwazulu-Natal*, ed. Philippe Denis, Scott Houser, and Radikobo Ntsimane (Pietermaritzburg: Cluster, 2011), 20–30.

new meaning in them that they start in earnest the work of healing."[60] The importance of the *re* is both in terms of another story and in terms of re-iterating a story. "Telling one's story may trigger change," says Denis, "but to be effective the transformation requires more time." This is why, Denis continues, "Michael Lapsley and his colleagues of the Institute for Healing of Memories speak of a 'journey towards healing.'"[61] This is also why the Ujamaa Centre works with the Siyaphila network of support groups in an ongoing manner, collaborating with them since 1998. Duration—endur-ing safe space, enduring opportunities for articulation, enduring valida-tion—is an important element in the building of resilience and in the heal-ing of trauma.

Several resources combine to facilitate the reordering of the "struc-tural disorder" that so much of trauma is a part of. These include the het-erotopic space created by the Siyaphila support groups in collaboration with the Ujamaa Centre,[62] together with the Bible's capacity through the processes of the Contextual Bible Study methodology to construct connec-tions across sacred time and space. An additional dimension goes beyond the elaboration of the traumatic experience and its validation through empathetic listening, which, important as they are, are insufficient.

> Addressing the social or relational dimension of the traumatic expe-rience is equally important. How can a storytelling workshop bring healing to the victim of rape if, for instance, the power of the abuser remains unchallenged in the family? How can children of a woman who died of AIDS feel comfort in telling their stories if the death of their mother has plunged them into poverty?[63]

Psychosocial change is directly related to and intersects with socioeco-nomic change. Since their formation in the mid-1990s, the Siyaphila net-work of support groups has devolved into a network of loosely related but independent groups, each with its own social location and constituency. Many of these are now community-based organizations (CBOs) or non-governmental organizations (NGOs) in their own right and have devel-

---

60. Denis, "Storytelling and Healing," 15.
61. Ibid.
62. Gerald O. West and Bongi Zengele, "Reading Job 'Positively' in the Context of Hiv/Aids in South Africa," *Concilium* 4 (2004): 112–24.
63. Denis, "Storytelling and Healing," 16.

oped their own networks with other CBOs and NGOs who offer them resources for engaging with the social structures/systems that so often frame trauma in South Africa.

Significantly, most of these now-independent Siyaphila support groups continue to relate to the Ujamaa Centre and continue to invite us to do Contextual Bible Study with them. At our most recent workshop, in August 2014, with representatives of more than ten different Siyaphila support groups, we probed why they continued to want to do Contextual Bible Study work.

Since our initial Contextual Bible Study on Job 3 we had reworked that Contextual Bible Study into a fairly stable form that could be done more widely with other communities. We had also worked on a follow-up Contextual Bible Study on Job 9 and another on Job 19, through which we explored more deeply the enduring lament of Job (and of those struggling to live positively with HIV). But Job 42:7 continued to beckon us, so at a recent workshop (cohosted with the Collaborative for HIV and Aids, Religion and Theology [CHART])[64] with representatives of the Siyaphila network we offered a Contextual Bible Study that focused on the "resolution" of the book of Job, working together on Job 42:7–11, in which Job is "restored." Through this Contextual Bible Study we reflected together on the capacities that Contextual Bible Study offered to people living with HIV.

The overwhelming response we received to this implied question was that rereading the Bible in this way built theological capacity and in so doing made a significant contribution to the religio-spiritual dimension of psychosocial resilience. On the journey toward healing for many who have been traumatized in South Africa, theological resilience is a significant resource. Most public forms of the Christian tradition (as with the Islamic tradition and traditional African Religion)[65] are part of the problem, religiously retraumatizing the HIV-positive. Recognizing and participating in the theological contestation of Job has provided a form of theological resilience, building the religio-spiritual capacities required to live positively in a religious landscape dominated by theologies of retribution.

---

64. See http://www.chart.ukzn.ac.za/.

65. Gerald O. West, "Sacred Texts, Particularly the Bible and the Qur'an, and HIV and AIDS: Charting the Textual Territory," in *Religion and HIV and AIDS: Charting the Terrain*, ed. Beverley Haddad (Pietermaritzburg: University of KwaZulu-Natal Press, 2011), 135–65.

Interpretive Resilience

Because the Ujamaa Centre works with a wide constituency, most of whom are from marginalized communities, we can reflect across our work more generally on the kinds of capacities that Contextual Bible Study offers. Among these is the capacity to recognize that our sociocultural, Christian, and biblical traditions are not monovocal; they are contested. Psychosocial resilience has been recognized as a substantive resource in trauma theory. For those struggling to live positively with trauma in a context such as South Africa, where the Bible is both an obstruction on the journey toward healing and a potential resource for restoration, the work of the Ujamaa Centre indicates the following: building the capacity of marginalized sectors to interpret the Bible from and for their own experience, recognizing that there are contending biblical theological trajectories or voices, nurtures the religio-spiritual dimensions of psychosocial resilience.

Bibliography

Adamo, David Tuesday. "The Use of Psalms in African Indigenous Churches in Nigeria." Pages 336–49 in *The Bible in Africa: Transactions, Trajectories and Trends*. Edited by Gerald O. West and Muse Dube. Leiden: Brill, 2000.

Aristotle. *Poetics*. Translated by Gerald F. Else. Ann Arbor: University of Michigan Press, 1967.

Bediako, Kwame. *Christianity in Africa: The Renewal of a Non-Western Religion*. Edinburgh: Edinburgh University Press; Maryknoll, NY: Orbis, 1995.

———. "John Mbiti's Contribution to African Theology." Pages 367–90 in *Religious Plurality in Africa: Essays in Honour of John S. Mbiti*. Edited by Jacob K. Olupona and Sulayman S. Nyang. Berlin: de Gruyter, 1993.

Bonino, Jose Miguez. *Doing Theology in a Revolutionary Situation*. Philadelphia: Fortress, 1975.

Cochrane, James R. *Circles of Dignity: Community Wisdom and Theological Reflection*. Minneapolis: Fortress, 1999.

———. "Questioning Contextual Theology." Pages 67–86 in *Towards an Agenda for Contextual Theology: Essays in Honour of Albert Nolan*. Edited by McGlory T. Speckman and Larry T. Kaufmann. Pietermaritzburg: Cluster, 2001.

Comaroff, Jean, and John Comaroff. *Christianity, Colonialism and Consciousness in South Africa*. Vol. 1 of *Of Revelation and Revolution* (Chicago: University of Chicago Press, 1991

Denis, Philippe. "The Healing of Memories and Reconciliation Consortium." Pages 18–30 in *A Journey towards Healing: Stories of People with Multiple Woundedness in Kwazulu-Natal*. Edited by Philippe Denis, Scott Houser, and Radikobo Ntsimane. Pietermaritzburg: Cluster, 2011.

———. "Memory Work and Resilience." Pages 1–18 in *Never Too Small to Remember: Memory Work and Resilience in Times of AIDS*. Edited by Philippe Denis. Pietermaritzburg: Cluster, 2005.

———, ed. *Never Too Small to Remember: Memory Work and Resilience in Times of AIDS*. Pietermaritzburg: Cluster, 2005.

———. "Storytelling and Healing." Pages 5–17 in *A Journey towards Healing: Stories of People with Multiple Woundedness in Kwazulu-Natal*. Edited by Philippe Denis, Scott Houser, and Radikobo Ntsimane. Pietermaritzburg: Cluster, 2011.

Field, Sean. "Beyond 'Healing': Trauma, Oral History and Regeneration." *Oral History* 34 (2006): 31–42.

Foucault, Michel. "Of Other Spaces: Heterotopias." http://tinyurl.com/SBL0689f.

Freedman, Jill, and Gene Combs. *Narrative Therapy: The Social Construction of Preferred Realities*. New York: Norton, 1996.

Herman, Judith. *Trauma and Recovery: The Aftermath of Violence—From Domestic Abuse to Political Terror*. Rev. ed. New York: Basic Books, 1997.

Holloway, John. "Dignity's Revolt." http://tinyurl.com/SBL0689g.

———. "Dignity's Revolt. Pages 159–98 in *Zapatista! Reinventing Revolution in Mexico*. Edited by John Holloway and Eliona Peláez. London: Pluto, 1998.

Kaminer, Debra, and Gillian Eagle. *Traumatic Stress in South Africa*. Johannesburg: Wits University Press, 2010.

Kayser, Undine. "Creating a Space for Encounter and Remembrance: The Healing of Memories Process." Centre for the Study of Violence and Reconciliation and the Institute for the Healing of Memories, 2000.

Mbiti, John. "Christianity and Culture in Africa." Pages 272–84 in *Facing the New Challenges: The Message of Pacla (Pan African Christian Leadership Assembly); December 9–19, 1976, Nairobi*. Edited by Michael Cassidy and Luc Verlinden. Kisumu, Kenya: Evangel, 1978.

Riches, John. *What Is Contextual Bible Study? A Practical Guide with Group Studies for Advent and Lent*. London: SPCK, 2010.

Ricoeur, Paul. "The Hermeneutical Function of Distanciation." *Philosophy Today* 17 (1973): 129–41.

Sanneh, Lamin. *Translating the Message: The Missionary Impact on Culture*. Maryknoll, NY: Orbis, 1989.

Scott, James. *Domination and the Arts of Resistance: Hidden Transcripts*. New Haven: Yale University Press, 1990.

Spivak, Gayatri C. "Can the Subaltern Speak?" Pages 271–313 in *Marxism and the Interpretation of Culture*. Edited by Cary Nelson and Lawrence Grossberg. London: Macmillan, 1988.

West, Gerald O. *Biblical Hermeneutics of Liberation: Modes of Reading the Bible in the South African Context*. Maryknoll, NY: Orbis; Pietermaritzburg: Cluster, 1995.

———. "Contextual Bible Study: Creating Sacred (and Safe) Spaces for Social Transformation." *Grace and Truth* 16 (1999): 51–62.

———. "The Contribution of Tamar's Story to the Construction of Alternative African Masculinities." Pages 184–200 in *Bodies, Embodiment, and Theology of the Hebrew Bible*. Edited by Tamar Kamionkowski and Kim Wonil. London: T&T Clark, 2010.

———. "Deploying the Literary Detail of a Biblical Text (2 Samuel 13:1–22) in Search of Redemptive Masculinities." Pages 297–312 in *Interested Readers: Essays on the Hebrew Bible in Honor of David J. A. Clines*. Edited by James K. Aitken, Jeremy M. S. Clines, and Christl M. Maier. Atlanta: Society of Biblical Literature, 2013.

———. "Do Two Walk Together? Walking with the Other through Contextual Bible Study." *Anglican Theological Review* 93 (2011): 431–49.

———. "Newsprint Theology: Bible in the Context of HIV and AIDs." Pages 161–86 in *Out of Place: Doing Theology on the Crosscultural Brink*. Edited by Jione Havea and Clive Pearson. London: Equinox, 2011.

———. "The Not So Silent Citizen: Hearing Embodied Theology in the Context of HIV and AIDS in South Africa." Pages 23–42 in *Heterotopic Citizen: New Research on Religious Work for the Disadvantaged*. Edited by Trygve Wyller. Göttingen: Vandenhoeck & Ruprecht, 2009.

———. "The Poetry of Job as a Resource for the Articulation of Embodied Lament in the Context of HIV and AIDS in South Africa." Pages 195–214 in *Lamentations in Ancient and Contemporary Cultural Contexts*.

Edited by Nancy Lee and Carleen Mandolfo. SBLSymS 43. Atlanta: Society of Biblical Literature, 2008.

———. "Reading the Bible in the Light of HIV/AIDS in South Africa." *The Ecumenical Review* 55 (2003): 335–44.

———. "Sacred Texts, Particularly the Bible and the Qur'an, and HIV and AIDS: Charting the Textual Territory." Pages 135–65 in *Religion and HIV and AIDS: Charting the Terrain*. Edited by Beverley Haddad. Pietermaritzburg: University of KwaZulu-Natal Press, 2011.

West, Gerald O., and Bongi Zengele. "The Medicine of God's Word: What People Living with HIV and AIDS Want (and Get) from the Bible." *JSTA* 12 (2006): 51–63.

———. "Reading Job 'Positively' in the Context of Hiv/Aids in South Africa." *Concilium* 4 (2004): 112–24.

White, Michael. *Re-authoring Lives: Interviews and Essays*. Adelaide: Dulwich Centre Publications, 1995.

White, Michael, and David Epston, *Narrative Means to Therapeutic Ends*. New York: Norton, 1990.

Whitfield, Charles. *Memory and Abuse: Remembering and Healing the Effects of Trauma*. Deerfield Beach: Health Communications, 1995.

Toward a Pastoral Reading of 2 Corinthians as a Memoir of PTSD and Healing

Peter Yuichi Clark

When people endure times of crisis or trauma, they often search for meaning and hope by engaging in a bidirectional reading of texts. One direction involves hearing, reading, or witnessing the stories of others in analogous circumstances. Doing so can help people to know that they are not alone in their suffering, thus fulfilling Donne's axiom that "no man is an island, entire of itself."[1] The other direction points toward texts and rituals in one's religious faith and spiritual practices, seeking a linkage between one's own story and a larger, transcendent story: one that recounts what is sacred or ultimate. A devout Jew or Christian might scour the Psalms or Job, for example, while asking, Am I alone in my pain? Does God even care what happens to me? Pursuing these parallel yet sometimes interwoven narrative tracks—one aimed toward connecting with one's fellow humans, the other toward connecting with the *mysterium tremendum et fascinans*—can serve as contextualization, as a basis of commiseration, as fuel for contemplation, as inspiration, and even as a model for emulation.

---

1. John Donne, "Meditation XVII" (1623) from *Devotions upon Emergent Occasions*, in *The Norton Anthology of English Literature*, 4th ed., ed. Meyer Howard Abrams et al., 2 vols. (New York: Norton, 1979), 1:1108–9. A relevant vignette involves Bryan Doerries, who stages adapted Greek tragedies for audiences of soldiers and veterans who may be dealing with PTSD. These reenacted plays stir much feeling and conversation, with Doerries's explicit goal being: "The experience of two hundred people in a room spending two hours together is a different way to combat isolation. Most importantly, if we had one message to deliver to you, two thousand four hundred years later, it's simply this: You are not alone across time." See Wyatt Mason, "You Are Not Alone across Time: Using Sophocles to Treat PTSD," *Harper's Magazine* 329, no. 1973 (October 2014): 62.

In an extremely raw season, care-seekers can find a salutary balm in this dual narrative approach.

Not surprisingly, this propensity is evident as people cope with post-traumatic stress disorder (PTSD), an illness estimated to affect almost 7 percent of adult U.S. Americans, with women nearly three times as likely as men to confront it at some point in their lives.[2] Personal stories of people with PTSD and their caregivers abound in the Western press and social media, which suggest the first vector I described. The other narrative vector—to discern psycho-spiritual comfort through a sacred narrative—can be observed in the manner by which Paul the apostle construes his own experience. For example, Kenneth Jones speculates that Paul might have faced PTSD. He argues that Paul uses the perfect tense when recounting life-threatening events, indicating that they are "still a vivid memory ringing in Paul's mind," and that the same tense in 2 Cor 12:9 conveys the enduring comfort of the divine voice.[3] Drawing upon Jones's meditation as an impetus, I apply a pastoral-theological lens to interpret 2 Corinthians as a memoir of Paul's struggles with traumatic experiences and his recovering process, thus exemplifying the kind of consoling textual duality I have observed. For traumatized readers, Paul's letter provides a story of a fellow sufferer and a model of how they can turn toward the sacred. Such is not the primary aim of Paul's letter,[4] but it offers a testimony of his human journey through illness, with an emerging awareness of his own vulnerability, and it illustrates how relying on the power of divine grace has led him (and, by extension, can lead us) toward healing and wholeness.

---

2. Ronald C. Kessler et al., "Lifetime Prevalence and Age-of-Onset Distributions of *DSM-IV* Disorders in the National Comorbidity Survey Replication," *Archives of General Psychiatry* 62 (2005): 593–602; and the National Comorbidity Survey Replication, "Appendix Table 1: Lifetime Prevalence of DSM-IV/WMH-CIDI Disorders by Sex and Cohort," http://tinyurl.com/SBL0689h.

3. Kenneth Jones, "Post Traumatic Stress Disorder and Paul's Life: Finding Strength in Christ Alone," http://tinyurl.com/SBL0689i.

4. For convenience I refer to 2 Corinthians as it appears in the canon and generally avoid the debate about whether the letter is a compilation of letters and textual fragments or a compositional whole crafted for a distinct rhetorical objective.

About the Interpretive Lens

The lens I utilize is not of my own creation. Indeed, I gladly follow in the footsteps of other pioneers, such as Erik and Joan Erikson's efforts to understand the characterological nuances of Martin Luther and Mohandas Gandhi.[5] More recently, pastoral theologians Donald Capps and Kathleen Greider have illuminated the spiritual dimensions of people coping with mental illness by examining first-person published accounts.[6] This exploration of the intersection of spirituality and mental health enables soul-sufferers (Greider's term) to speak in their own voices, with the theologian functioning as companion to the memoirists and guide to the readers. Greider expresses well the goal:

> We will seek to better and more compassionately understand what many of us do not have to face—living with extreme and often disabling brain disorders and other anguish of soul…. We will work according to the principle that analytically considered anecdotal human experience has heuristic value through the revelation of particular and thematic insights that thoughtful readers neither disregard nor universalize.[7]

My approach is also indebted to Clarence Barton, my first Clinical Pastoral Education supervisor, whose chaplaincy in a state psychiatric facility taught me to attend to profound hints of meaning couched within the often-confusing utterances of severely ill adults. I am not insinuating that Paul was psychologically disabled in the same ways that some whom I served clearly were, yet this theme in the Pauline letters may benefit from the close listening I attempted to do there and aspire to do now.

---

5. See Erik H. Erikson, *Young Man Luther: A Study in Psychoanalysis and History* (New York: Norton, 1958); and Erikson, *Gandhi's Truth: On the Origins of Militant Nonviolence* (New York: Norton, 1969). It is commonly accepted that Erik's wife Joan was a full collaborator in his theoretical and literary work throughout their lives together.

6. Donald Capps, *Fragile Connections: Memoirs of Mental Illness for Pastoral Care Professionals* (St. Louis: Chalice, 2005); Kathleen J. Greider, *Much Madness Is Divinest Sense: Wisdom in Memoirs of Soul-Suffering* (Cleveland: Pilgrim, 2007).

7. Greider, *Much Madness*, 14, 42.

Describing PTSD

Before I begin that task, delineating the symptoms of post-traumatic stress disorder seems worthwhile, as does acknowledging that neither the apostle Paul nor anyone alive in his time was diagnosed with PTSD.[8] Although psychiatry can be traced to India in the seventh century BCE and Greece a century later, PTSD as a recognized psychiatric illness is of recent vintage. The first description of PTSD-like symptoms in Western medical literature occurred in 1879; the diagnostic category of PTSD was formally established in 1980 and has been validated cross-culturally. The World Health Organization defines PTSD as "a delayed and/ or protracted response to a stressful event or situation (either short- or long-lasting) of an exceptionally threatening or catastrophic nature, which is likely to cause pervasive distress in almost anyone."[9] Crucial to that definition is that the precipitating event overwhelms one's adaptive and integrative capacities, thus breaching one's basic concepts of safety. Given the frequency of traumatic events within human history, it is reasonable to assume that over the centuries many thousands have suffered the effects of PTSD without the "benefit" of a standardized medical term.[10]

Building upon criteria in the WHO's *International Classification of Diseases* (10th ed.) and the American Psychiatric Association's *Diagnostic and Statistical Manual of Mental Disorders* (5th ed.),[11] clinicians categorize PTSD symptoms into three clusters. The reexperiencing cluster incorporates intrusive memories (flashbacks) and nightmares; the hypervigilance or hyperarousal cluster includes combative behavior and sleep distur-

---

8. Because I am neither a biblical exegete by profession nor a trained psychologist, I rely throughout this essay on the insights of numerous commentators and researchers, to whom I am greatly indebted. Interested readers may request a complete list of these sources from me via e-mail at peter.clark@ucsf.edu.

9. World Health Organization, "Posttraumatic Stress Disorder [F43.1]," in *The ICD-10 Classification of Mental and Behavioural Disorders: Clinical Descriptions and Diagnostic Guidelines* (Geneva: World Health Organization, 1992), 120.

10. These effects could include comorbidities such as cardiovascular disease, diabetes, and substance dependence, since research studies show a strong association between a PTSD diagnosis and these conditions.

11. American Psychiatric Association, "Posttraumatic Stress Disorder [309.81]," in *Diagnostic and Statistical Manual of Mental Disorders: DSM-5*, 5th ed. (Washington, DC: American Psychiatric Association, 2013).

bances; and the avoidance or numbing cluster encompasses phenomena such as affective blunting, a diminished interest in people, anhedonia, indifference about goals and future plans, and shunning activities and situations that remind one of the original traumatic event. I contend that, if Paul was coping with PTSD, he likely experienced symptoms in the first two clusters, but there is no indication of those in the avoidance/numbing cluster, based on how he depicts himself in his letters.

By adopting a more granular perspective, I concentrate on the eight criteria and twenty-four subcriteria listed for PTSD in *DSM-5* and speculate that Paul's condition could meet three of the former and six of the latter, namely:

- Exposure to actual or threatened death, serious injury, or sexual violence in one (or more) of the following ways:
  - Directly experiencing the traumatic event(s) [Criterion A1]

- Presence of one (or more) of the following intrusion symptoms associated with the traumatic event(s), beginning after the traumatic event(s) occurred:
  - Recurrent, involuntary, and intrusive distressing memories of the traumatic event(s) [Criterion B1]
  - Intense or prolonged psychological distress at exposure to internal or external cues that symbolize or resemble an aspect of the traumatic event(s) [Criterion B4]
  - Marked physiological reactions to internal or external cues that symbolize or resemble an aspect of the traumatic event(s) [Criterion B5]

- Marked alterations in arousal and reactivity associated with the traumatic event(s), beginning or worsening after the traumatic event(s) occurred, as evidenced by two (or more) of the following:
  - Hypervigilance [Criterion E3]
  - Sleep disturbance (e.g., difficulty falling or staying asleep or restless sleep) [Criterion E6]

Substantiating this assertion requires delving into Paul's missive and searching for possible clues.

READING FIVE PASSAGES

In at least five pericopes Paul either alludes to or explicitly describes his personal experience: 2 Cor 1:3–10; 4:7–12, 16; 6:4–10; 11:21–33; and 12:7–10. I reflect on each in turn, beginning with Paul's *exordium*, a rhetorical term for an introduction that reveals the central theme of a speech or argument.

Paul opens the letter not with his customary thanksgiving to the recipients but instead with a *berakah*, offering a blessing to God "for what God has accomplished for and through *him*."[12] A motif that occurs is the tension between affliction and suffering (Greek *thlipsis* and *pathēma*, respectively) and cognates of the noun *paraklēsis*, rendered in English as "encouragement," "comfort," or "consolation." For Paul, this comfort arises while one is given courage and endurance to face suffering; it is not so much being rescued *out of* affliction as it is receiving sustenance *within* affliction. Paul seems to derive resolve from affirming that sufferings and consolations are linked and shared—identifying Christ's suffering with his and the Corinthian believers' as well—and he avers that God's comfort is not only meant for oneself but ought to spill out in compassion toward others.

Here I would direct attention to Paul's declaration that "the affliction we experienced in Asia" felt devastating: "We were so utterly, unbearably *crushed* that we *despaired of life* itself. Indeed, we felt that we had received *the sentence of death* so that we would rely not on ourselves but on God who raises the dead" (1:8b–9, emphases added).[13] This description could be evidence of *DSM-5*'s Criterion B4 in that, while he may be speaking hyperbolically,[14] it also may point to his psychological distress. As Paul recalled his tribulations, they may have gained even more emotional intensity, especially if his memory associated them with earlier crises in his ministry, and thus he may have endured symptoms that felt crushing, leading to despair, and portending death. At the same time, Paul quickly reminds readers that leaning into such distress is an occasion to acknowledge weakness and take refuge in divine grace and power, an awareness he reiterates throughout 2 Corinthians.

---

12. David E. Garland, *2 Corinthians*, NAC 29 (Nashville: Broadman & Holman, 1999), 53, emphasis original.

13. Unless otherwise noted, biblical quotations are from the NRSV.

14. Intriguingly, Paul himself uses the word *hyperbolēn* in 1:8.

From this exordium I proceed to 4:7–12 and 16, in which Paul takes an apologetic tack and attempts to demonstrate his apostolic sincerity, in contrast to his opponents. What merits notice here are the well-known phrase "treasure in clay jars" in 4:7 and the "hardship catalog" in 4:8–10.

Alluding to clay jars likely hearkens to texts such as Gen 2:7, Isa 45:9, and Jer 18:1–10 and 19:1–11, in which God is portrayed as shaping humanity (or judgment on it) like a potter. These *ostrakinoi skeuē* were either expendable containers, like modern glass or plastic bottles, or had thin, translucent walls to function as lamps.[15] Either way, if they cracked, they were usually discarded rather than repaired. The parallel between this metaphor and how many PTSD victims describe themselves as "broken" or "shattered" by their trauma is powerful. Yet Paul believes that God entrusts unspecified treasure into fragile (and perhaps traumatized) human vessels, which are held together through divine power.

This discourse leads directly into what commentators describe as the first hardship catalog in the epistle. Such catalogs were a rhetorical device employed by contemporary Stoics and Cynics to illustrate how their outlook allowed them to trump adversity, or *peristasis*, with tranquility, or *ataraxia*, thus proving their philosophical superiority.[16] Paul, by contrast, does not make a case for his own equipoise. Rather, he creates four sets of antitheses, often with wordplays, in order to allude to his travails and argue that he survived due to divine power: for example, *aporoumenoi-exaporoumenoi*, akin to "stressed, but not stressed out" (4:8),[17] and "we may be knocked down but we are never knocked out!" (4:9 Phillips). I contend that these two pairs respectively point toward Criteria B4 (the psychological effect of suffering hardships) and B5 (a physiological reaction to internal or external traumatic cues). Further, alongside Paul's dependence on his theology for meaning, his use of paronomasia is a subtle form of humor, which can bolster resilience and contribute greatly to one's healing.

---

15. John T. Fitzgerald, *Cracks in an Earthen Vessel: An Examination of the Catalogues of Hardships in the Corinthian Correspondence*, SBLDS 99 (Atlanta: Scholars Press, 1988), 167–68; Ben Witherington III, *Conflict and Community in Corinth: A Socio-rhetorical Commentary on 1 and 2 Corinthians* (Grand Rapids: Eerdmans, 1995), 387.

16. Fitzgerald, *Cracks in an Earthen Vessel*, 47–116.

17. Garland, *2 Corinthians*, 229.

Following this repurposed catalog, Paul states that "[we are] always carrying in our body the [dying][18] of Jesus, so that the life of Jesus may also be made visible in our bodies" (4:10), and that, "even though our outer nature is wasting away, our inner nature is being renewed day by day" (4:16). What Paul seems to declare is that enduring these traumatic situations entails embracing his finitude and fragility; identifying his ministry with Christ's life, passion, and resurrection; and continuing his work while awaiting God's resurrecting power. As Guy Nave succinctly phrases it: "Living with confidence in the midst of suffering is not the same thing as passively accepting suffering and waiting for one's 'pie in the sky when I die.'"[19] Indeed, it means envisioning ourselves as "wayfarers and pilgrims," to borrow from Saint Jerome.[20]

In 2 Cor 6 Paul constructs a second hardship catalog or "résumé of ministry"[21] that supplements 4:8–10. The content of this catalog is more detailed, and its structure is rather elaborate. The catalog begins with three sets of three hardships each, including general suffering, suffering at others' hands, and occupational hazards (6:4–5). Then Paul lists eight qualities of his ministry (6:6–7), followed by three combinations (right hand/left hand, honor/dishonor, ill/good repute; 6:7–8). Finally, Paul gives seven antitheses either describing paradoxes of his ministry or differentiating between his adversaries' mistaken views and his apostolic vindication.

As for trauma and possible PTSD, I suspect several precipitating events in the list of hardships, especially when Paul mentions "beatings, imprisonments, [and] riots" (Criterion A1). Moreover, the reference to "labors, sleepless nights, hunger" might imply bouts of hyper-vigilance and sleep disturbances (Criteria E3 and E6; see also 7:5). Of course, Paul was literally a tentmaker, a dual-career minister, and much of his rationale for writing 2 Corinthians arises from his preference to work for his wages, rather than rely on the Corinthian believers' patronage, as the so-called super-apostles

---

18. NRSV translates *nekrosis* in 4:10 as "death," but I am persuaded to read this dynamically rather than statically.

19. Guy Nave, "2 Corinthians," in *True to Our Native Land: An African American New Testament Commentary*, ed. Brian K. Blount (Minneapolis: Fortress, 2007), 316.

20. Jerome, "Homily 63 on Psalms," in *1–2 Corinthians*, ed. Gerald Bray, ACCS NT 7 (Downers Grove, IL: InterVarsity Press, 1999), 242.

21. Garland, *2 Corinthians,* 303.

were doing.[22] Working multiple jobs, Paul would have had to sacrifice sleep to make ends meet. I grant this point. Yet at the same time it is not uncommon for PTSD sufferers to attempt to distract themselves from the memories of the traumas, with overworking as a distinct possibility.

Skipping over Paul's appeal for a collection for Jerusalem's poor (8:1–9:15) and his so-called bragging rights polemic (10:1–18),[23] eventually I arrive at the third hardship catalog, which is even more detailed than its predecessors (11:21–33). Paul's strategy here is brilliant. He notices the intruding missionaries' boasting and crafts his own, but he subverts their logic. Rather than crow about how many churches he founded or the number of people who followed the Way because of him, Paul decides that "the only thing worth boasting about is what the Lord empowers."[24] Consequently, he itemizes discrete experiences that easily correspond to Criterion A1: imprisonment, being beaten with scourges and rods, a stoning, three shipwrecks, being adrift at sea, deprivation of food and clothing, and seven kinds of dangers, both natural and human. He also names insomnia again, which links to Criteria E3 and E6 above.

However, in addition to hearing Paul's recollection of traumatic exposures, it is pivotal to highlight the sardonic humor that suffuses his rhetoric. Once again Paul adopts the debating tactic of the hardship catalog and upends it to fit his theology. However, he also capitalizes on two other Roman cultural artifacts and transforms them to suit his purposes. One is the Res gestae divi Augustus, a funerary inscription published widely after Caesar Augustus's death in 14 CE in which Augustus enumerates what he has achieved and then tells how the Roman people celebrated him as *pater patriae*. Paul's audience would hear his list as resembling and then reversing that triumphalist imperial narrative.[25] This becomes even more obvious in 11:31–33, when he swears an oath—typically a precursor to an anecdote of heroic exploits—and then admits to the indignity of escaping from Damascus at night, lowered in a basket (see Acts 9:25).[26] It has been

---

22. David Rensberger, personal communication at Society of Biblical Literature Annual Meeting in San Diego, November 2014.

23. The phrase "bragging rights" comes from Witherington, *Conflict and Community*.

24. Thomas D. Stegman, *Second Corinthians*, Catholic Commentary on Sacred Scripture (Grand Rapids: Baker Academic, 2009), 253, 255.

25. Witherington, *Conflict and Community*, 451; Stegman, *Second Corinthians*, 256.

26. To be fair, Paul stands in good biblical company: Rahab helped Hebrew spies

argued that Paul is satirizing a second tradition called the *corona muralis,* a crown given to the first centurion who scaled an enemy city's wall. Rather than earning this tribute, "Paul ... describes a reversal of military bravery and another token of his humiliation and weakness."[27] What I would emphasize is that Paul takes an incident in his early ministry in which his life was in danger—a paradigmatic Criterion A1 event—and fashions the story as a parody. Displays of such humor indicate an adaptive capacity that Paul has demonstrated before, and it serves him well both personally and in advancing his ministerial agenda.

The fifth pericope appears after Paul reports on an out-of-body mystical experience. "To keep me from being too elated, a [stake] was given me in the flesh," Paul writes (12:7), using the word *skolops,* meaning either a "thorn" or a "stake." Much ink has been spilled speculating on this "thorn," leading one scholar to quip: "In each case men supposed that St. Paul's special affliction was akin to what was a special trouble to themselves."[28] The affliction referenced may have been a visually apparent malady, enough to weaken Paul but not enough to prevent him from traveling and fulfilling his duties. If so, it would have created an ironic situation. As an apostle, Paul could perform miracles, including healings, but to his opponents' eyes he would have been a pitiful miracle worker if he himself could not be healed. Facing the reality of what could be another Criterion A1 situation, Paul implored God three times for its removal—a pattern seen in the Hebrew scriptures, Jewish ritual, Greek literature, and Christ's Gethsemane prayer. Then, for the only time in his letters, Paul documents the risen Jesus's words: "But he [has] said to me, 'My grace is sufficient for you, for [my] power is made perfect in weakness'" (12:9).[29] Having received this word from the Lord, Paul welcomes his weaknesses, "so that the power of Christ may dwell in [*episkēnoō,* literally "pitch a tent upon"] me," and then he adds a final, abbreviated hardship catalog:

---

to escape from Jericho, using a rope through a window (Josh 2:15); and Michal similarly helped David to flee from Saul's troops (1 Sam 19:12).

27. Garland, *2 Corinthians,* 506.

28. Alfred Plummer, *A Critical and Exegetical Commentary on the Second Epistle of St. Paul to the Corinthians,* ICC (Edinburgh: T&T Clark, 1915), 350.

29. NRSV renders *eirēken* as simple past tense, but I concur with Stegman and Jones that this should be translated as perfect tense, since it is an enduring insight for Paul.

"Therefore I [delight in][30] weaknesses, insults, hardships, persecutions, and calamities for the sake of Christ; for whenever I am weak, then I am strong" (12:10). Paul confesses his divine surrender, and therein he recapitulates two prior themes: the "clay jars" theme of 4:7; and his argument in 1 Corinthians that God chooses the foolish, the weak, and the poor, "so that no one might boast in the presence of God, [who] is the source of your life in Christ Jesus, who became for us wisdom from God" (1 Cor 1:29–30a). Amidst many traumatic events, Paul joyously affirms a conviction that harmonizes well with the Canadian songwriter Leonard Cohen:

> Ring the bells that still can ring
> Forget your perfect offering
> There is a crack, a crack in everything
> That's how the light gets in.[31]

If it is reasonable to believe that Paul wrestled with PTSD, it seems clear by the end of his letter that he gained remarkable healing. What, if any, parallels might there be between Paul's path and what women and men can do now to seek relief and recovery?

Paul's Recovery and Current Treatments

Upon examining these passages more closely, I find it compelling to assert that Paul found (or, he probably would say, was led into) a journey of recovery from these significant traumas that incorporated five distinct elements. The first involves the apostle's reliance upon, and recasting of, the rhetorical device of the hardship catalog. It resembles treatment methods such as cognitive processing therapy, prolonged exposure therapy, and stress inoculation training. An objective of these therapies is to allow sufferers to reclaim their experiences without being paralyzed by the impact of past traumas, thus equipping them to stay engaged in present-day situations and relationships. With therapeutic support, PTSD sufferers gradually face feared stimuli, while attempting to reduce anxiety by displacing it with new corrective information that counteracts avoidance behaviors and

---

30. NRSV translates *eudokō* as "I am content with," but that is too timid. See Nave, "2 Corinthians," 327.

31. Excerpted from Leonard Cohen, "Anthem," *The Future* (New York: Columbia Records, 1992).

with techniques such as muscle relaxation, breathing, and guided imagery. In order to create the conditions for controlled reexposure, people often write a diary or recounting of the original event and then are asked to read and reread that narrative regularly. Guided by a counselor, a patient can explore irrational thoughts and unpleasant emotions evoked by those memories and thus learn "to differentiate the trauma event from other non-traumatic events, thereby rendering the trauma as a specific occurrence rather than as a representation of a dangerous world and of an incompetent self."[32] This component also can reinforce a sense of mastery in having survived the original trauma and in successfully coping with current "trigger events." While this modality does not suit all sufferers' needs,[33] the exercise of writing seems to help convert highly emotional memories into a linguistic form that makes events easier to process. Furthermore, for those who include positive religious references in their stories, there is evidence to suggest a mood benefit from doing so.[34]

The parallel between this treatment approach and what I read in 2 Corinthians is striking. Even without a trained therapist's counsel, Paul tells and retells stories about his traumatic experiences, and, in the letter's canonical form, these accounts grow more elaborate with each telling (with the possible exception of 12:7–10). Regardless of whether the epistle is a compositional whole,[35] this progressively evolving and detailed narrative

---

32. Barbara Olasov Rothbaum and Edna B. Foa, "Exposure Therapy for PTSD," *PTSD Research Quarterly* 10.2 (1999): 3.

33. Mott et al. report that not all patients with PTSD are appropriate for such therapy, particularly if there is an imminent threat of homicide, suicide, or external danger; see Juliette M. Mott et al., "Characteristics of U.S. Veterans Who Begin and Complete Prolonged Exposure and Cognitive Processing Therapy for PTSD," *Journal of Traumatic Stress* 27 (2014): 265–73. Even without those threats, though, there are some patients for whom it simply does not provide tangible relief; see David J. Morris, "After PTSD, More Trauma," *The New York Times*, New York edition (18 January 2015): SR1.

34. Julie J. Exline et al., "Religious Framing by Individuals with PTSD When Writing about Traumatic Experiences," *International Journal for the Psychology of Religion* 15 (2005): 17–33.

35. See note 4 above. I appreciate David Rensberger's reminder that the unity of 2 Corinthians is not a settled question in New Testament scholarship. Yet my assertion does not hinge on the provability of a coherent, cohesive single letter. For many trauma survivors, it is not unusual to have a "cycling" element to their narratives— at times being vague and nonspecific, at other times being very concrete. Thus, not insisting on 2 Corinthians as a unified letter actually bolsters our hypothetical case; it

presents readers with an example analogous to what PTSD sufferers gain in a successful therapeutic outcome: the ability to recall their traumatic memories with greater clarity, without feeling overwhelmed. In addition, Paul seems to derive a sense of context and comfort from rehearsing these stories. Contra Barbara Rothbaum and Edna Foa, he does not seem less convinced of "a dangerous world and of an incompetent self"; rather, he takes refuge in a positive religious reference: his confidence in God's power, even when he feels powerless.[36]

This assurance helps to nourish an internal sense of religious coping, which is a second dimension of his recovery. Paul often testifies to enjoying an intimate relationship with God. His encounters with the risen Christ (1 Cor 15:8–10; see also Acts 9:1–9) and ecstatic visions (2 Cor 12:1–10) together contribute to a sense of identity as a minister and to a purpose that sustains him in the midst of his traumatic experiences. Yet beyond the benefit to himself internally, Paul's religious coping also has an external focus. This is apparent throughout 2 Corinthians, when Paul defends his bona fides as an apostle. His paradoxical defenses are not self-aggrandizing, like those of the super-apostles, but are motivated rather by concern for his Corinthian sisters and brothers.

Paul's religious coping illustrates the importance of spirituality in health generally, but more specifically in PTSD sufferers' treatment and recovery. A victim's religious beliefs can shift negatively after a trauma, often leading to worse clinical outcomes. However, researchers suggest that people who assign greater positive meaning to stressful events usually are more resilient and adaptive and that therapies with an explicitly religious aspect can reduce symptoms for certain PTSD sufferers. Furthermore, a person's baseline level of spirituality can predict later symptom severity. As Joseph M. Currier, Jason M. Holland, and Kent D. Drescher state:

> Veterans who endorsed more daily spiritual experiences, practiced prayer or meditation in a more regular manner, endorsed greater levels of forgiveness (for self, others, and from God or Higher Power), incorporated positive religious coping strategies (e.g., collaborating with God or Higher Power to solve problems, look to divine realm for strength), or

---

allows us to perceive Paul as a human being whose coping capacity persists yet fluctuates from day to day.

36. This would be consistent with the conclusions of Exline et al., "Religious Framing."

CLARK

were engaged in a church or other community all showed lower levels of PTSD symptomatology at discharge.[37]

Although Paul's religious calling was a primary reason for why he was victimized, it also enabled him to cope both when the traumas occurred and later when he recalled them.

A third aspect of Paul's recovery emerges in the quotation above. Paul was intensely involved in his faith community. On numerous occasions he voiced his longing to be present with his churches, and his care for those congregations typified his accountability. This appears to reinforce what counselors are discovering about PTSD treatment, namely, that whether the social milieux in which sufferers seek to recover are welcoming or shame-inducing will play a large role in how they will cope. Clearly for Paul, the grounding he felt with other believers afforded him deep rootage.

The fourth and fifth aspects can be considered jointly, in that Paul's humor represents an adaptive strategy, as does his skill in reframing unhelpful thought patterns in Greco-Roman culture and within his own religious context. People with a robust sense of humor are more likely to reappraise stressful situations by reinterpreting their meanings for personal growth and self-protection and to regulate their emotions during stress, thus supporting the conclusion that "humor is often integral to a sense of hope, well-being, and humanness."[38] Moreover, Paul's inversion—insisting that divine power is visible within his humiliation rather than in prowess, as the surrounding society and even the Corinthians expected—manifests a cognitive flexibility that enhances self-efficacy. Both of these attributes are prized in present-day PTSD treatments, and clearly they assisted the apostle in his own time, enduring his own traumas.

Conclusion

As in the beginning of this essay, I again suggest a bidirectional movement within the apostle's story of traumas and his ability to survive them through God's sustaining grace. One direction is communitarian, turn-

---

37. Joseph M. Currier, Jason M. Holland, and Kent D. Drescher, "Spirituality Factors in the Prediction of Outcomes of PTSD Treatment for U.S. Military Veterans," *Journal of Traumatic Stress* 28 (2015): 62.

38. Jacqueline Garrick, "The Humor of Trauma Survivors: Its Application in a Therapeutic Milieu," *Journal of Aggression, Maltreatment and Trauma* 12 (2006): 181.

ing toward others. Paul asserts this when he links his own travails with the Corinthians' situation, then connects both his and their trials to God's consolation as a shared theme (1:3–7), thus emphasizing their interconnectedness as a healing resource. Then, in the remainder of the letter, he submits evidence of his own trauma and survival, and in so doing he joins the "communion of saints" who were and are soul-sufferers.[39] This lens for reading 2 Corinthians might aid some PTSD sufferers by reminding them that they, too, can thrive in the midst of their affliction—just as Henri Nouwen's friends convinced him to publish his journals by imploring him: "Wouldn't [others] find it a source of consolation to see that light and darkness, hope and despair, love and fear are never very far from each other, and that spiritual freedom often requires a fierce spiritual battle?"[40]

The other interrelated healing direction is toward the sacred, and for Paul it entails an incarnational turn. The traumatized apostle discovers comfort through his reliance on God's power, made evident through his weakness, and by identifying his ministry with that of the risen Jesus, who suffered and endured while trusting in God's love. David Rensberger phrases it well:

> Perhaps we might say that Paul saw Christ as a fellow trauma sufferer, one whom God had rescued from death, and whose trauma God had turned to good for the redemption of others.... This is the point that he believes the Corinthians are missing in their evaluation of apostles, which is the underlying issue in much of [his letter]. The Corinthians are looking for trauma-free power, and are impressed by people who claim to possess it. Paul believes that after the crucified Messiah, "power is made complete, reaches its goal, through weakness" (2 Cor 12:9).[41]

Hence the apostle, Christ his Lord, and PTSD sufferers can join hands as a congregation of trauma survivors and commence a dance of healing and wholeness, energized by grace.

---

39. John Gillman, personal communication at the Society of Biblical Literature Annual Meeting in San Diego, November 2014.

40. Henri J. M. Nouwen, *The Inner Voice of Love: A Journey through Anguish to Freedom* (New York: Doubleday, 1996), xviii–xix.

41. David Rensberger, e-mail communication received on 9 December 2014.

Bibliography

American Psychiatric Association. *Diagnostic and Statistical Manual of Mental Disorders: DSM-5*. 5th ed. Washington, DC: American Psychiatric Association, 2013.

Bray, Gerald, ed. *1–2 Corinthians*. ACCS: NT 7. Downers Grove, IL: InterVarsity Press, 1999.

Capps, Donald. *Fragile Connections: Memoirs of Mental Illness for Pastoral Care Professionals*. St. Louis: Chalice, 2005.

Cohen, Leonard. "Anthem." *The Future*. New York: Columbia Records, 1992.

Currier, Joseph M. Jason M. Holland, and Kent D. Drescher. "Spirituality Factors in the Prediction of Outcomes of PTSD Treatment for U.S. Military Veterans." *Journal of Traumatic Stress* 28 (2015): 57–64.

Donne, John. "Meditation XVII" (1623) from *Devotions upon Emergent Occasions*. Pages 1108–9 in vol. 1 of *The Norton Anthology of English Literature*. 4th ed. Edited by Meyer Howard Abrams et al. 2 vols. New York: Norton, 1979.

Erikson, Erik H. *Young Man Luther: A Study in Psychoanalysis and History*. New York: Norton, 1958.

———. *Gandhi's Truth: On the Origins of Militant Nonviolence*. New York: Norton, 1969.

Exline, Julie J., et al. "Religious Framing by Individuals with PTSD When Writing about Traumatic Experiences." *International Journal for the Psychology of Religion* 15 (2005): 17–33.

Fitzgerald, John T. *Cracks in an Earthen Vessel: An Examination of the Catalogues of Hardships in the Corinthian Correspondence*. SBLDS 99. Atlanta: Scholars Press, 1988.

Garland, David E. *2 Corinthians*. NAC 29. Nashville: Broadman & Holman, 1999.

Garrick, Jacqueline. "The Humor of Trauma Survivors: Its Application in a Therapeutic Milieu." *Journal of Aggression, Maltreatment and Trauma* 12 (2006): 169–82.

Greider, Kathleen J. *Much Madness Is Divinest Sense: Wisdom in Memoirs of Soul-Suffering*. Cleveland: Pilgrim, 2007.

Jones, Kenneth. "Post Traumatic Stress Disorder and Paul's Life: Finding Strength in Christ Alone." http://tinyurl.com/SBL0689i.

Kessler, Ronald C., et al. "Lifetime Prevalence and Age-of-Onset Distributions of *DSM-IV* Disorders in the National Comorbidity Survey Replication." *Archives of General Psychiatry* 62, (2005): 593–602.

Mason, Wyatt "You Are Not Alone across Time: Using Sophocles to Treat PTSD." *Harper's Magazine* 329, no. 1973 (October 2014): 57–65.

Morris, David J. "After PTSD, More Trauma." *The New York Times*. New York edition. 18 January 2015: SR1.

Mott, Juliette M., et al. "Characteristics of U.S. Veterans Who Begin and Complete Prolonged Exposure and Cognitive Processing Therapy for PTSD." *Journal of Traumatic Stress* 27 (2014): 265–73.

National Comorbidity Survey Replication. "Appendix Table 1: Lifetime Prevalence of DSM-IV/WMH-CIDI Disorders by Sex and Cohort." http://tinyurl.com/SBL0689h.

Nave, Guy. "2 Corinthians." Pages 307–32 in *True to Our Native Land: An African American New Testament Commentary*. Edited by Brian K. Blount. Minneapolis: Fortress, 2007.

Nouwen, Henri J. M. *The Inner Voice of Love: A Journey through Anguish to Freedom*. New York: Doubleday, 1996.

Plummer, Alfred. *A Critical and Exegetical Commentary on the Second Epistle of St. Paul to the Corinthians*. ICC. Edinburgh: T&T Clark, 1915.

Rothbaum, Barbara Olasov, and Edna B. Foa. "Exposure Therapy for PTSD." *PTSD Research Quarterly* 10.2 (1999): 1–3.

Stegman, Thomas D. *Second Corinthians*. Catholic Commentary on Sacred Scripture. Grand Rapids: Baker Academic, 2009.

Witherington, Ben, III. *Conflict and Community in Corinth: A Socio-rhetorical Commentary on 1 and 2 Corinthians*. Grand Rapids: Eerdmans, 1995.

World Health Organization. *The ICD-10 Classification of Mental and Behavioural Disorders: Clinical Descriptions and Diagnostic Guidelines*. Geneva: World Health Organization, 1992.

Appendix
Program Units of the Society of Biblical Literature Annual Meetings 2012–2015 for Which Session Listings Included the Keyword "Trauma"

	2012	2013	2014	2015
Academy of Homiletics	x			
African Biblical Hermeneutics			x	
African-American Biblical Hermeneutics				x
Bible and Cultural Studies				x
Bible and Pastoral Theology	x			
Bible and Practical Theology		x	x	x
Bible and Film			x	
Biblical Hebrew Poetry				x
Biblical Criticism and Literary Criticism		x		
Biblical Literature and the Hermeneutics of Trauma		x	x	x
Children in the Biblical World			x	
Chronicles-Ezra-Nehemiah			x	
Contextual Biblical Interpretation		x	x	x
Ecological Hermeneutics	x			
Ethiopic Bible and Literature	x			
Exile (Forced Migrations) in Biblical Literature	x			x
Extent of Theological Diversity in Earliest Christianity	x			
Feminist Hermeneutics of the Bible	x		x	
Formation of Isaiah				x

	2012	2013	2014	2015
Gender, Sexuality, and the Bible		x		x
Hebrew Bible and Political Theory				x
Ideological Criticism			x	
Israelite Prophetic Literature	x	x		
Minoritized Criticism and Biblical Interpretation				x
Paul and Politics	x			
Postcolonial Studies and Biblical Studies		x		
Psychology and Biblical Studies	x	x	x	
Reading Theory and the Bible	x	x		x
Religious Experience in Antiquity; Mind, Society, and Religion in the Biblical World			x	
Social History of Formative Christianity and Judaism			x	
Social Sciences and the Interpretation of Hebrew Scriptures	x			
Theology of the Hebrew Scriptures	x			
Women in the Biblical World		x		
Writing/Reading Jeremiah			x	x

CONTRIBUTORS

Samuel E. Balentine (sbalentine@upsem.edu) is Professor of Old Testament and Director of Graduate Studies at Union Presbyterian Seminary (Richmond, VA). He serves as General Editor of the Smyth and Helwys Bible Commentary series, to which he contributed a volume on Job (2006), as General Editor of *Interpretation: Resources for the Use of Scripture in the Church*, and as Editor of *The Oxford Handbook of Ritual and Worship in the Hebrew Bible* (forthcoming). His most recent publications include *Have You Considered My Servant Job? Understanding the Biblical Archetype of Patience* (University of South Carolina Press, 2015) and *The Oxford Encyclopedia of Bible and Theology* (2 vols., Oxford University Press, 2015), for which he served as Editor-in-Chief. He is currently writing an introduction to wisdom literature.

Elizabeth Boase (liz.boase@flinders.edu.au) is Head of the Department of Theology at Flinders University in Adelaide in South Australia, and Senior Lecturer at Adelaide College of Divinity and Uniting College, where she has taught since 2009. She is the author of *The Fulfilment of Doom: The Dialogic Interaction between the Book of Lamentations and the Pre-exilic/Exilic Literature*, and has published in the fields of Lamentations, Jonah, Isaiah, Psalms, and ecological readings. She has a particular interest in questions of hermeneutics. Along with Christopher Frechette, she is founding co-chair of the Biblical Literature and the Hermeneutics of Trauma program unit of the Society of Biblical Literature. She is currently writing the Earth Bible commentary on Lamentations.

Philip Browning Helsel (phelsel@austinseminary.edu) is Assistant Professor of Pastoral Care at Austin Presbyterian Theological Seminary (Austin, TX). He was born and raised in Bangkok, Thailand. He is interested in linking the macro- and micro- worlds in the care of trauma, offering a framework for the pastoral care of stories, systems, and self. He is co-chair of the Interreligious and Intercultural Pastoral Theology group at The Society for Pastoral Theology. His publications include *Pastoral Power Beyond Psychology's Marginalization* (Palgrave, 2015), an in-depth exploration of social class and mental illness since the recession. The author of many articles and book chapters, he serves on the editorial board of *The Journal of Pastoral Care and Counseling*. His current research focuses on how immigrant adolescents use graphic novels to subvert bullying and work through their identifications with multiple cultures.

L. Juliana M. Claassens (jclaassens@sun.ac.za) is Professor in Old Testament with a focus on human dignity at the Faculty of Theology, Stellenbosch University, South Africa. Prior to this she studied and taught in the United States for thirteen years. Her most recent book is *Claiming Her Dignity: Female Resistance in the Old Testament* (Liturgical Press, 2016). She is also the author of *Mourner, Mother, Midwife: Reimagining God's Liberating Presence* (Westminster John Knox, 2012) and *The God who Provides: Biblical Images of Divine Nourishment* (Abingdon, 2004).

Peter Yuichi Clark (peter.clark@ucsf.edu) serves as Professor of Pastoral Care at the American Baptist Seminary of the West (Berkeley, CA) and Director of Spiritual Care Services at UCSF Medical Center and UCSF Benioff Children's Hospitals at the University of California, San Francisco. Peter is an American Baptist minister, a board certified chaplain in the Association of Professional Chaplains, and a certified supervisor in the Association for Clinical Pastoral Education. He has contributed essays to several books including *Asian American Religious Cultures* (ABC-CLIO, 2015), *Religion: A Clinical Guide for Nurses* (Springer, 2012), *Revealing the Sacred in Asian & Pacific America* (Routledge, 2003), and *Generativity and Adult Development* (American Psychological Association, 1998), as well as the *Journal of Pastoral Care, Semeia, Pastoral Psychology*, and the *Journal of Supervision and Training in Ministry*.

Christopher G. Frechette (christopher.g.frechette@gmail.com) is Visiting Assistant Professor in the Department of Theology at St. Mary's University (San Antonio, TX). He has also served on the Ecclesiastical Faculty of the Boston College School of Theology and Ministry. With Elizabeth Boase, he is founding co-chair of the Biblical Literature and the Hermeneutics of Trauma program unit of the Society of Biblical Literature. He is an associate editor for the *Catholic Biblical Quarterly*. His recent publications include "The Old Testament as Controlled Substance: How Insights from Trauma Studies Reveal Healing Capacities in Potentially Harmful Texts," *Interpretation* 69 (2015); and "Destroying the Internalized Perpetrator: A Healing Function of the Violent Language Against Enemies in the Psalms" in *Trauma and Traumatization in Individual and Collective Dimensions: Insights from Biblical Studies and Beyond* (Vandenhoeck & Ruprecht, 2014).

Margaret S. Odell (odell@stolaf.edu) is professor of religion at St. Olaf College in Northfield, Minnesota, where she teaches Bible and theology and writes on the Hebrew prophetic literature, particularly the book of Ezekiel.

Ruth Poser (ruth.poser@staff.uni-marburg.de) is an academic staff member for Old Testament Studies in the Department of Protestant Theology at the University of Marburg (Germany), where she earned her Dr. theol. in Old Testament (2011). She is the author of *Das Ezechielbuch als Trauma-Literatur* (Brill, 2012), and she has translated multiple chapters of the book of Ezekiel in the context of the project "Bibel in gerechter Sprache" (Bible in just language). Currently, she is working on the subject of shame in the psalms.

Robert J. Schreiter (rschreit@ctu.edu), a Catholic priest and member of the Missionaries of the Precious Blood, is Vatican Council II Professor of Theology at Catholic Theological Union (Chicago). He has published seventeen books in the areas of inculturation, world mission, and reconciliation. Among them are *Constructing Local Theologies* (Orbis, 1985); *The New Catholicity: Theology between the Global and the Local* (Orbis, 1987); *Reconciliation: Mission and Ministry in a Changing Social Order* (Orbis, 1992); and *The Ministry of Reconciliation: Spirituality and Strategies* (Orbis, 1998). For twelve years he served as a theological consultant to Caritas Internationalis for its programs in reconciliation and peacebuilding, and he continues to work with organizations and groups around the world in peacebuilding. He lectures in academic and church circles on inculturation, intercultural communication, reconciliation, religious life, and world mission.

Brent A. Strawn (bstrawn@emory.edu) is Professor of Old Testament at the Candler School of Theology and in the Graduate Division of Religion of Emory University, where he has taught since 2001. His published research includes works on ancient Near Eastern iconography, Israelite religion, Old Testament theology, and legal and poetic texts of the Hebrew Bible. With reference to the Psalter, he coedited (with Roger Van Harn) *Psalms for Preaching and Worship: A Lectionary Commentary* (Eerdmans, 2009) and has authored numerous essays on the psalms—and their psychological import—including most recently, "Poetic Attachment: Psychology, Psycholinguistics, and the Psalms" in *The Oxford Handbook of the Psalms* (Oxford University Press, 2014) and "The Psalms and the Practice of Disclosure," in Walter Brueggemann, *From Whom No Secrets Are Hid: Introducing the Psalms* (Westminster John Knox, 2014).

Louis Stulman (stulman@findlay.edu) is Professor of Religious Studies at The University of Findlay (Findlay, OH). He is the author of *The Prose Sermons of Jeremiah* (Scholars Press, 1986), *Order Amid Chaos* (Sheffield, 1998), *Jeremiah* (Abingdon, 2005), and the coauthor, with Hyun Chul Paul Kim, of *You Are My People: An Introduction to Prophetic Literature* (Abingdon, 2010). He has co-edited several volumes, including most recently one with A. R. Pete Diamond, *Jeremiah (Dis)Placed: New Directions in Writing/Reading Jeremiah* (Bloomsbury, 2011). He is general editor of the series Core Biblical Studies (Abingdon) and has served on the editorial board of the *Journal of Biblical Literature*. He has written commentaries on the book of Jeremiah for *The Common English Study Bible* and *The New Oxford Annotated Bible* (forthcoming).

Gerald O. West (West@ukzn.ac.za) is a Senior Professor in Biblical Studies, in the School of Religion, Philosophy, and Classics, at the University of KwaZulu-Natal, South Africa. His particular research interest is African Biblical Hermeneutics. He is also Director of the Ujamaa Centre for Community Development and Research. The work of this Centre is reflected in his essay in this volume. His most recent book is *The Stolen Bible: From Tool of Imperialism to African Icon* (Brill, 2016).

Index of Ancient Sources

CPSIA information can be obtained
at www.ICGtesting.com
Printed in the USA
FFHW021311091019
55431442-61205FF

9 781628 371451